W9-COE-291

REA

FRIENDS
OF ACPL

3 1833 00156 9364

"*Birth, education, marriage, tragic deaths, successes, failures—eternal life—heaven. Never static.*

"A Christian family is a mobile blown by the gentle breeze of the Holy Spirit. This is not a romantic idea; it is in accordance with what the Bible teaches is possible. Each member of the family, as he or she is born again, is indwelt by the Holy Spirit. If this takes place, one can picture. . . the Christian family as constantly changing from month to month, year to year, with the mix never the same—agewise, interestwise, talentwise, intellectwise—never static, with always new fascination in discovering new points of communication as human beings are growing and developing. A mobile—blown by the breeze of the Holy Spirit."

By *Francis and Edith Schaeffer*

EVERYBODY CAN KNOW

By *Edith Schaeffer*

L'ABRI
HIDDEN ART
CHRISTIANITY IS JEWISH
WHAT IS A FAMILY?

# WHAT IS A FAMILY?

## Edith Schaeffer

**Power Books**

**FLEMING H. REVELL COMPANY**
Old Tappan, New Jersey

All Scripture references are from the King James Version of the Bible.

Excerpt from the hymn "Great Is Thy Faithfulness" by Thomas Chisholm is Copyright © by Hope Publishing Company and is used by permission.

Allen County Public Library
Ft. Wayne, Indiana

*Library of Congress Cataloging in Publication Data*

Schaeffer, Edith.
    What Is a Family?

    1. Family.        2. Conduct of life.        I. Title.
HQ734.S3767        301.42'7        75-29057

ISBN 0-8007-5088-8

Copyright © 1975 by Edith Schaeffer
Published by Fleming H. Revell Company
All Rights Reserved
Published in the United States of America

2260961

My gift to Fran for
our fortieth wedding
anniversary . . . 1975

# Contents

# Acknowledgments

The writing of this book was an unexpected surprise to me during this year which marks the sixtieth year of living in a family (starting as a baby and continuing now as a grandmother) and also marks the fortieth year of being a wife and the thirty-eighth year of being a mother! If ever I was to write a book about what a family is, this seems to be the logical time. Although who knows what "too young" or "too old" really refers to? I would never have thought of writing it, if my good friends Billy and Marilyn Zeoli had not urged me to put a lecture into written form — the lecture entitled "What Is a Family?" My hesitancy was shoved aside when time and place opened up to write. There were hindrances, such as bruised muscles and concussion of ribs resulting from a fall, but nothing that stopped the writing.

A theoretical book about the family could not come from me. It had to be what had been lived through or observed. Therefore, I need to thank my husband and children and children-in-law and grandchildren for allowing me to use examples from their own lives and experiences. I also want to thank Marry Berg-Meester for allowing me to tell her story. Additional thanks need to be given to my husband for agreeing to our working in two rooms on two projects, side by side, when it would have been easier for him had I concentrated on being an "ear." Writing a book cannot be separated from the other parts of life. The period of writing time is threaded into the lives of all who are in the family, and affects them in many ways. The finished product — and its results among the scattered places it goes — also affects the lives of those who are mentioned.

And so a book is written, and another pebble dropped into the lake! Ripples result which affect various people, including the writer and those who inspired the writing. "Thanks" on my part would be inadequate, but may God fulfill the needs of any who have helped put forth this volume by urging it on or walking in and out of the pages.

# WHAT IS A FAMILY?

# 1

## A Changing Life Mobile

Browsing through a handcrafts shop, one's eye is caught by paper-thin chips of grained wood, shaped as birds flying together, ships sailing in a breeze, fish moving through transparent water. "How lovely to bring alive the dullness of the baby's room, and for the breakfast nook with its dead view of bricks instead of trees."

"I must have *that* for the hospital children's ward." — "What a good thing for the nursing home people I visit each Wednesday." — "Whooee — Look! — Wheeeee — Just a tiny breath of air and they come alive." *Mobiles.*

Lingering before a painting, standing afar off to look at a statue, and then moving close to feel the smoothness of the marble, one turns to step into the next room of the art museum and the eye is caught and held by a mobile, twisting, turning, moving, changing — form and freedom demonstrated vividly in the space of a few square feet — a mobile! Whether copper or brass, wrought iron or blown glass, silver or dark wood, the threads that hold this artwork are almost invisible, and the combination of angles and arrangement are never the same at any moment. An almost-living artwork — the mobile.

Spring — chartreuse-colored leaves on the long, thin, stem-like branches of blowing willow trees dip into the lakes and

bob up again, spraying drops of water. The movement becomes doubled as the rippling lake reflects the branches and
breaks into a whole series of concentric circles as each drop
becomes a center of its own widening little momentary world.
Fascinated, one sees that this movement and reflected movement is increased by swans and ducks swishing through the
water, making their own V-shaped wakes, moving to their
own important destinations. The eyes move to include the
dipping, bobbing, black-and-white diving birds mysteriously
appearing and disappearing in their search for proper food
below the lake's surface. Without realizing that one's look
has caused the head to be suddenly thrown back to catch
another quickly moving set of forms, eyes are now riveted
on the wonder of lake gulls swooping and whirling as if in
practised ballet formations guided by some fantastic chore-
ographer. And the lighting keeps changing as clouds drift
and gather, disperse and float into sight, covering the sun,
bringing its rays in spotlight emphasis to brighten the shift-
ing shadows in the water, and to be itself reflected drama-
tically beside a bobbing sailboat tied to a post. Mobiles of
nature.

Walking along the Montreux quay, we see the view of the
lake framed in stone-bordered gardens interspersed by trees.
Spring flowers stand straight and proud, gloriously diverse
tulips — reds, dark purples, apricots streaked with white,
orange tipped with deep rust — mingle with daffodils in
fresh, bright-yellow shades and white-cupped jonquils. Passing a hotel lawn, one sees the drifting petals of a heavily
loaded magnolia tree carpeting the green grass with curls of
pale pink. And suddenly there is Castle Chillon, silently
guarding its stories of centuries within the stones, moss-
covered at the base where the moat's water darkly flows,
moving the fronds of bushes which have pushed out between
cracks in the wall.

After passing the boat dock, we come to a widening in
the quay, just under the wall which securely holds back the
earth well enough to keep the railroad tracks up where they

belong. Perpetual movement seems to be taking place in this
widened area on the promenade. Two little girls are con-
centrating on keeping their arms moving in the same rhythm
as they turn a long rope, while a third one, braids flying
and cheeks pink, is jumping expertly, missing the rope as
it skims under her feet — jump, jump, jump-jump-jump —
while voices chant a singsong verse. Adult voices, male voices,
female voices, young voices, older voices, childish voices,
baby voices adding odd syllables, together in unison the
chant comes forth:

> Baby in the high chair,
> Can't sit still.
> Ma-Pa OOOooo-la-la —
> How many hours can the baby sleep?
> One, two, three, four, five, six,
>     seven, eight, nine, ten, eleven,
>     twelve, thirteen, fourteen, fifteen —

"Ohhh, that's good — Margaret did fifteen — I'm next,
I'm next — I'm next."

"No, let me be."

"No, let Uncle Ran!" — "Let Franky!" — "No, John wants
to!" "Then Udo is next after that!"

Now the adults enter in. The chant begins again, the counting goes on, "Ran did seventeen. Uncle Ran did seventeen.
Hey, Kirsty, you weren't watching; Uncle Ran did seventeen."

Kirsty, with her curly, dark red hair bobbing up and down,
is jumping with her own little rope, biting her lip in fierce
concentration as she keeps track of her own count and nar-
rowly misses being hit by a trio of three-year-olds trying to
race each other on their tricycles. "Watch out — ooo —
ouch!"

"I know another jump-rope song!" — "I do, too; mine has
different things to do in it, like turn around, touch the ground,
kick the can, get out of town!" — "Mine has red-hot pepper
at the end, and then you have to turn the rope fast, fast, fast!"
— "Let's do that one!" — "Look, look how fast Genie can go!"

Amazed now, you — as you have become an invisible part of the background — determine to follow this grouping of people to try to determine *what* they are. Why this combination? Is it a school? How many are there?

The rope jumping finally comes to an end, but not the perpetual motion. You have to run to keep up, then slow down to a stroll. There is a gray-bearded man, looking like a professor, with hair ruffling in the flow of air as he pushes himself along on a scooter, raced by a young fellow with a mustache on another scooter. Behind them, wobbling a bit, comes a five-year-old on a bicycle a little too big for her. "Look, look! I can ride Becky's bike." An eight-year-old is on roller skates, and there goes a tall, thin fellow, his hair thinning on top, a mustache, too — but look at his knees pushed out in that ridiculous fashion as he rides the three-year-old's tricycle, careening down a slight incline.

"OOOoooo — Samantha fell in the lake, Samantha fell in the lake." A sharp squeal causes several to move over to look at a projection of a few rocks at the shore, where, sure enough, a perspiring young woman, her hair falling around her shoulders, having escaped its pins in her quick movements, is hauling up a curly-haired three-year-old from the slippery ledge of rock where she had gone in up to her shoulders, but happily had been reached in the nick of time. Cameras are quickly pointed in that direction, on the part of a couple of adults, but not quick enough, as she has already been dried in someone's T-shirt, and is being dressed in an assortment of clothes quickly loaned. "Here, put my extra jersey on her." — "My socks will do." — "Yes, her shoes are soaked completely." — "Isn't it good Sue was watching." — "It was the moss, slippery all the way up to there." — "Look, look, she doesn't seem to mind at all. Doesn't she look funny dressed in all those things too big for her, riding the tricycle again to catch up with Jessica and Fiona?"

"Look at John on the grass over there. He can stand on his head!" — "Oh, well he may be able to do that in his late thirties, but look at me! I can still stand on my head and do my legs back and forth like this. See? And I'll be sixty this year." — "Uncle Ran, lift *me* up, too." — "Look, Uncle Ran is lifting Giandy up, way up over his head!" — "How funny. Look, he can lift Uncle Franky up, too. He's strong." — "How many pushups can you do?" — "Look at Nony. She really *is* standing on her head."

Your invisible following of this group of people takes you through a lunch-table discussion with three high chairs added to the miscellaneous collection of ages. You try to hear all the conversation at one time. Children talking about school experiences — English school, Swiss school — they seem to study in two different countries. Adults are heatedly discussing world news of the moment, interspersed with philosophy and sports, stopping to order desserts, or to take a child to the toilet. You've decided now that here are a collection of parents. You have counted ten adults, twelve children. Why together? What is going on?

The evening comes on. A baby is being nursed, then fed some baby food and yogurt; toddlers are having boiled eggs and toast with their yogurts. You watch amazed as each one clutches a clothbound notebook. "Do you have paste for today's postcard?" — "Look, I'm going to put these leaves in mine!" — "I'm pressing this clover I found in the grass for mine." As you follow through the next hour, you find the twelve-year-olds, the eleven-year-old, the eight-year-old, and the six-year-old writing away, pasting cards and bits and pieces of the day's treasures in these notebooks, with mothers taking dictation.

"Put this — Manthy fell in the lake! Did you put it? Let me see!" — "We rode tricycles; Manthy wore Margaret's jersey after she got wet. We had a nice walk. Giandy fell down on his knee. I love the family 'union." Going back to where the children are writing, you would see pages of diary — impressions, ideas, thoughts as well as facts of what happened that day.

What are you looking at? *A family reunion.* A mobile. A human artform.

*What is a family?* A family is a mobile. A family is the most versatile, ever-changing mobile that exists. A family is a *living* mobile that is different from the handcraft mobiles and the art-museum mobiles, different from the mobiles of lake and trees and from the mobiles of birds, fish, and animals — different from any mobiles of machine, animal, or plant. A family is an intricate mobile made up of human personalities.

In so many ways a family is a mobile — an artwork that takes years, even generations, to produce, but which is never finished. The artwork of this mobile called "family" continues, and imagination, creativity, originality, talent, concern, love, compassion, excitement, determination, and time produce a diversity which is a challenge to any intelligent human being who has been given understanding of how to begin in the studio of life itself.

In what sense is a family a mobile? Just in that people blended together can run, jump, skate, tumble, swim, sail, and play together? Is it in the sense that an ever-increasing exchange of ideas can take place in communication? Is it in the sense that study and recreation can be shared in an increasing variety of ways? How is a family a mobile?

A mobile is a moving, changing collection of objects constantly in motion, yet within the framework of a form. The framework of a family gives form, but as one starts with a man and woman, a mother and father, there is never any one day following another when these two, plus the children that come through adoption or birth into the home, are either the same age or at the same point of growth. Every individual is growing, changing, developing, or declining — intellectually, emotionally, spiritually, physically, and psychologically. A family is a grouping of individuals who are *affecting* each other intellectually, emotionally, spiritually, physically, psychologically. No two years, no two months, or no two days is there the exact same blend or mix within the family, as

each individual person is changing. If people are developing
in a variety of creative areas, coming to deeper understanding
spiritually, adding a great deal of knowledge in one area or
another, living through stimulating discoveries of fresh ideas
or skills — they are affecting each other positively. The mobile of the grouping of toddlers with young schoolchildren,
of ten-year-olds with teenagers, of young married couples
with middle-aged married couples, of grandparents with two
generations coming along under them, is as amazingly real,
vivid, and *living* as any possible mobile one could imagine.

*What is a family?* A family is a mobile. A family is an
art form. A family is an exciting art career, because an art
form needs work.

Come again, and look at the mobile of this particular time
within family life, the family reunion. It is an only-once-a-
year special gathering which everyone has been awaiting for
a long time. There is an older couple, the grandparents; then
four couples, each with children. A cake will tell you something of the number of years each couple has been married.

"Ohhhh, look at the cake, the candles on the table, the
lovely bouquets. What is it? Tell us, Nony."

"This is an anniversary cake. It is Sue and Ran's wedding
anniversary today, so I planned this party in the middle of
our reunion to celebrate all our wedding anniversaries. The
numbers on the cake are: FORTY for the years Nony and Av
have been married, EIGHTEEN for Pris and John, FOURTEEN
for Susan and Ranald, ELEVEN for Debby and Udo, and
FIVE for Franky and Genie. The five bouquets are as close
as I could get to the flowers each couple had for their wedding
bouquets, and the new dresses for the brides — all made from
the same pattern and similar materials — are to give us the
fun of dressing up tonight for snapshots and memories we'll
never lose!"

"Let me take a picture of all the brides and grooms." —
"Oh, Margaret, you're cutting off the tops of our heads. Here,
let me show you." — "Take one of the cake with Sue and Ran;

it really is their anniversary day." "Here, Elizabee, you hold Baby Naomi and I'll take that. I've got Giandy in it, too, and the table with the flowers. Good!"

"Now everybody sit down here; we have a surprise. We're going to look at slides projected on that screen; so sit where you can see. These are pictures taken throughout the years when your parents were little, starting twenty-eight years ago."

"Oh, look! I'd forgotten what Switzerland looked like then. Look at those fields. Why, there is an apartment house now where those cows are grazing!" — "Oh, how cute! Debby is only three years old in that one, just the age of Samantha now. Don't they look alike?" "Mummy, was that *really* you? I can't believe it!" — "Tell me, Mummy, how old were you when you met Daddy?" — "Did you ever hear how Av and Nony met?"

Tea, hot Ovaltine, and cake are served, and conversation covers a tremendous diversity of subjects as the children ask questions; changes of not only countryside, but of world conditions, and philosophy and morals are discussed.

The fire is stoked with more wood, hot water is added to the half-full pots of tea, and nuts and raisins passed around to munch on as subjects blend, shift, change — covering education, history, sports, projection of possible happenings in the future, biblical prophecies, music, bringing up children, psychology, art, literature, historical novels, science, theater, mystery stories, creativity, television, and the wonder and marvel of having a growing, changing family to share with. Conversation grows hot with differing opinions at times, and even more heated with strong agreement at others. People pound their fists and walk out of the room, come back and start again, and either modify a point, or "suddenly see" something they didn't see before — or go to bed disturbed or mad, to get it sorted out in the next discussion or perhaps alone with someone. This is not polite surface conversation, but an exchange of growing, developing ideas which are often a result of much reading, thinking, praying, and struggle. Each one has something to relate concerning the imperfection of himself or herself, of human relationships as a whole, and relationships in marriage in particular. But each one has something to say in the direction of the unmistakable worthwhileness of fighting to have the continuity which cannot be had outside of a family — a family which is not shattered, scattered, fragmented, splintered, but together in a growing unity throughout the years and generations.

The conversation is one of the central fulfillments taking place among other fulfillments satisfying the expectations of a year of waiting for and looking forward to the family reunion. Everyone in the middle of difficulties, disappointments, distresses, shocks, illnesses, hospital experiences, depressed moments, as well as in the middle of exciting projects, new ideas, creative works, practiced-upon skills, looks forward to the family reunion.

When Giandy, aged four, broke his leg and spent a month in traction in the hospital, one of his satisfactions came in thinking of how he could tell all about it at the next family reunion. He could just picture the satisfying expressions of sympathy and horror on the faces of his English cousins as he would embellish the story. Jessica, having had a double hernia at the age of three, would not need to be outdone in having her own memories of the hospital and nurses to describe. And the pleasure of having four stitches in her forehead for Samantha, aged four, is largely made up of having a story to tell, too, — a story worth everyone's concentrated and quiet interest at the next family reunion.

The invitations to the next year's reunion go out at Christmastime, to be opened with the gifts on Christmas Day. They consist of tiny calendars with the dates of the reunion circled in the week they occur, and the invitation written on that page, under the picture, just before the name of the month, or at the beginning of the calendar (if there is no other room). YOU ARE INVITED TO THE FIFTH ANNUAL FAMILY REUNION TO BE HELD. . . . As the new year begins, the calendar is usually beside the children's beds, on the wall or on a desk — or kept in a drawer with precious possessions.

To the saving up of things to tell is added plans of "things to do," and the preparation of not only music, poetry, and games, but drawings to present to everyone the first night, or a little letter of welcome — written in the handwriting of Becky, Natasha, Kirsty, and embellished with each individual's idea of good design.

There is much preparation involving the desire of expressing love for cousins, aunts and uncles, grandparents, and parents in some visible form. There is an incentive that is very strong in preparing surprises for others to enjoy. Naturally, the youngest ones, Baby Naomi, little Francis, the small Ranald John, are not yet ready to prepare for the reunion, although the four-year-olds are full of memories and have their own ideas of elaborate planning on their own level.

Children who have had the waiting period come to an end in the reality of the arrival of the moment, and have found possible the sharing of hard things in the past year, the relating of exciting things, the satisfying fulfillment to the curiosity of what new projects others have been starting — by being told in full — are much more able to understand what it means to "Wait, for the coming of the Lord draweth nigh" (*see* James 5:8). This is the time ahead of us, *all* who are children of the Lord, and it will be a tremendously real and perfect *family reunion* when the dead shall rise and we who are alive and remain shall be caught up to be with Him in the air. There is a reunion ahead which is to be absolutely perfect and will be full of sharing. We can find out how Abel felt being the first martyr, and how David felt as he stood before Goliath. There will be lots to share!

Families are meant to be a mobile, a growing, changing, beautiful art form which will in some tiny way picture the beauty of the gigantic art form of the complete "Family" of those who have come to God in His given way, and been born again. There is beauty ahead, when we shall all be dressed alike, in linen pure and white, the "dress" He is preparing for that reunion.

Not only for little ones, but at every age, the knowledge that there are people close to you — family — who want to "hear all about it" is a double blessing. First, it is a protection against doing the most devastating thing that occurs to you in the midst of anger, self-pity, the danger of placing the drive to fulfill one's immediate desire above the long-term continuity of life; and second, an inspiration to "keep on." It helps to know that somebody, another human being, really cares whether you keep on or not!

It is good to have a healthy honesty on the part of those married longer years, as they relate that awful moment of anger when the wedding ring was thrown on the floor and rolled into a crack and took two hours to find and put back on. It is good for the ones married just a short time to know that a marriage can weather "down" moments and rough places, as well as coming to know that it is important to *work* at relationships with some measure of unselfishness and understanding because the end product is worth it! Time for protected, uninterrupted conversation, with freedom to express oneself without the danger of being completely misunderstood, is needed in this cross-relationship with its variety of people, of a variety of ages and experience, as well as in the one-to-one relationships or those within the small two-generation individual family. Courage to go on, as well as ideas concerning how to deal with situations that arise between children of various ages, between father and child and mother and child, are gained by exchange of problems or ideas that have proved helpful in the history of actually dealing with problems.

Conversation times in this family reunion include the exchange of a great many creative ideas. Ideas of how to use time, or how to fit in the practise of piano, cello, recorder, or violin into  busy school schedules and even busier parents' schedules, can be a tremendous help and inspiration in sending people back to the next year with the feeling that it is *not* impossible to add a few more things. Or people can feel, "When the baby gets older," or, "When they are all in school."

There is a demonstration and reminder of the fact that no two years are the same, and that the mobile which is the family has many new patterns and combinations ahead.

Looking at old pictures, having an anniversary party, long conversations, active time outdoors — riding children's scooters and tricycles with them, jumping rope, and standing on our heads — is that the sum total of a family reunion? No, there is also the concert when Becky plays her violin — year by year showing her progress — accompanied by Uncle Ran on the piano. Elizabeth plays the piano; each year the leaps ahead are heard and observed. Natasha recites poetry in French and English. Kirsty plays the piano at her own level of progress. Margaret amazes us all with her recorder music, long, complicated sonatas, with Ran accompanying her on the piano. John plays his cello with Ran, also. Plans are laid for another year, with perhaps a chamber-music quartet practised separately, with four playing together at the reunion. The little ones look forward to the time when they will play or recite. Then we relax and just enjoy the music of Bach, Brahms, Vivaldi, and marvel that all this can come forth within such a tiny number of people — a blowing, growing, changing mobile that started with just two persons!

God's mobile — a human being — two human beings — a family of human beings. Mobiles that can reproduce. Constantly changing patterns, affected by each other, inspired by each other, helped by each other. A family which is real in space and time and history, with roots in the past and stretching out into the future. Is this something to be dropped, broken, kicked, cut down, belittled, despised, lost to the twentieth century, unheard of by the twenty-first century?

There is an evening of square dancing. The Virginia reel with someone doing the calling from a tape (on a cassette) while everyone dips and bows and jumps, marveling at the energy of eight-year-old Kirsty and the ability of six-year-old Natasha to remember the calls; puffing, perspiring Franky wondering how the farmers could have done this after a day of digging potatoes! There is another time of playing games:

The Farmer in the Dell, Musical Chairs, Drop the Handkerchief.

There is the excitedly awaited time when all the dresses (and overalls and blouses for the little boys) are spread out. Genie has cut them out and made them, with help on hand sewing from Nony or someone else — and there they all are at last! *Oh*s and *Ah*s come from big and little throats. "Hasn't Genie done a great job. How could she get it all done?" Each one quickly takes off the outside clothes he or she has on, anxious to get into the annual family-reunion dress. "I want my family 'union dress," cries each little one, and Giandy has to be reminded that his is a suit. They *want* to be in the alike clothes. Never mind if anyone thinks we are a school out for a walk, the fun of all having the same material (well made and classic in style) is the fun of belonging. All year long when there is a concert, a wedding, a birthday party, a special occasion, the family-reunion dress is worn again (and handed down when outgrown). Memories of feeding the ducks, skipping stones across the lake, riding bicycles through the woods across the valley, whispering secrets to cousins, being frightened when Samantha fell into the lake, dancing the square dance together, cutting the wedding cake, looking at pictures of the mothers and daddies when they were younger, are all somehow bound up in the dresses. Snatches of the warm feeling of oneness in a family come back time after time as the dresses are worn through the years. There is an importance to the family-reunion dresses which surpasses by far any surface idea that Grandmother has supplied a new piece of clothing and Genie has given time to make it. Memories are worth working for.

The books, cheap loose-leaf notebooks, covered carefully with the material identical to the family-reunion dresses of the current year, are not just an added gift to make the time pleasant. Nor are the notebooks just to amuse the children at the end of the day. The story of the day, written each evening, and the stubs of the boat tickets for the annual boat ride on the lake, the postcards, the leaves, and pressed flowers

— all serve to bring back good memories which are a preparation for future life and a protection at times of future temptation to "blow it." Twentieth-century children, with all that works against lasting relationships, and everything that is for breaking all ties to prove freedom, need all the help they can be given. The growing row of notebooks in each child's drawer or bookcase is a kind of insurance. Of course, it is not foolproof; in itself it will not be enough to stop each child from ever getting into twentieth-century problems and dangers, but the books can be helpful. Fingering over the books five years hence, ten years hence — and seeing one's own hopes and aspirations, pleasures and private ideas, notations of what was enjoyed in the family relationships of that time — can be invaluable in making a difference in some decision where two paths could lead to very different futures. It isn't that a decision can never be rectified, but so much of life can be spoiled and wasted if a person turns toward the whole relativistic view of no morals, no absolutes, no base, no purpose, and then begins to try to live that way by smashing the things which are founded on a base!

Family reunions, memories, little things to help keep the memories alive are *not* a luxury that takes too much time and effort and money, but a definite necessity on someone's part, if the mobile is to be beautiful and not lopsided and broken.

How does a family reunion come about? First of all, time is a central ingredient. It takes time to become a grandmother and grandfather! It takes time to have three generations! To have the five marriages represented on that cake means that the grandparents had to live forty years in sickness and in health, during better and worse, weathering each other's fair treatment and unfair treatment. There will have been times of birth and death, caring for older family members of the previous generation and the new babies as they came along, through the growing and teenage years of their children, the marriages of each child, and then the one-by-one arrival of the grandchildren.

A wedding anniversary like the one described cannot suddenly be pulled out of the air by a conjurer. One cannot start with a full-fledged three-generation reunion, without having lived through the ups and downs of all that the years held.

The problem with most people is that they want instant food with the containers thrown away, and the food, too, if it burns or doesn't suit — and the same desire for "instant happiness" permeates their daydreams of a family or a family life. If one family half-begun does not work out — "Toss it out and start again!" — but with a few extra problems added, of course, because there is no neat little package of time which is brand-new and not invaded by memories of the past. Nor is the world big enough to wipe out the crisscrossing of space and people.

This family reunion did not come about because of perfect people, nor because of having had perfect relationships every moment of every day, nor because of having always made right decisions, nor because of calm perfect dispositions and easy-to-live-with characters. There has been a long succession of mistakes and sins, forgiveness asked for and given, troubles and feelings of hopelessness, discouragement to the point of wanting to give up, hard lessons learned, and a fresh learning from each other. The older ones have learned from the younger, as well as the opposite way around. The Bible says, ". . . tribulation worketh patience; And patience, experience; and experience, hope: And hope maketh not ashamed; because the love of God is shed abroad in our hearts by the Holy Ghost which is given unto us" (Romans 5:3).

You don't find any instant formula for living with the reality of showing forth love, whether within a personal family, or in the larger Family of those who are the children of the Lord, or in the "family of man." Showing love that has depth and is real comes along in the succession of events given us: tribulation — patience — experience — hope. Hard things — broken legs, hospital experiences, illnesses, disappointments, having to skimp on food because of having lost money or spent too much, making one's own yogurt and cheese, economizing in creative ways, finding a lack of under-standing, being attacked from outside, going through floods and avalanches, car accidents, fires destroying part of the house, having mean, untrue accusations thrown at us by others (or thrown at one of the other members of the family) — every kind of tribulation is what is meant. *Tribulation worketh patience*. It is after a certain amount of tribulation has been lived through, and that takes time, that a person can acquire some patience not to burst into: "Oh, not again! You didn't forget again, did you? I told you —" but rather just bite one's tongue and give a loving reply, with *some* demon-stration of patience. Patience cannot be shown unless there is a circumstance which would make us impatient.

Then, after lots of opportunity to have patience, *experience* results. Time after time, patience is demonstrated (not for other people to remark about, but to be noticed with a com-forting little feeling inside, knowing what one is *not* saying), and then comes the experience of knowing how to get along with another imperfect human being, which makes it possible to have a continuing relationship with the same person (and the same person*s*, as the family becomes plural). Patience following tribulation and experience following patience carry no labels as to whether they are for father or child, mother or grandchild, husband or wife. This is how *people* are to get along with other people. And it applies in the family first of all, equally for each to strive for.

After the experience comes *hope*. You may say, "Oh, of course, there is hope for the coming of Christ." Yes, that too — hope for the coming of the Bridegroom Christ, our perfect bodies, and removal from all tribulations. But I think it is a present hope for this life, too. This hope is the hope that "maketh not ashamed," because the result of it is the love of God being "shed abroad in our hearts." As we go on being patient or steadfast during various kinds of tribulation in our family experiences together, the love of God grows, and His love *in* us becomes more apparent *through* us to each other,

as well as our natural love for each other growing and mellow-
ing into a richness that could never exist without the long succession of ups and downs, better and worse situations. These
can be labeled as tribulations followed by times of hope
which are practical, everyday things — verbalized by "I love
you," demonstrated by a red rose or a surprise plan for a
special period of time together.

The universe is a spoiled universe, and people have been
really made "abnormal" by sin. There is no possible way of
having good relationships, nor of having a whole grouping
of good relationships in the framework of a family, if there
is *no* one who understands that it takes time, patience, hard
times, unselfish work, sacrifice of a variety of sorts, and planning on the part of someone to insure memories of beauty
sprinkled all through the difficulties. Some*one* has to feel
the wonder and dignity of having the mobile of the family be
the artwork which that person is interested in seeing develop.

What a mobile! It is Sunday now, during the family
reunion, and the twenty-two people are alone for that one rare
Sunday (out of the whole fifty-two in the year) of being
together for a worship service. The middle generation takes
charge of the services. The two youngest are being fed,
ready for a nap, the three-year-olds shift their chairs around
a bit, the older children have their notebooks ready to take
notes, while younger ones decide to draw pictures in theirs
as they are "keeping quiet," but everything is put quietly
aside while Udo prays. An excitement is felt by each one, as
we realize that here we are *alone*, a family really together
in so many ways in addition to being physically together. It
hasn't just happened — it has come as a result of years of
prayer and living, misunderstanding, forgiving, and growing
— and it is not static now. It is in the midst of being blown
into new, fresh arrangements together. We thank God together as Udo prays, for the reality of what He has given
us, really so deeply meaning it, each in his own capacity of
understanding, each with yet so far to go. Then Franky

gives us a study from the Book of Psalms, and we listen seriously, our Bibles open, marveling at the freshness of the Word of God as it comes with no trite phraseology. Then Ranald teaches a whole series of new children's hymns, with motions to be made with the hands and words straight from Bible stories. He then plays the piano while Susan holds the printed cards with words and illustrations on them. We all sing more heartily as we learn a new song, and then another one is taught. Fiona, Jessica, and Samantha hitch their chairs a little in excitement, and now sing with much enthusiasm, song after song after song.

Now it is time for Udo's message, before another song, and then comes John's. Each young father has given a portion of Bible study, and the memory carried away is of a unity of belief and an assurance that each individual is being led by a human father who has a base. Through the year ahead there will be family prayers in the individual homes, but time after time the memories of the togetherness of grandparents and four families, gathered in one room at one time, will underline the oneness.

Unity and diversity. Form and freedom. Togetherness and individuality. *A family*.

Age. youth, childhood, infancy — strung together on tiny threads. Blowing in delicate movement independently, yet together. A family — belonging to each other, affected by each other, compassionate for each other, concerned about each other, interested in each other — a living mobile, never static. *A family*.

Birth, education, marriage, tragic deaths, successes, failures — eternal life — heaven. Never static. *A Christian family* is a mobile blown by the gentle breeze of the Holy Spirit. This is not a romantic idea; it is in accordance with what the Bible teaches is possible. Each member of the family, as he or she is born again, is indwelt by the Holy Spirit. If this takes place, one can picture not perfection, but a measure of reality in thinking of the Christian family as constantly changing from month to month, year to year, with the mix

never the same — agewise, interestwise, talentwise, intellectwise — never static, with always new fascination in discovering new points of communication as human beings are growing and developing. A mobile — blown by the breeze of the
Holy Spirit.

No, not one member of any family will *always* be directed
or blown by the Spirit, nor will all the members be directed
every day in perfect balance to His plan, but there is an
exciting possibility of knowing something very real in some
*measure*, as there is recognition of the importance and centrality of the living artwork, the mobile which the family
can be..What is a family? An artwork — a mobile.

Walk once again through the handcrafts shop to see what
vandals have done to the mobiles. The threads have been cut,
the ships are sagging in ugly disorder. Look at the grained
wood of the fish, split and dirtied by an angry boy's pen-
knife. Come into the art museum and gasp with dismay as you
look at the once-ethereal beauty of blown-glass forms cracked,
and one on the floor smashed into powder. See the copper
forms dented with a hammer, now hanging dizzily from one
sagging silver wire, the others cut to drop the rest to the
marble floor. Walk by Lac Léman and imagine the scene
after senseless destruction has splintered the trees, torn up
the gardens, shot at the swans who kept on swimming with
broken, blood-streaked wings — unable to fly or make a
beautiful wake again.

Mobiles — smashed, torn, sagging, all balance gone, the
delicate interplay finished — turned into something too ugly
to keep around, too paintful to see. Broken marriages, smashed homes, splintered relationships, shattered families, these
have become the norm in this twentieth century. No generation to follow a generation in the beauty of balance threaded
together like the mobile! Senseless breaking up of priceless,
living, balanced beauty over — so often — nothing.

The present atmosphere is like a smog that seems to creep
in the door of the church when the organ is playing the
wedding music and the roses are still fresh with the florist's

dew. Voices seem to be chanting behind the music. "Only
do what you want to do — Don't do anything that is hard —
Fight for your own rights, even if it means destroying everything — Put yourself first — Never mind what anyone else
thinks — Pay the other person back — Get even — Do your
own thing — Express yourself — Get fulfilled one way or
another — Be free — Get rid of old mores and customs —
Break out of the prison of social opinions — There are no
lasting relationships possible, so walk out as soon as you
feel like it — Nothing is worth working for — Be open-
minded — Follow the crowd — Everything is relative, anyway." The expectation is for keeping on only as long as it is
fun, makes you happy, or is convenient.

There are no beautiful mobiles, works of art in the form
of families, which have never been in danger of being broken.
Frustration, anger, impatience, the feeling of being misunderstood, the giving in to daydreams of perfection — these or
other forms of dissatisfaction invade every human relationship for at least minutes, if not hours or days. Have any two
people *never* felt like walking away from each other? The
difference is that the deep underlying sense of the importance of family continuity must be stronger than the insistence
on having perfection. People throw away what they could
have, by insisting on perfection which they cannot have, and
looking for it where they will never find it. Everyone has been
in danger of this, but many more each year are giving in to it.

There is a beauty and continuity which can *never* be had
unless someone in the family has the certainty that the whole
art form is more important than one incident, or even a string
of incidents. To smash a Ming vase which is absolutely irre-
placeable — just to satisfy a violent feeling of wanting to be
emphatic in making a statement, when there is a five-and-
ten-cent-store plate which could be smashed just as well to
suit the need — is a minimal picture of what it is to smash
the living artwork of a family, and then to spend the rest of
one's life paying for it and seeing other people pay for it,
too. Wasted lives.

People need to experience the beauty of being part of a mobile art form, and people who have never known such beauty exists need to see it taking place. If human relationships are to be beautiful on a wider form, in church and state, the individual families making up society have to be really worked on by someone who understands that artists have to *work* to produce their art. It doesn't just fall down ready-made from the sky!

# 2

## An Ecologically Balanced Environment

Dip, creak, dip, creak, splash. "Isn't this just about perfect? A rowboat, a sunset streaking the water with rosy light, and look, look! A new moon over there. See?" Dip, creak. Plop, plop. "What did the oar hit? Look, a dead fish!" — "Two dead fish, no three. Ugh — another. Who said this was perfect?" — "I guess it is just an ugly reminder of all that we are told about pollution of lakes and streams — fish dying everywhere. What an unromantic sight, let alone the waste of all that fish."

"You know, I haven't been in Southern California since I was a very small child, and I can't wait to drive through the orange groves around Monrovia where I used to live. I walked through wonderful orange groves going to school at Orange Avenue School. I still remember the marvelous odors of blossoms and leaves."

"*Orange groves*, that really dates you. Didn't you know that pollution has so spoiled things around here that orange trees won't grow properly anymore?"

The Chinese Communists started to kill all the sparrows because they were eating so much rice and seed that they thought the country would be better off without them. Later they found out to their alarm that when an amazing number of birds had been destroyed they were losing more food than ever before. Why? Well, because the sparrows had been eating insects as well as rice and seed, and the insects attacked the crops with unhindered vigor after the sparrows were out of the way, resulting in more loss of rice and grain than before. It was just demolished *before* harvest time, instead of when stored!

Today we are discovering the interrelationships of plant and animal life to such an extent that the extermination of any species brings risk to the well-being of human beings. There is much written, studied, lectured about, and attempts are being made to do something about all the complex ecological relationships which exist. However, while many are trying to preserve wild life and restore environments conducive to animals reproducing and growing naturally (some of which are in danger of becoming extinct), other human beings are purposely killing the very same species, interested only in the personal gain from selling the skins, tusks, or whatever it is that might bring cash. Human beings are, so to speak, creeping or rushing through jungles and forests, fields and seashores, rivers and lakes — at cross-purposes! Some preserve and protect, others molest and kill for their own livelihood.

The conservationists have a measure of understanding that they are doing something with a lasting effect, something that will really help far more people in the end, even if many wouldn't thank them for it. The others are sure it is their right to make a living now by grabbing and killing the animals wandering wild and free, and selling what is salable to others who want to buy. And so these two sections of humanity work at cross-purposes. In addition to this destructive situation (not quite so personal as two groups of people stalking through the jungle, but taking place because of choices of *some* sort), air, water, soil, and environment are being polluted in an incredible variety of ways by people — to their own detriment.

There is a very serious discussion concerning the tragic imbalance being produced in one way or another in the

world today. There *was* a balance at some time! There existed a balance at one point in history in areas where now the
imbalances are disturbing people. The charts, examples, and
experiments always show what took place *before* something
came along and upset the previous balance. We're told that
when villagers in Brazil and Argentina destroyed jungle cats
and owls, their living places were overrun by disease-carrying
rats. Many examples are given of the upset of balance, whether in soil or because algae have been destroyed in the sea.

The important thing to notice, I believe, is that there is an
environment which is crucial to the well-being of human
beings. There is an ecological balance that is essential to life.
Disease-ridden rats, seed-destroying insects, polluted water
in which fish cannot live, are a threat to human life, but there
is something even more basic to human beings — and that
is the proper ecological balance and natural environment
for the life and production of truly significant, balanced
human personalities. Human beings sicken and die emotionally, psychologically, and intellectually if they don't have
the right environment or balance in which to grow.

Babies have been left in hospitals with all the proper nutrition, sanitation, temperature, water, sleep and scheduled
attention as to physical needs. We are told of the amazing
difference in physical and intellectual development when such
children were given love (in the form of people taking the
job of rocking and cuddling and playing with a child so
many hours a week) and others were not. At one period in
recent history, child-care books told mothers to pay special
attention to strict schedules and never to pick up a baby.
Then experts began to tell of the tremendous harm done by
such harsh schedules and urged that babies be rocked, sung
to, and loved in sympathetic response to their crying. It was
found that babies stimulated by bright bits of cloth put close
to their beds, given a music-box lamb to feel and listen to,
and talked to and read to long before they could be expected
to understand, would talk earlier and have a higher IQ than

the babies left too long alone with no stimulation intellectually or emotionally. Not only intelligence but personality is affected by the early environment. Everyone who has had anything to do with children who have been wandering the streets (in certain parts of the world, in "packs") knows something of the amazing changes which have taken place when such children were placed in a totally different place with a different set of balances in their environment.

What is a family? A family is an ecologically balanced environment for the growth of human beings. It came into existence for that purpose. It was God whose idea it was to place a man and woman together to begin the first family. It was God who told them that the next family would come about by a man and a woman leaving their parents, and the man cleaving to his wife to become one flesh. The perfection of the universe — perfectly balanced in every minute, as well as in a gigantic way — came about not by chance, but because a perfect, brilliant, all-wise, infinite, eternal God created it that way. The Lord God formed man of the dust of the earth and He made him in His own image — a personality which could think and act and feel. God created Adam, as He has told us in Genesis, and as Jesus underlined in Matthew. And God saw that it was not good for a man to live alone. Adam had God with whom to have communication, but God is infinite and eternal. In some ways Adam was very alone in his finiteness, and in his limitedness. So God, in understanding of Adam's needs, made Eve, that Adam might have a finite, limited human being with whom to have a relationship in a horizontal way and on a finite level.

It was not by mistake that God made two very different kinds of people, a man and a woman. Eve was made from a rib in Adam's side. This is a marvelous fact in history to prepare us for the statement later in the Bible, as Paul wrote God's explanation to us of the relationship of the believers — the church — to Christ the Bridegroom. "For we are members of *his* body, of *his* flesh, and of *his* bones. For this cause shall a man leave his father and mother, and shall be joined unto his wife, and they two shall be one flesh. This is a great mystery . . ." (*see* Ephesians 5:30–32).

In Genesis we are told that Adam said, "This is now bone of my bones, and flesh of my flesh . . . " (2:23). And the next verse was quoted by Jesus in Matthew (saying that it was something the men He was speaking to should have read in Scripture): "Have ye not read that he which made them at the beginning made them male and female, And said, For this cause shall a man leave his father and mother, and shall cleave to his wife: and they twain shall be one flesh" (*see* Matthew 19:4, 5).

What kind of an environment and proper balance was the first child to be born into? *Oneness.* There was meant to be oneness as an atmosphere. There was meant to be oneness as security. God made Adam and Eve as two very different people who could become one unit. Male and female created He them — on purpose. God made woman to be physically beautiful in the eyes of man. God also made man to be beautiful in the eyes of the woman. Two kinds of beauty, complementing each other, fulfilling each other. God gave man and woman capacity for love and someone to love, capacity for gentleness and someone to whom to be gentle, capacity for communication and someone with whom to communicate, capacity for worshiping Him and having communication with Him — their God — and someone with whom to join for worship, capacity for learning and someone with whom to discuss all the new discoveries and understandings, capacity for physical oneness and someone with whom to be become one in a mysterious and very real way. God also gave man and woman the capacity to be a family and the marvel of being able to reproduce, so that the man could place his seed within the woman and she could conceive and bring forth a tiny human being who would be part of each of them. Wonder of wonders! The *first* family. Diversity and unity in the oneness of human beings. Diversity in the marvelous variety — male and female — a variety to be always a thing of wonder to any two people discovering each other's minds and emotions and reactions, exciting in the effects of their oneness, as well as the marvel of the oneness of their bodies. Then the diversity of the tiny full-blown little human being coming forth after nine months — no two ever exactly alike, not even twins. Variety, diversity, each human being to be different from all the others.

What would it have been like if sin had not come into the universe? What would it have been like if Eve and Adam had believed the Word which God had spoken to them in understandable verbalization. If Eve and Adam had only asked God questions before deciding to believe Satan, how different it would have been. But the coming of the Fall took place before the birth of the first new little human being, the first baby ever to be born. The first family was already an imperfect, spoiled, abnormal atmosphere for that first baby! No baby has ever been born into a *perfect* situation, a perfectly balanced atmosphere, a perfect family. Since Adam and Eve chose to believe Satan's lie, rather than what God spoke to them, there have been *no perfect people*. The perfect balance of nature was also upset. We live in a spoiled abnormal universe. It is not the perfect place which God created, but one day it is to be restored — perfectly.

Meanwhile, many discoveries have been made concerning the need for ecological balance in nature, and some people try very hard to do something in the area of conservation or restoration on a human scale — imperfectly, but making a real difference. All this is very good, but the most important and most delicate balance of all is being shoved aside by many of the same people. The balanced environment for tiny, living, growing human beings is the family, and some people who would give their efforts tirelessly for fauna and flora let their own children become warped, withered personalities by shoving them into a completely unbalanced, polluted environment in which to grow into adults. So many today seem not to feel any responsibility for the children of their own wombs, let alone for producing an atmosphere for other people's children. Strangely, the reason given is that they want "happiness."

You see, if the family is meant to be the basic atmosphere for people, then a whole community of families and a whole state of families and a whole nation of families is important also — in many far-reaching ways. Something is going to go wrong with people if the scale is tipped so that the majority of them are born into a setting, an atmosphere, an environment which is completely out of whack with what they need. Somehow or other the emotional, psychological, spiritual, esthetic, moral, creative "seeds" are going to be eaten up *before* the harvest stage, if you see what I mean! It may not be possible to carry out the illustration to the full, but it seems to me that it shows what I want to say about tragic and unexpected results being in the offing when people forget the importance of the family. Unhappily, it is already taking place. Psychiatrists' offices are already overfull. People are already going to pieces. Children are already mixed-up to the point of having no norm from which to deviate! And it will get worse.

How balanced? What ingredients go into making something in the direction of an ecologically balanced environment for the growth of a new human being? First of all there is to be a mother and a father, a male and a female — one who had the baby grow inside her for nine months, and one who placed the seed within her — equally responsible, equally interested, each with a part to contribute which the other cannot give. Motherliness and fatherliness, separate but blended in a marvelous oneness called "parents." Natural childbirth is a great new understanding of blending parents at the moment of birth. But it really, I believe, is closer to what birth was meant to be like in the beginning — the father and mother as close as possible in cooperating with the different parts they play in this high point of bringing forth a child. The baby is born almost directly into the hands of the father, to be held to the mother's breast a moment later. Both welcome the new human being with every kind of welcome that is natural to their two personalities, sharing in the struggle of bringing forth and sharing in the receiving of the child with loving welcome demonstrated in some vivid way. But whether by natural childbirth or not, the first ingredient that makes up a balanced environment is the very human necessity of *people,* other people to whom to relate, and who care — not efficient machines which will provide all the necessary elements listed scientifically. It is a "people universe," created by a Personal God, and it was He who made a man and a woman with the capacity for being a father and a mother, before He brought a tiny, helpless baby into the world. Parents are the first ingredient. Parents have a responsibility to stay together to provide this ingredient.

There are modern drives for *fulfillment,* for *happiness,* for *equality,* for *freedom,* for peace at any cost, for "doing what comes naturally," for "doing what feels good," for "existential living," for "open marriages", for "denying standards," for abandoning "stuffy words and concepts" such as responsibility, loyalty, faithfulness, sacrifice, trustworthiness, endurance. These drives stir up such pollution in the area of interhuman relationships that there are dangers, ecologically speaking, of far more important species than certain birds becoming extinct. Some of the very people giving their lives to preserving a certain species of birds are apparently without understanding as to what essentials they have thrown away in their own environment and that of their children.

The Bible gives what might seem a very contradictory list of words we need·to think about daily in the practical business of living. "He that loseth his life shall find it" (*see* Matthew 10:39). Yes, it is for the Gospel's sake, but on further reading one realizes that here is a truth which takes place in many ways. It is the bread-cast-on-the-water-returning kind of thing. A woman who puts aside "happiness and fulfillment" as primary, and begins to think of the needs of husband and children, finds herself amazingly more fulfilled (if there is time to notice) as days go on. A man who puts his children and wife and home first, before falling into the arms of somebody who seems to "understand" him, will find that, as time goes on, the total of what he has *found* can't be compared to what he has *lost*. *Reaping what you sow* is another thing that simply turns out to be true. Continuity is something that is absolutely priceless, and if one sows a series of divorces and remarriages or promiscuity, there is no continuity to be had. Nothing takes the place of the security each individual needs (the parents and the grandparents, as well as children) in having a continuity of life. To sit together and look over past photographs (which show shared history which has meaning to the whole family) demonstrates something that cannot be purchased at any price! It isn't just a question of being morally right — that is another matter. What I am saying is that the environment a new baby needs is that of having a mother and father, but the environment which human beings need is also one of continuity, of being conscious of being in the stream of history in a way that can be personally experienced.

Yes, we are part of the human race. In that sense we are a part of the family of man. As Christians we have been born into the Lord's Family, and God is our Father. This is true and marvelous. If we are in a church or a grouping of Christians, this, too, is in a smaller way our family with some reality. But our own-sized piece of reality, something small enough to teach us what all the other relationships are about, is the individual family. It is supposed to be a fact small enough for us to understand and experience, and gradual enough for us to absorb in all the days of growing. A human being is meant to be able to grow in a very real personal family of people that belong to him or her, and to whom he or she belongs. This is the "natural" human environment — personal — for a person.

One shattering aspect of slavery was the breakup of homes. Human beings were sold out of their families, never to have contact and sometimes never to meet again. Quite rightly, this is spoken of as a shadow spoiling the history of a nation wherever it occurred. But the staggering thing in the twentieth century is the abandonment of responsibility to keep a family together, on the very part of the two adults whose family it is. What a hue and cry there would be today if men and women were put on a block and auctioned off, leaving behind weeping babies, and children in the split which would be taking place as they were carted off to two different geographic locations! But the same people *take themselves off,* expecting to give some sort of substitute for the continuity they should be providing, by dividing the children's time or in some cases sending the children off to foster homes. Homes of today — shattered and split as thoroughly as any in slave-auctioning times — by cold choice.

From birth to death, a human being needs shelter. A physical shelter can be one of many diverse possibilities, from a castle to a tent. The physical shelter which is "home" to a person may be a tiny hut on a South Seas island, a Swiss chalet on the side of an alp, a tent in the middle of a camping lot, an old railroad car on a sidetrack long since rusted, a clapboard house in Pennsylvania, a Cape Cod cottage, a wood-and-stone-and-glass architectural triumph on a California cliff, an apartment in the middle of a high-rise building in the midst of a huge city, a junk in Hong Kong, a houseboat in a Dutch canal. Slum or palace — it does not matter much — the basic need is the existence of a shelter into which one can run to be separated from the rushing world outside, protected and welcomed to some degree, a place to go out of and come back to! The balanced environment for a human being includes a home of some variety as a shelter from stormy blasts of weather or unbearable heat. But for the four walls or flapping canvas sides, or the jagged rock sides of a cliff home or balconied enclosures of a chalet to really become "home," there needs to be a home*maker* exercising some measure of skill, imagination, creativity, desire to fulfill needs and give pleasure to others in the family. A home can't come ready-made from any kind of commercial source, no matter how expensive or cheap. Something must be added to furniture and walls to turn a house into a home

Birds make a variety of nests, and the offspring feel at home in that particular kind of nest. It makes a difference in their being able to grow properly. Somebody has to be the nest maker, the artist, the interior decorator, the imaginative person with a dignity born of understanding its importance, as well as a desire to produce a home — as differentiated from merely a house. A home combines the shelter from physical storms and floods and physical attack of bandits with the reality of tiny, growing or adult human beings finding the shelter they need from intellectual, emotional, and spiritual attacks. The family and home are *meant* to be the environment where human beings can find shelter, warmth, protection, and safety in each other. There is the total giving to a tiny infant, which quickly shifts in what is taking place as months and years go on. A mother finds she is given understanding protection by a son or a daugther, as well as by her husband. A father finds that the love and loyalty of a little girl is something as real in keeping the driving rain of criticism outside as is the roof in keeping out the hailstorm. A balanced family environment is meant to be a very real shelter to be "run to" at times of need in life. These are two-way relationships growing up from two-way sensitivity, but never equal at any one moment. Don't forget that there are no perfect people and no perfect balances in a spoiled universe. The *giving* without expectation of return is important for an unlimited section of time. *Unlimited?* Where are your "rights"? It is important to establish principles in the imperative need of rethinking some things that are too easily on people's tongues and in their attitudes. We are all in danger of being shipwrecked because of not doing a bit of basic thinking.

What is most important in human relationships? The winning of a point in an argument? Or the building of a growing, lasting relationship? The gaining of a victory, in making the other person do his or her share? Or the beauty of an emerging artwork which is rare in a day of "splits" — the artwork of a deepening, continuing togetherness? I've met a man who goes to untold trouble and discomfort to feed an almost-extinct species of birds, climbing rocks over the Bermuda seas, setting alarm clocks to do the right thing at the right time. He doesn't ask the birds to give him his fair share of return! Why are people so blind as not to see the dangers facing an almost-extinct reality of families which go on, which continue, which produce human beings with a certain amount of balance — psychologically, physically, spiritually, emotionally, intellectually, culturally — with diversity of interests, talents, and excitement — families which enjoy each other. How precious a thing is the human family. Is is not worth some sacrifice in time, energy, safety, discomfort, work? Does anything come forth without work?

Have you exclaimed over gorgeous English gardens with their clipped lawns, precise flower beds, sunken pools with water lilies? And have you found that the family couldn't afford a gardener, so that the father or mother of the household got up before everyone else — to plant and keep the garden in this state? Somebody has to get up early, stay up late, do *more* than the others, if the human garden is to be a thing of beauty.

No person is perfect. The one doing much for the sake of the others can explode suddenly, and spoil a whole patch of time and results! No results are perfect. The work can suddenly seem to be of no avail. Why bother? It is worth fighting for, the environment that is slowly disappearing, since it produces lasting human families which produce more stable, balanced human beings.

Do you feel like saying, "Fine, but I can't be that example. Last night I got so sick of doing the dishes alone, that I threw five plates on the floor in sheer frustration and anger. So I blew it! No feeling of willingness to sacrifice my time to let the others sit in there playing the piano or putting a jigsaw puzzle together!" What about such an episode? Does it finish something? Not at all, if there is a constant attempt at honesty in communication. When the surprised faces come to the door to look, the dish-thrower is perhaps still furious and spits out, "I'm *sick* of doing these while you all enjoy yourselves." And someone will probably sheepishly stoop over to help pick up the pieces. Or if the smashing has relieved the feelings, perhaps the response to the faces would be, "I'm sorry. I just blew up inside, while I was trying to be a bit too sacrificial for myself; I really wanted to be in there with you." And someone helps finish up, even if it is awkward.

Whether it is over that quickly or drags out into walking off into the woods (or up and down the elevator or into the fields, depending on where you live), there must be a time of being willing to say, "I'm sorry," or "I really blew up because I was trying to be more noble than I could," or "I *wanted* to let you all have a good time, but I guess I expected one person to notice all the clash of dishes, and I suddenly blew up." Something needs to come out, right away, or an hour later, two hours later. And there needs to be some exchange of forgiveness, understanding, and an ending to the day at *some* point — fixing a cup of tea or coffee or a milk shake or apple juice and cookies or toast and sitting down together to talk, or read a book or play a game of checkers, and going to bed together.

Why bother? Because is it *not* letting big things grow out of little things which is important in keeping an environment of togetherness. The anger, sharp words, outbursts, frustrated feelings, and swift wave of wanting some sort of revenge may boil over like cream of chicken soup all over the stove, lifting the lid and making a mess of brown ugliness all over the sides of the pan and the stove. Just as with the icky mess of soup — the need is to take a deep breath and plunge in to clean up. As a Christian, at some point one says, "I'm sorry, Lord. I wanted to be the kind of person Your Word tells me to be, always giving a soft answer to turn away wrath, always being willing to wash people's feet, always being willing to serve. Now I've made a mess of it. Please help me. Help me to put my pride aside and be the one to say I am sorry, even though I would rather that the *other* person or persons would take the initiative and make *me* some tea and toast!" Yes, as a Christian, somewhere along the line we talk honestly to the Lord and ask for His help. But the basic resolve to consider the total relationship of husband and wife through the years and the total relationship of the family as an environment for growing new people, children, and grandchildren is more important than any one incident, more important than human words can express. Over and over again, *someone* in a relationship needs to consider. the family as a career, a project, serious enough to be willing to be the one to "scramble up over jagged rocks to feed the birds, so that they won't become extinct." The family is even more important than rare species of birds, and taking on the career of being a mother and wife is a fabulously rare lifework in the twentieth century, and a very challenging job. A wasted effort? A thankless job? An undignified slave? No, a most exciting possibility of turning the tide, of saving the species, of affecting history, of doing something that will be *felt* and *heard* in ever-widening circles.

One family? "How ridiculous," you may think. How can one family affect anything? One person battling away to put selfish interests aside, to put other people before herself or himself, even for a fraction of time, day by day, how could that help?

Adam and Eve were one couple, one family. Eve was one woman rebelling against the Word of God, choosing to believe Satan's word as true. What a result! Noah and his wife and his married children were one family after the Flood — one family at that time who had believed God and were given the opportunity to start with a fresh world, to bring children into an environment of knowing and believing true truth about God. Abraham was given a promise that from his one family, actually from one son, Isaac, the generations of people who would follow would be born of Abraham's seed one day in the future. The family into which the Second

Person of the Trinity was born, fulfilling the promise to Abraham, was one little family. Mary was one young Jewish virgin, who experienced the unique Virgin Birth as the Messiah came forth. But the Messiah, Jesus Christ, was born as a baby in a family environment, with Joseph and Mary and later other brothers and sisters with whom to relate in childhood. The family was real, not artificial, but an ordinary family of believers in the Living God, willing to do His will in this unusual task, but opening their home to the Son of God for all those years of daily life in His human growing-up years, along with the children born later. A daily interrelationship involving all kinds of work, sacrifice, financial sharing, compassion, love, and understanding took place in that one family.

One family and the children of that family can do marvelous things to affect the world or devastating things to destroy it. Hitler was one man born in one family. We could use many contrasting examples to emphasize that the old-fashioned saying "The hand that rocks the cradle, rocks the world" is not just a group of quaint, idiotic, romantic words —it just happens that they are true. The problem today is that people want to have computers rock the cradles, institutions take over from that point on, and have no human influence involved at all. What career is so important as to allow the family to become extinct? The family which has continuity for not just one lifetime, but for generations, gives solidity and security and environment that cannot be duplicated and which spreads in a wide circle.

Who can make the family a career? The natural person provided with the attributes for that is the woman. The mother, who brings forth the child and can feed it for a year at her breasts, is versatile in the fantastic diversity of talents she can develop. In the rest of the book will be unfolded some of the variety in this career, and the excitement of the challenge in pioneering in an age when women are in danger of becoming extinct in the drive to be neuter. To be a mother and homemaker and an environmental expert in designing a place for the particular blend of people which will be your family — to grow and develop — is an amazing possibility. To be at the same time a wife and a companion, an interesting, growing, changing, developing person in the eyes of the man you married — not for just two years nor twelve nor twenty nor thirty, but forty and fifty years — is an added portion of this career.

The family is the environment in which a human being may develop as he or she should. But the mother-wife is a big part of the environment, and the husband will be affected by her environment, even as the children will. What about the intereffect upon each other? Right! Not one of the five or six people will be the same as they would have been without each other. What a responsibility for each person in the years during which they will be each other's environment! Will each one be perfect for each other? Of course not. But the humanness of the situation — the mistakes, the faults, the weaknesses, the times of recognizing the mistakes and being sorry, the imaginative "love offerings," the awkward attempts to communicate and to explore the reality of changing ideas and opinions — will give what the human being needs. Sterile air is not healthy to breathe for a body in a normal state; fresh outdoor air (with some germs in it as well as sunshine) is better, we are told. The psychological, emotional, spiritual, intellectual air, imperfect though it may be, of a family really attempting to live as a family and to stop looking for perfection elsewhere, will provide not only what is needed for a baby to grow, but for an adult as well.

Human adults make such stupid mistakes in spending a lifetime chasing rainbows. They chase an elusive thing called "happiness" which they have vague daydreams about and picture in unrealistic ways, while wasting what they *could* have had if they had spent time and imagination and work and all their talents in developing what they did have to start with. Amazing things can be made by some people out of raw material, while others are throwing away as "junk" the same material, always looking for a more perfect starting material before they begin. Given the same length of time, the longer one waits and searches before starting, the more impossible it will be to build, carve, design, produce in the time that is left! This is true of any art project, any creative work, and true of the family!

Reports are coming to us now, through all kinds of news magazines, which tell of the failure of the "swinging couples." Failure in what way? Well, we are told, it "just doesn't work." It is said that "energy and interest wear out, and it all becomes boring." There is a thought that working out some way of more lasting relationships which include more than sex, might help out! The same thing is taking place among young people who try to live totally promiscuously and find that somehow nervous breakdowns result from having no security in more complete relationships. It seems that discoveries are being made that there is more to a human being becoming fulfilled by another human being than just the physical satisfaction of a momentary oneness. Adult humans need the shelter of another human being — intellectually, spiritually, emotionally, psychologically in a lasting way — as well as needing the shelter of the arms of another human being. A child needs the shelter of a parent's lap and arms, but also the shelter of communication and understanding. A family is needed by the adult as well as the child.

Confusion exists among many girls today because of some of the things put forth by the women's-liberation movement. There are girls who fear that they are giving in to a weakness if they show longing or interest in being mothers and homemakers. There are others who, already married, have become so "turned around" that right seems wrong, and wrong seems right, and they feel that a split in the home is what they must head for if they are going to be really liberated and free. As a result, homes that were once secure are breaking and shattering. Saddest of all is the knowledge, from an understanding of *true truth,* that God has made man and woman as people with capacities and needs for a continuity in relationships, and that life is all too short anyway, so that a terrible loneliness is ahead for people who have torn up their homes with their own hands. Armand Nicolai has recently said that the number-one mental health problem is resulting from the effects of certain women's-lib teachings among married girls. The reaction to be felt is not one of "shock" in the sense of condemnation, but of sorrow that such unnecessary suffering is being inflicted upon people who are trying to twist themselves out of the reality of *who they really are,* and who are trying to plunge themselves into an alien environment which is all out of ecological balance for them.

A family — parents and grandparents and children, the larger combination of three or four generations, or one little two-generation family — is meant to be a picture of what God is to His Family. "Hear my cry, O God; attend unto my prayer. From the end of the earth will I cry unto thee, when my heart is overwhelmed. Lead me to the rock that is higher than I. For thou hast been a shelter for me, and a strong tower from the enemy" (Psalms 61:1–3). Our earthly family should be the ones to whom we want to run, cry, telephone, telegraph — when we feel overwhelmed by failure! An earthly family is meant to be a shelter, a solid, dependable "ear" that will hear and understand, as well as a place to which to run. Then this family, these parents, this father and mother are to make clear to their children the understanding of the faithfulness of God. We should be able to say, "You know something of the way we love you. You can always come to us in any kind of trouble. You will always find forgiveness and understanding and help. Yet we are nothing in comparison to God, our Heavenly Father whose faithfulness is *perfect* compared to our imperfection."

The concept of *parents* should not split a child at any point in his or her history. To have to choose whom to call, because they are not together, is a shattering decision to have to make. *Home* and *family* are "togetherness" words with a connotation of oneness, the environment into which the first baby was born, and each baby should be born.

Happily, there *is* a Perfect Family, a completely "one" Family, and a home that is waiting for each member of that Family, where the environment will be without flaw for all

eternity. "I go to prepare a place for you . . . that where I
am, there ye may be also," says Jesus the Bridegroom to each
one who has become a part of His bride through accepting
Him as Saviour (*see* John 14:2, 3). "In my Father's house
are many mansions . . ." (v. 2). There is a home ahead, for
each one of the children of the Lord who have been born
into His Family. We are told that "God is not ashamed to
be called their God: for he hath prepared for them a city"
(*see* Hebrews 11:16). God is not ashamed to be called the
God of those who have suffered all kinds of illnesses, persecu-
tions, imbalances of the abnormal universe, and improper
environment bringing sorrows as well as the agonies of martyrdom, *because* He has prepared a city which is real and
forever. That makes it possible for Him to say that the suf-
ferings of this present time are not to be compared with the
glories that are ahead. By comparison, the present is but a
moment.

We have a home ahead and we have something to be certain about when we tell homeless people this good news,
whether they are street urchins or neglected old people. There
*is* a Family — with a Heavenly Father to whom they may
belong and where they may go — into which birth is by
choice. However, if we have time left in the land of the living
and any opportunity at all, we should make a resolve, God
helping us, to make our human family as close as possible
to what it should be. Or if we have no mother or father, sister or brother, aunt or uncle, grandmother or grandfather,
niece or nephew, husband or wife, child or grandchild, then
we should "adopt" others who have no family. Our concern
and compassion, interest and care, cards, letters, flowers,
gifts, and prayers can be a help in producing a "family environment" for them.

If ever a "movement" were needed, it is a movement to
reestablish real family life. As one can imagine the world
becoming a dry desert devoid of plant life because of ecological imbalances, one can also imagine families shriveling up
and leaving a desert, too, as far as human personalities are

concerned. Any one family is an oasis. A springing up of many green spots in the desert is needed, at the cost of people putting other people before their own search for happiness. The mere existence of an oasis is important to the traveler in a desert. The mere existence of a family, even a widely scattered family, is important to people — even from the viewpoint of being aware of what they have *not* had.

There are artificial fruit flavors to be added to water to make a drink, but never to have experienced the flavor of real orange juice, rich grape juice, fresh pineapple juice, tree-ripened grapefruit juice, is to have absolutely no basis of judgment as to the deviation from what is being imitated. As conservationists set forth to educate the world (whatever section of it they can reach with their books, articles, broadcasts), people also need to be filled with some sort of strong drive to have a family life no matter how much work and sacrifice it may take, to demonstrate what it is that is being lost!

A living, growing, changing *real* family is as thoroughly an ecological demonstration of what human beings thrive in as any "experimental farm." It is as noble a career as can be entered in the ecological field! Profession? "Housewife." No! "Ecologist" — in the most important area of conservation — the family.

# 3

## The Birthplace of Creativity

God created. The Personal God who has always existed has always been creative. The evidence of His creativity we are able to see, day by day, all of our lives. We did not hear His stars which sang together eons of time ago, but we do hear the variety of notes in birdsongs in almost original beauty in woods, jungles, along lakeshores and mountain streams, and then we hear them copied in wind and string instruments. We have never seen His unspoiled planets and stars, moon and sun, mountains and seas, flowers and trees. But the leftover beauty which we *do* have in these creations of God is all that our own spoiled nervous system can stand — more than the most beautiful sunrise over the hills, and the full moon lighting snow-covered mountains. More than whatever was the height of beauty in our own experience would be *too much,* until our capacity is restored and made perfect.

God made man in His own image, in the image of the Creator made God man, with the capacity to create, and also the capacity to enjoy and respond to Creation — God's Creation — and the horizontal response to the creations of other human beings.

"Let us make man in our image" (*see* Genesis 1:26). The plural speaks of the Triune God who brought man into a universe in which there were Three to appreciate man's first creative acts, as well as the angelic hosts. The Father, Son, and Holy Spirit provided the audience for man's naming of the animals. "And whatsoever Adam called every living creature, that was the name thereof. And Adam gave names to all . . ." (*See* Genesis 2:19, 20). It seems to me that the naming of the animals was the first opportunity for poetry and prose. What imagination could be fulfilled in choosing poetic, humorous, lyrical, diverse, descriptive names for the animals! "And the Lord God took the man, and put him into the garden of Eden to dress it and to keep it" (v. 15). What a scope, limited only by the limits of Adam's finite yet-unspoiled imagination, intelligence, and creativity, as he was given the perfect and fantastic array of plants, trees, grasses and mosses, flowers and leafy ferns, fruits, berries, and vegetables to develop his horticultural and landscape artist's capacities. And there was an inspiring possibility of communication with the Creator who would appreciate and comment on what had been done, with personal response and attention.

Yes, creativity was born in a family setting with a perfect environment — vertically in the relationship between God and human beings, and horizontally between man and wife. Into this setting the way was prepared for new human beings to be born, and for diverse, creative people to come forth, begin to create, and to influence each other.

Freedom of choice, an absolute necessity for creativity, was there from the beginning. Being able to think, have ideas, and then to choose to make or do something, is essential to creativity. Choice is not only involved in taking raw material and making something else out of it, but in *choosing* to run, instead of walk, in *deciding* to leap and twirl as a talented ballet dancer can do, instead of simply running. Adam and Eve, being created perfect, would physically have been able to dance and leap in amazingly beautiful, unhindered movement in the Garden of Eden, as part of their expression of sheer joy. They had been given choice so that creativity, from the very first, could take many directions.

After the Fall, when Adam and Eve chose to believe Satan's lie, denying what God's Word had been to them, their choices were never again *all* right in any area. Nor have the choices of their children nor their children's children been *all* good, down through the centuries of mankind. Creativity can be constructive, and take what "is" and cause something new to spring forth which will be fulfilling and helpful and give birth to more beauty, to fresh ideas in another person or persons. Or it can be destructive and have a destructive influence upon other people.

God who is perfect — perfect love, perfect justice, perfect goodness, perfect wisdom, perfect holiness — also created perfectly all that He created. But angels and human beings were created with choice, and some angels followed Lucifer and others remained loyal to God. The choice in creativity goes in one direction or another, in that individual creative works can be constructive or destructive.

Constructive creativity not only affects other human beings, but brings glory to God by being in the stream of His creativity. Creative works which blend with the real universe, whether made by men who are in communication with God or not, are fulfilling what God gave man capacity to create. Cain and Abel had creative ideas in building altars in an arrangement of some special pattern of selected stones. Cain had a creative idea in arranging all his fruits and vegetables on his altar, but Cain's creative act was a destructive one. Why? Because the arrangement was not beautiful? No, because he was defying what was the given way of coming to God, through the lamb. Beauty as contrasted with ugliness is not a criterion for judging as to whether a creative work is destructive or constructive. A very beautiful work of art can be totally destructive in its effect, and in leading a stream of people to take a defiant position, denying truth. It really is important to understand that creativity is marvelous, but can also be terrible. The choice involved and freedom needed for bringing forth art, music, literature, architecture, scientific projects, and so on, means that the results will affect other human beings and influence them, at times without their knowing how powerfully they are being influenced. If God really exists, there is an absolute truth. Therefore, creative expression which denies God's existence, and denies that there is an absolute, and denies truth and even the existence of truth, denies His Creation — and is destructive creativity.

Destruction has been Satan's aim for himself and any man he can influence. Human beings can destroy other human beings by their destructive creative acts, even as Satan destroys. In a certain sense, artworks can "kill" more thoroughly than bombs! Certain kinds of architecture can rule out the possibility of family life, as cleverly as certain kinds of history books can rule out the possibility of even searching for God. Influence can be in two directions. Atmosphere and environment for creativity can affect people in either direction.

The family should be the place where each new human being can have an early atmosphere conducive to the development of constructive creativity. Parents, aunts and uncles, grandparents, and sisters and brothers can squash, stamp out, ridicule, and demolish the first attempts at creativity, and continue this demolition long enough to cripple spontaneous outbursts of creation. These things can take place carelessly, and we might be astonished at what we have unconsciously spoiled.

There is a double responsibility, therefore, in being a family, in being the birthplace for creativity. First, there is the need to be aware of the fact that creativity can be either destructive or constructive. Second, there is the need to be aware of the conscious preparation of the seedbed for the first seeds of creativity to sprout. Creativity needs the right atmosphere and encouragement. Naturally, heredity has a part in who comes forth from a family. One cannot expect a child to be a Mozart just by playing symphonies on the record player and having wonderful instruments in the music room. Nevertheless, the atmosphere or seedbed has a great deal to do with the growth of a person, even as with a plant!

Given a tiny new human being, how can you know what encouragement to give? Is this a musician, painter, writer, mathematician, or zoologist who will do something magnificent in one of these areas, given the right beginning? The knowledge of what talents lie within the seed is hidden, but an atmosphere can be conducive to developing in many directions, until later one or another becomes obvious as some special talent. The environment in a family should be conducive to the commencement of natural creativity, as natural as breathing, eating, and sleeping. A balanced, creative person can come forth, developing and branching out in a wide number of areas, if some amounts of imagination and care are used. The first requirement is a dignity of attitude toward the family. This dignity involves accepting the seriousness and excitement of having your own home be a very specific creativity center. Given one, two, three, or more new little beings, one at a time, adopted or born to you, you have an opportunity to develop a growing, changing, constantly better environment for budding and blossoming creativity.

Does it take two people, each contributing 50 percent to this project to achieve results? No, there is no perfect balance of fifty-fifty in any human relationships, not even in business offices and school faculties, let alone in marriages and families. Someone will have to put in a larger percentage, perhaps 99 percent in the beginning, although a shared interest and determination is always better than a lopsided one. It is good to realize, however, that someone has to have time to give to this. A creativity center doesn't just spring forth with one day's work. There is a need for developing ideas, fresh new starts, trying again with a different set of things, and so on. An effort on the part of one can inspire the other adult involved into giving time, too, and also inspire some ideas. If a wife has been doing 99 percent of arranging creative projects, and the husband suddenly has a new idea, the danger is in squashing the idea just because of the unfair balance — and destroying *his* first "sprout."

The family as a creative birthplace is not just a statement that the family is the place where *children* should have their first acts of creativity inspired. The family should be the birthplace of the wife's creativity and the husband's creativity, encouraged by each other, by the children as they get old enough to encourage their parents, by sisters and brothers, aunts and uncles. All too often, when a baby takes its first step, there is a burst of laughter that practically knocks him down, and fear to try again hinders for a length of time. This can be true of any first step in cooking, gardening, drawing, carpentry work, making a mud pie, playing a piano or recorder, making a rag doll, sewing, making a lamp or whatever. Whether it is a tiny child's first creative effort or an adult's timid beginning of something new, that first step can be turned into a full stop because of the very wrong kind of reaction on the part of others. It is important to be aware of what is needed to encourage creativity, and what is to be avoided which might squash it altogether or at least for a long time.

Just what *is* needed? An atmosphere of two-way communication, which involves listening as well as talking, and taking an interest in the other person's thoughts and ideas. A mutual trust is built up in carefully listening to even the wildest and the most impossible-sounding projects. If the response is always, "Oh, that's impossible," then the communication doesn't continue. A person, even a five-year-old, gets discouraged in setting forth an idea if it is immediately ruled out, and if the ideas continue, they will be taken to somebody else outside the family!

"I'm going to make a raft!" — "Really? What are you going to use to make it?" — "This wood, see? I found it in the woodshed. Please?" — "Well, okay, go ahead and try, and then you can see if it will float." The six-year-old boy will work all afternoon, getting what help he can commandeer. Perhaps you can make a sail for him, if that seems to be the encouragement he needs. The crooked pile of sticks will sink, if there is any water to try it on, or perhaps float for a few moments, but it can be a marvelous raft with a sail right there in the garden, and a meal can be supplied to eat "on board." The very trust inspired by the cooperation and serious treatment of the project can pay off, not only in more creative attempts, but in a closer relationship. Now, if boat making continues to be his interest, the cooperation may include buying some books on the subject, or getting information as to what are the basic things to be understood. Perhaps the interest will switch to making a tree house, and then the father's help will be an important part of the work. Discouragement can come in attempting something too "impossible," yet to stop the project altogether is more discouraging. There is needed a shift in direction, some help in achieving at least a partial result of what was aimed at without any variation of saying, "I told you it wouldn't work." If indeed it does not work, a plan to divert the disappointment with some special treat, a hot-dog roast in the garden, a special day off together, a longer story that night — whatever scale of diversion is needed — is helpful in not allowing the disappointment to "kill something." Soon a new idea will come tumbling out from the child's lips, if he or she knows the failure won't be rubbed in or laughed about.

An atmosphere of trust brings forth a sharing of ideas and an attempt to make things, with an expectation that the most wonderful thing is just about to come forth. This atmosphere comes if the basic attitude is one which takes mistakes and fresh attempts as quite expected. "That parachute [a cloth tied in four knots with a rag doll descending from the balcony rail] isn't letting her down very well. Ooops! But I'm sure the kite will work well if we put a bit more tail on it."

If creative projects are to follow one after another, there must be a balance in priorities. A clean and orderly house is a joy to everyone, yet there is a need to be sensitive to the greater importance of freedom to paint, mix clay, scatter pieces of cloth in cutting out a dress or a sail. The possibility of getting soil on a waxed floor is suddenly far less important than the wonder of a tiny box with an exciting mist of green showing that the plants are coming up. Cotton stuffing for a wobbly sewn cotton or wool animal can be in danger of scattering wisps of fluff all over the couch, but there is a moment when the four-year-old's help in pushing in the cotton for the eight-year-old's elephant must be recognized as as a high point in her day. The priorities mustn't get mixed up. An atmosphere conducive to creativity must be one of respect for the young (or old) artist — however talented or clumsy the attempt has been — respect for the need for making a mess!

Creativity needs an audience, some appreciation, the response of another human being, as well as the freedom to be accomplished and some raw materials to work with. It may be easy enough to hang up the drawings and paintings of a small child, to make a shelf for the early rough shapes formed in Plasticine or clay, or to provide a temporary museum for the collection of shells, stones, leaves, butterflies or bugs, stamps or buttons. However, to stop your work and be an audience may seem a nuisance or just too inconvenient. Again comes the "balance" which will be referred to all through this book, the importance of recognizing an important moment when you see it. Be sensitive to the need of bringing your phone conversation to a close, putting your book aside, deciding to do an easier dessert for supper, stopping your cleaning chores. With perhaps some knitting in your hand, come and sit down to watch the "all-important" circus, wedding, play, concert, set of magic tricks, reading of an original book, replay of an event in history! No matter how clumsy the production is, this long-planned or suddenly-put-together event of two or three or four (or just one child) needs an audience and appreciation and reaction.

Creativity needs the availability of reaching the attention of a sympathetic friend at just the right moment. This is true in the budding of creativity in an early childhood moment, but it is just as true in the serious creativity of a genius. Someone needs to come and watch, listen, look, *respond*. If there is helpful criticism to be given, the first flush of excited completion of a work is not the moment to give it.

A good rule to remember (whether you are dealing with a three-year-old person, a thirty-three-year-old, or a sixty-three-year-old) is that right after the baby song, play, picture has been presented, right after the mature painting, lecture, music has been introduced, right after you have read the most important book chapter, heard the sermon, listened to the cello solo, looked at the statue — anything you say must be positive. The human being looking for understanding needs to find it at this moment. The need for sharing what has been exciting in bringing this forth — whatever *this* is — needs response. The spark must meet another spark, or the fire dies out and dark discouragement can flood in.

Discussion, constructive criticism, presentation of some thoughts on what has been done, cannot be given to anyone at the wrong moment. The right moment comes later. If a family is to be a birthplace for creativity, there must be some practical attention given to not repeating mistakes in this area. Of course mistakes will be made, and sometimes the response will be wrong, but it is good to know what has brought about the slammed door, the running upstairs or out of doors, the disgusted "You *never* will understand" that bursts forth. It is good to know what to avoid the next time. The right response is central in importance in encouraging the next step of growth.

The inspiration of freedom, communication, and trust needs also the *example* of adult creativity within the family. Each parent should be "doing his own thing" in music, painting, dressmaking, tailoring, furniture making, curtain making, the sewing of bits of leftover pieces together to make quilts, writing, flower-and-vegetable gardening, producing of a fantastic garden in a huge bottle, wood carving, metalwork, writing, weaving, making rush-bottom seats for old chairs, needlepoint, baking bread, making Indian and Chinese meals, branching out in all sorts of fresh ways of cooking as an art, making puppets, and so forth (with a list too long to write).

However, there should also be an example of how the creativity can be a way of expressing love within the family, father to mother, as well as parent to child. The children will soon be following examples of not only saying, "I love you," but making something with love all sewn up in it or painted on it or arranged in flower patterns!

Thoughtfulness expressed in shining the silver on a gray Sunday afternoon to make a tea wagon of sandwiches and tea a thing of special beauty, or the family never forgetting the arrangement of ivy, flowers, a wee plant, or a tiny fish-bowl as a centerpiece for the tea table, can be a very early lesson in creating an atmosphere of special preparation for each other's "down" days. "Why are you making the teapot and pitcher and those spoons so shiny?" comes the four-year-old's question. "Oh, because it is so gray outside and Sunday tea will be more like a sunset time without the sunset if we have this shininess to reflect the candles. Look, Jessica, can you see the flames in the teapot? Daddy and Av [the Hebrew name for *father* which her grandfather likes to be called] will feel more cheerful with all the shininess and candles, don't you think?" Then the little sandwiches, with as much variety and care as if a wedding party were being served, are made and cut in dainty shapes and placed out on the table, while the child dances in pleasure and rolls over a stool in sheer joy, calling out, "Tea is ready, Sunday tea — and I just love Sunday tea."

Simple gestures of thoughtfulness bring forth natural and spontaneous creative acts on the part of little human beings growing up where these things are a part of everyday life — the norm. Beauty should be important as an inspiration to doing the best with what is at hand for the Christian home-maker. God put the first family in inspiring surroundings. As much as possible, each new family (no matter what deprivation or squalor either or both parents may have known in their own childhood) — which has become a family of two children of the Living God — should prepare a home with as much to inspire as possible. The Garden of Eden can't be duplicated, but that was God's choice place to put the first family. Plastic and tawdry and tinselly things which are far from God's Creation do not provide a conducive atmosphere for understanding and appreciating real beauty. What is *good taste*? This is as controversial a question as "What is good art?" But allowing for differences in taste, "Something that fits in with the real universe," seems one standard that could be a help. Real wood, linen, wool, cotton, silk, metals and stone, living plants, trees, bushes, fish, flowers — all these need to be included in whatever measure is possible in the twentieth century. Handmade things of all sorts — hand-thrown pottery, handwoven cloth, crocheted or knitted things, carved wood, objects made personally by the family or friends — not only make a difference in atmosphere, but present the idea that it is possible to make things. Expensive equipment for making things is out of reach for most individuals and families, but the realization that the most beautiful things can be made by *hand* should come very early in life and should come from within the family.

A bracket should be put in here to say that some families and some homes are like cement prisons or boxed-in places without air, as far as creativity is concerned, and some of the people of genius in the world's history have been inspired by people outside of the family. Thus, only when escaping from the family and being taken in by understanding people, has their creativity burst forth from the "dormant seed." However, this is not what a Christian family should ever be. The austere, barren atmosphere of hard benches, ready whips, dominant, crushing authority, bare tables, lack of pleasant food, and an attitude of harshness towards creativity (as if it were all a frivolous waste of time) is not what the Bible has shown.

Does the Bible rule out creativity as an unspiritual thing? Think of all of the marvelous things which God commanded to be made for the tabernacle, and for the Temple. The exact directions given to Moses for the tabernacle, and to Solomon for the Temple, included fantastic artworks — and meant that people needed to have the creative skills to produce these things. It should not surprise us to read of the wonderful embroidery, silverwork, pure gold candlesticks, and bowls in these metals made with marvelous designs of almonds, with branches and flowers specified in the design. Someone had to weave the fine linen. Someone had to embroider with the "cunning work" described as showing the cherubims in a tapestry form. Someone made the veil for the Temple. Someone made the wonderful robes for the priests. Beauty, as well as spiritual meaning, was combined in God's given pattern. This is not the place to discuss the artwork of the Bible, but only to remind us that families were involved in this creative work. Fathers and mothers taught sons and daughters and inspired them as the children watched the artwork. Their tents and homes simply had to be the birthplaces of creativity as these skills were handed down and copied. God's House was to be made beautiful; the building took place among the families involved and gave them scope for creativity.

Is the family a utopia? Not in a fallen world. Can there be perfection of beauty and perfection of atmosphere for creative work? *No!* Interruptions, frustrations, misunderstandings — the hindering of each other's work takes place in every family. But the togetherness in projects is more important than the perfectly protected place for each individual's work. Some kinds of work in creative areas need a studio with the right light, a room without noise, a darkroom, a room without dust, protection from interruption "until the tape is made" or "until the surprise is ready." However, with the use of imagination and originality there are things that can be done *with* each other as well as *for* each other. There is simply not enough time in life for all the combinations and possibilities to be accomplished.

It cannot be said too frequently that *no family situation is static*. The creative possibilities will be different five years from now for any family. The ideas and projects of growing children soon become the ideas and projects of teenagers and then of adults and later families. By that time you have three generations inspiring each other, discussing ideas, swapping skills, stimulating each other. No individual stands still, and no blend remains the same. Something is lost as an older couple is alone in a house, and no stimulation comes from younger, more energetic ideas. But something is gained in having freedom to do things that have been put off before.

I know of a seventy-five-year-old man who is making a set of needlework chair seats for some wonderful antique chairs he inherited. When the needlework gets tedious he practises his violin or goes out for a run on his cross-country skis. Retirement from business or law or insurance or farm work does not have to mean retirement from creativity. The creativity born in a family setting can continue as long as there is strength to do anything at all.

Who can know — as they walk away from each other, smashing their families into splinters, making a search for personal happiness the basic drive in life — what balanced, creative people who "might have been" have been squashed and stepped on and turned into uncertain, fearful, bitter ones who will need much help before their creativity will come forth? The children? Yes, but the danger is to the parents as well.

People feel a drive to "do something for society," to undertake huge projects — having been liberated from the "limitations" of their homes and families. What society needs more than anything else is a glimpse through a window into the family life of people who are becoming creative in amazingly diverse ways and who haven't time to be bored. The natural sequence is a spilling over into a wider area affecting other people, even without meaning to do so.

"What are you?" — "Just a housewife." *No!* "What are you?" — "I'm involved in a co-op of creativity called a family."

"What are you?" — "Just an office worker." *No!* "What are you?" — "I'm a father involved in an amazing co-op of creativity known as a family."

Form, freedom, unity, diversity — demonstrated in original ways! What a real challenge for the immediate moment.

# 4

## A Formation Center for Human Relationships

"She is head of the personnel department of that large company." — "He is really tops in the public relations affairs of the country." — "That ambassador is a born diplomat." — "The president of that company knows how to handle people." — "You can't imagine the delicate balance that rests in the understanding which that newspaperman has in dealing with people." — "He is more than surgeon-in-chief; that man's way of treating people is the key to the whole atmosphere of that hospital!" — "You may not know the name, but that person has more effect on people than anyone in the Pentagon — just a way of treating each as significant." — "Sounds strange, perhaps, but my day is *made* if I get on the bus with a certain ticket taker. It's hard to explain, but the smile and little remark that goes with the punch of the hole in the ticket changes my whole attitude towards the day."

*Human relations. Public relations.* Are these subjects to be taken for a semester in some college or university in preparation for certain jobs? Who needs to know how to get along with people, deal with people, work with people, handle people? Presidents? Secretaries of State? Ambassadors? Generals? Heads of departments? Doctors? Lawyers? Judges? Teachers? Professors? News editors? A list of important world leaders who need to know a lot about human relationships would be long, indeed. However, as one thinks a bit longer, what coal miner, ditchdigger, street sweeper, or employee at the so-called bottom of the scale is not having some sort of relationship with other human beings — day by day in work, as well as day by day wherever each one lives? What clerk in a grocery store, waiter in a restaurant, and janitor scrubbing the hall floor in a hotel or office building is not having an effect on other people?

Human relationships are taking place whether or not anyone stops to label them. Good or bad human relationships and constructive or destructive human relationships take place at every level of life. Whether people treat people as human beings or machines, people are treating people in *some* way. Whether people treat everyone as having importance, dignity, significance, or whether people treat others on a sliding scale of importance — everyone is reacting to other people in some way. Human relationships start at birth and continue to death, whether or not anyone consciously thinks about it. Adults have been teaching children lessons of how to treat other people, in devastatingly horrible ways or in biblically right ways, whether or not they have ever thought of themselves as teachers. Teaching takes place by example, every minute of every day for every new human being, by whoever is with that baby human being — hour after hour, day after day, month after month.

We carefully select music teachers, art teachers, math teachers, skating teachers, horseback-riding teachers, or cooking teachers for our children, and forget that, in addition to whatever else is being taught, baby-sitters, day-care centers, and everyone else with whom we are placing our children are teaching the whole basic idea of human relationships. Should we hurry and start classes, organize seminars, and add the subject of human relationships to the curriculum? It's not that easy. You and I and no one else can shove it off.

Where should the formation center for human relationships be? Should there be a camp, a conference, a set of tapes placed in a centrally located room to teach the basics of human relationships? As one reads the daily newspapers giving blood-curdling stories of how human beings treat each other, do we wonder what the cruel ones at age thirteen, thirty-three, or fifty-three were seeing at *three?*

It seems to me that this is a very important answer to the question "What is a family?" *A family is a formation center for human relationships.* The family is the place where the deep understanding that people are significant, important, worthwhile, with a purpose in life, should be learned at an early age. The family is the place where children should learn that human beings have been made in the image of God and are therefore very special in the universe. In other words, one is not simply to sit with a set of sentences to teach by rote memory, while every action and example is denying the words.

The sets of words to be taught should be the true Word of God. The Bible tells of the things which children should be learning at an early age in order to find out how human beings are to treat other human beings — whether they are in the personal family, in God's Family, friends, neighbors, or are enemies. God gives every basic teaching, and guidance by example is supposed to be in line with what the Bible teaches. Can parents be perfect? Of course not. Can grand-parents be perfect? Of course not. Can brothers and sisters be perfect? Of course not. Can aunts and uncles be perfect? Of course not. Children should learn very early that we are all sinners and we all fall into times of misbehaving. They should know that adults don't carry out what they should, in keeping with what the Bible teaches them to have as a basic rule of behavior. Children should know that mistakes are made and that parents fall into sin at times. Apologies should be made to small children by parents. The under-standing of what an apology is and what forgiveness is should be a two-way street from the very beginning.

Pretending perfection immediately teaches falseness and rationalization of mistakes as the very first lessons taught.

The biblical teachings should be given and discussed with day-by-day pointing out of where one or another teaching can be practical, and where we may have acted contrary to the Bible. Reality in the area of difficulties in human relationships must be lived in daily experiences. The importance of "putting first things first" in human relationships should also be experienced together, as well as talked about. The expectation that "tomorrow we'll do better" lends an important atmosphere, even though we need to allow for a repetition of mistakes on our own part and the child's. While making it clear that the understanding of how to deal with and live with human beings takes a lifetime, the fact that progress is to be expected should give a feeling of excitement to the whole relationship within the family, which will naturally spread out beyond the little family to touch other people.

If families were even partially what they should be, dotted all over the world would be some very effective centers for the formation of good human relationships. The drive for restoring families which have continuity through generations of togetherness is a drive for doing something basic about the whole problem of human relationships. The solution to a fight, argument, difference of opinion, unthoughtfulness on the part of another person, unfair treatment, selfishness, egoism, disregard for another person's rights, is *not* splitting up and finding other human beings to live with, but understanding must be taught, time after time, through seeking to find solutions which are not perfect, but which are *possible*. Someone must be challenged to pray, or to plan something really lovely as a surprise (or to pray for an idea and then prepare the surprise), even before the disagreeable situation has come to an end. The reaction of "I wonder what would help to change this!" and expecting an idea, and recognizing the creativity involved in the area of human relationships must take place on the part of at least one person involved! The realization that this (whatever *this* is) is not the end of all things, should be a growing, deepening realization which begins in childhood during the diversity of demonstrations of a flowing number of solutions to difficulties which are always changing and popping up to spoil things!

Elizabee and Becky had a precious forty-five minutes at home each school day. The bus deposited them at the foot of the hill, and they ran breathless up the dirt road to get into the chalet kitchen for lunch, to be met with shouts of welcome from little brother, Giandy. Priscilla felt this forty-five minutes was the central family time of the day, dividing the long day at school with not only food, but real communication. As mother of the family she felt it was her part to go to tremendous lengths to have the meal ready and everything in order for a special time together.

Pris's morning work is to teach a group of nursery-school children in her kitchen, which is also the only dining room. Her part of *L'Abri* work in the mornings is to have games, songs, finger painting, and a great variety of lessons for the preschool-age children of the many other *L'Abri* Workers. In this tiny Swiss Alpine chalet kitchen the scene changes several times a day. Often the evening meal is made up of twenty-five people, so that the forty-five minutes alone as a family is central in importance.

Imagine Priscilla's preparation for the forty-five minutes. Early in the morning a casserole is made, noodles and tuna fish, macaroni and cheese, shepherd's pie, ravioli. Lettuce is washed and put away, or cabbage cut up for cole slaw. Jell-O is made for dessert, apples washed, or cookies baked and tucked away. At great cost in energy and efficiency, the meal is ready *before* the nursery-school children troop in — to cut scraps of paper all over the table and floor, get finger paint on chairs and table oilcloth, scatter toys, paper dolls, blocks, and puzzles all over the place. The last coat has been buttoned up, the last pair of boots pulled on, the toys picked up, the paper scraps put away, the finger paint wiped off, the table set, the oven turned on, the water poured, a candle lit in the table's center, and the scene is set. There are lovely smells issuing from the oven, and a good measure of calm order, as if all Mother had to think about was the arrival of two eager little schoolgirls.

What picture did Pris have in her imagination? All this order and pleasant food, with the girls' arrival followed immediately by Daddy's arrival, and forty-five unbroken minutes of family togetherness. Time to eat. Time to hear of school problems or pleasures. Time to exhange ideas. Time to read for a few minutes from a book. Forty-five minutes full of family togetherness. It must be unspoiled. It must be complete. It must be perfect. What actually was happening — day by day, week by week? Disappointment — time after time. Self-pity, fury, and frustration were being expressed in different ways, minute after precious minute. "Where is Daddy? Why doesn't he come?" — "How can he be so thoughtless? He knows when the bus comes and you have to go — This is just impossible, it makes me so sick — I'm furious, the food is all getting cold!" Interspersed between other bits of conversation would run the refrain of disappointed expectations for thirty or so minutes before John would appear. John is a busy person with an incredible number of interruptions added to his morning schedule. An amazing number of people ask him questions or stop him on his way home for lunch. When he would finally come to the door of the kitchen, three pairs of children's eyes looked at him with varying degrees of worry, and Pris greeted him with, "You've ruined our time again. There are only ten minutes left before the girls have to catch the bus!" or — "John, you don't care anything about our having a family life. Look at all I do to get ready for this time and you can't even get here in time to be with us."

Screaming, stamping of feet, tears, frustrations expressed over and over again, using up the precious fifteen minutes left, after the first half hour had already been spoiled by expressions of disappointment and counting of the minutes. Multiply those forty-five minutes by one hundred! Multiply the fifteen minutes by one hundred. What a fantastic amount of wasted time! What possible results could it all bring?

What is of basic importance? What kind of lessons in human relationships are being given to three children in the midst of this? Are they being taught to yell for their "rights," no matter what is destroyed during the yelling?

One day Pris had a talk with the three children and told them she had an idea. The word *idea* ought to have sparkles coming out to set it off, since it was a very special idea which was going to make a difference to all their lives during the next day. Also, it was going to be a lesson endless in its teaching effect. Pris didn't think of this when she shared the surprise with the three children. At the time she told them that it was simply, for her and for them, "a fun idea for a birthday present. I'm going to give Daddy a birthday present, but don't tell him ahead of time. It will be at his place for lunch on this birthday. It is this card which says: YOUR BIRTHDAY GIFT IS THAT FOR TWO MONTHS I WON'T SCOLD OR BE MAD OR SAY A THING WHEN YOU ARE LATE FOR LUNCH." Things changed at lunchtime. Day after day, there was an air of excitement and anticipation. First of all, conversation started on positive lines when lunch started — without Daddy. The promise meant that not only had the birthday been a fun time with a special kind of grin on Daddy's part and happy giggle on Mommy's part when the card had been read, but there was an expectation on the children's part to see how it would all work out. The time spent waiting for Daddy's late arrival (because he continued to be late) was without strain, and the conversation could be about the food, school, news about cousins which had come in letters, the weather report of rain or sun for "tomorrow's afternoon off," the possibility of getting a new hamster, the cat's latest escapade, and so forth. No longer was the waiting time wasted in mounting tension. When the door burst open, the children looked expectantly at Mommy to see whether she would have the "victory" to keep her promise. Would she really say nothing scoldingly, nothing about the time? Would she not even look at her watch? No, Pris said, "Hi, John, did you have a good morning? Becky got a good mark in math. Elizabee

got a ten in her *dicté* today. Here, have some tuna casserole."
The children's happy sighs or little giggles would bubble
over into the already-relaxed atmosphere. Then ten, twelve,
fifteen, or eighteen minutes would be positive ones, special
ones, minutes to be added, day after day, to a string of good
communications as a family.

Did it last for only two months? What is your guess? No,
it gave some very deep and fresh understanding to the reality
of the preciousness of time. Time can never be brought back,
and like money, it is spent one way or another. Once spent
it is gone — except for the memory. Time spent in yelling
for what is not possible means it is lost for the use of what *is*
possible. A principal thing to write in the notebook of our
minds in the area of human relationships is: When people
insist on perfection or nothing, they get nothing. When people
insist on having what they daydream as a perfect relationship, they will end up in having no relationship at all. When
people waste the time they could have — by screaming for
more — they will have no time at all. The waste of what
*could* be, by demanding what *cannot* be, is something we
all have lived through in certain periods of our lives, but
which we need to put behind us with resolve. Perhaps it does
not fit into our circumstances to write such a birthday note
as did Priscilla, but your life and mine is in danger of having
great globs of wrecked periods of time, simply because we
refuse to pay any attention to what God has so carefully
outlined to us in His Word.

Come to the Book of Proverbs: "Better is a dinner of herbs
where love is, than a stalled ox and hatred therewith" (15:
17). "The heart of the wise teacheth his mouth, and addeth
learning to his lips. Pleasant words are as an honeycomb,
sweet to the soul, and health to the bones" (16:23, 24)
What a difference to the whole family, to other people with
whom we are having contact — to all human relationships
— are the words which come forth from us. We can give an
ugly retort in answer to an ugly remark, but "A soft answer

turneth away wrath" (*see* 15:1) tells us what kind of result a pleasant answer will have. Proverbs gives teaching as to the kind of situation one can develop in the formation center for human relationships. Here we have a teaching situation, but a real-life situation at the same time. What opportunity to demonstrate what will happen. Right here, now, when can *pleasant words be as an honeycomb, sweet to the soul, and health to the bones?* When it would be easy to speak unpleasant words. That is when the reality shows up.

The vivid lesson which Pris's children are having concerns the two possible ways of meeting a situation, and the very different results of the two choices. "Pleasant words are as an honeycomb, sweet to the soul, and health to the bones" has a very practical meaning in contrasting the two different uses of words during these short periods of time. "A merry heart doeth good like a medicine: but a broken spirit drieth the bones" (Proverbs 17:22), coupled with "Heaviness in the heart of man maketh it stoop: but a good word maketh it glad" (12:25), are also illustrated specifically in the changed lunchtimes together as a family.

To make children memorize Scripture verses, without ever pointing out failure to live them and ways of changing the failures into victories in practical areas, is only to prepare children to dislike the Bible. Honesty in human relationships at this level has far-reaching effects in other areas as well. "I was wrong in reacting that way day after day, and it wasn't doing any of us any good. This other solution is something that is as helpful to me as to the rest of you." This will be a basic lesson in human relationships which will be remembered as an example in amazingly different sets of circumstances throughout life. This basic teaching of what is most important — a human being and the relationship with that human being — can be added to by another question along the same line, "What is more important — fighting for one's rights or developing a relationship, with an important response given at the moment when it is needed?"

You have just vacuumed the living-room rug, and the hall is spic and span; now you can turn to the next thing on your list. Suddenly the door bursts open, and little Susie or Johnny comes in happily with a fistful of dandelions and early spring violets with a few blades of grass and weeds mixed in. His or her eyes are full of delight, sparkling with assurance of bringing love in that grubby hand, expectant of a welcome for this treasured arrangement. Mud is mixed with leaves and dry blades of grass, as sandals or boots leave a trail across the clean rug. The outstretched hand is accompanied by a breathless "Look, Mommy, for you." What is going on inside? It started out in the garden or field, that sudden idea, that original burst of imagination which pictured a communication of love with the gift. This is a little three-year-old's budding understanding of giving some material evidence of a hard-to-put-into-words feeling. This is an important moment, long to be remembered, later to be added to with fresh understanding.

What is the response? — "Susie [or Johnny] how lovely! You picked those for Mommy, didn't you? Let's find a vase for them. They'll be put right on Mommy's bedside table to remind her that you thought of her when you were out playing." Or, "We'll put them on the lunch table. Thank you. Here, let me kiss you." The child has a warm feeling of success in communicating. Mommy understands what is going on. Perhaps there is a verbalization now — "I love you, Mommy," or perhaps just a turning to go out again, secure in a growing relationship. Then, as the child leaves the doorstep (or perhaps not until evening) a suggestion is made: "Next time, dear, try to remember to come in the kitchen door." After all, how long will it take to brush up the mud and leaves, to whiz the vacuum over the spots again? How expensive is this as a price to pay for responding to love with understanding?

Or is this what happens? — "Susie [or Johnny], you little monster! Look at all the mud and those dirty leaves and stuff on my clean rugs. Get out of here with your nasty little weeds; I'm getting ready for company. How many times do I have to tell you to come in the kitchen door!" All this is accompained by a rough shake and a shove toward the door. The light dies out of the child's eyes, the tousled head drops down in confusion, tears drip silently or with audible weeping, depending on the child. Something has been so thoroughly stepped on, squashed, hurt, that the withered drying of the little bunch of weedy flowers is only a picture of a worse withering taking place inside the child. What a costly price to pay for gaining that feeling of "Well, I told the child off. He [she] will remember the next time to do what I say. I don't vacuum rugs for nothing. I'm not to be imposed upon and made into a slave by my children or anybody else."

Whichever the response, a lesson has been given and learned concerning human relationships. Something has been taught more vividly than any lecture could teach it. An opportunity has been used — one way or another. It is not neutral. One person may be self-satisfied with the feeling, "I've told him off now. Let's see how he likes that. He won't dirty up my house again." But that person might be amazed that the rebellion of ten years later has had its seed sown at that moment. That person might be horrified that the inhuman treatment a thirty-three-year-old is one day going to give to another human being is being prepared for at this very time. Recognition of the family as a formation center for human relationships is needed in order to have an underlying seriousness about the scope of the day-to-day opportunities.

"What can possibly be the far-reaching effect of one incident?" True, one time is not sufficient to finish the job, but a succession of "one times" add up, especially if there is no apology given, no verbalized recognition that you have been thoughtless and cruel. Neglected mothers and grandmothers may perhaps have been preparing for their own neglect by teaching over and over again that people's sensitive feelings, and people's need of response is never as important as clean houses, schedules, or rules and regulations.

"Bill is going to love this chiffon pie; it's his favorite dessert, and I feel so accomplished in getting the bedroom

curtains finished and up. Ooops! There's his car now." Bill,
tired from a long day, has his mind on some things he asked
to have done that day: "Have you sewed the buttons on my
jacket, and put the zipper in my blue jeans?" The light in
Betty's eyes starts to fade, confusion takes the place of the
assurance that she was going to be able to show Bill the results of her day of loving preparation. "Ohhhh! I'm sorry. I
forgot; I'll do it tonight. But look, the curtains are finished,
and wait till you see what I've fixed for dessert, your favorite,
and it turned out perfect."

What is the response? Perhaps the children are waiting to
hear, and this is their lesson time in human relationships,
though no one is thinking of that. "Oh, Betty, the curtains
are lovely, you really sew so beautifully and it saves so much
money. Imagine what an interior decorator would have
charged for that! Mmmmm [a real kiss, not a peck], I'm glad
you are *you*. What's for dessert? I can't eat buttons, and
thanks for saying you'll do them tonight; I can read you the
news while I watch."

Or is this what happens? "I couldn't care less about those
curtains. I want those buttons on and now! I don't care what
you made for dessert. just get me those blue jeans in a ready-
to-wear state." The sewing has to take place after supper,
but the meal has been a nightmare for children as well as
parents, and the moment of accepting the day's loving work
is gone forever, down the drain. Yes, there will be forgiveness after an apology *if* it is made, and a new start. Yes,
one time does not finish off the relationship. Yes, being
willing to say quietly, "I'm sorry," and not to try to spend
the rest of the evening justifying oneself is the wife's part in
realizing the expense of proving herself right is too costly.
But in this story the man needs to see that he has paid a
price for winning, for yelling for his rights, the price of stepping on a loving communication that took hours to prepare.

"Darling, look what I've brought you." The satisfied voice,
pleased with having such a bright idea, accompanies the

handing over of a tissue-wrapped box of chocolates (but you are on a diet), or three red roses (but you want to save money and that would have bought some meat), or a filmy new nightgown (but you told him the teapot was broken, and could he please bring a new one tonight).

What is the response? This is the moment that counts — "Oh, thank you, it was so sweet of you to be thinking of me. Sometimes I wonder whether you remember I'm alive during the pressures of your work, and this means so much because you took time to go and look for it during the day. Tomorrow while you're gone, I can see this sitting here saying, 'Ran wants me to know he loves me.' " The response does not only bring satisfaction to Ran at the moment, but warms him the next day at odd moments in the midst of his pressures, continues the growth of something far deeper than the gift could express. The watching children have absorbed something, too. They have not only noted that gifts say, "I love you," but have had planted deeper in them the need for trying to express the fact that someone else's existence matters, by doing a variety of things — not just by verbalization, but by giving and accepting gracefully.

What a shattering moment can take place with the opposite response, whose effect on each person involved or within earshot can last longer than anyone would realize. "Oh, you idiot, you know we haven't enough money for meat, and you bring roses." (Or "You know I'm on a diet and you bring chocolates." Or "You know that I asked you to bring home a teapot and you bring me a silly nightgown.") "Besides, you're late and you didn't call me today. Hurry up and get ready for dinner."

Gone is the possibility of greeting love with the acceptance of its form, even if inappropriate. Gone is the possibility of showing an understanding of someone's attempt to express the fact that there was desire for communication during the time apart. Gone is the opening for communication springing from that moment. What a costly price has been paid for telling him off and showing him what he ought to have done. What costly use of a moment when the children could have learned something positive in their needed lessons that a person's feelings are more important than money "wasted."

Is any family going to be perfect in every moment of opportunity to make the right response in the midst of a struggle not to make the wrong response? No, of course not. But there is a difference between realizing that one has made a wrong response and hurt something deep inside, and trying to make some sort of gesture or verbal apology later, resolving not to repeat that mistake — and simply ignoring the seriousness of a whole succession of such incidents. To think of tiny, daily incidents as an unimportant string of dull happenings, rather than to remember that you have a major part in a formation center of human relationships which is going to have far-reaching effects — perhaps in world affairs as your children become government leaders, but certainly in some sphere of human relationships — is to be totally blind to one of the basic reasons for the existence of families.

One lesson I tried to teach my children from an early age, repeating over and over again the best explanation I could think of, in different ways at different times, was the fact that some things must never be said, no matter how hot the argument, no matter how angry one becomes, no matter how far one goes in feeling, "I don't care how much I hurt him [or her]." Some things are too much of a "luxury" *ever* to say. Some things are too great a price to pay for the momentary satisfaction of cutting the other person down. Some things are like throwing indelible ink on a costly work of art, or smashing a priceless statue just to make a strong point in an argument. Saying certain things is an expense beyond all reason. This is true for man, woman, and child. Proverbs says something in this direction which applies whether it is the mother or father, grandparents or aunts and uncles, children who are brothers and sisters, or cousins speaking to each other. "Every wise woman buildeth her house: but the foolish plucketh it down with her hands. . . .

In the mouth of the foolish is a rod of pride: but the lips of the wise shall preserve them" (14:1, 3).

What is it that can never be put into words, which can't be erased and forgotten? What is it that one can resolve and succeed never to say during the lifetime of relationship with one person? What is it that is like plucking your own house down, pulling your own family to pieces around your own ears, and creating a ruin of the most precious relationship? It is attacking the person in his or her most vulnerable, most sensitive, most insecure spot in life. It is pulling the rug out at a place where the other person felt there was a solid acceptance and understanding, without question. It is bringing up something from the other person's background which he has no control over and which carries with it painful memories of outsiders' lack of understanding. It is turning the one secure place in all of life into a suddenly exposed place of naked attack from which there is no place to run. At some point in the beginning of a relationship, it is of tremendous importance to decide inside yourself just what things are really "out of bounds," and to declare to yourself that you will never resort to saying anything about: his or her big nose, deformities, lack of cultural or educational upbringing, and psychological fears or special weaknesses. Naturally it can't be too big a list, but there must be certain specific areas you rationally decide not to let "wild horses drag out of you"! It is possible. It is a restraint that you can inflict upon yourself. It is a possible control.

Not only must you select the areas with some degree of exactness, and shy away from them, but children should be conscious that there is an absolute limit to what can be said to each other, to parents, friends, and in preparation for their own marriages. Have you ever broken ribs or badly bruised all the muscles in a severe fall directly on your rib cage? I have — just this week. It is amazing how suddenly controlled is my coughing. How gentle and limited in volume is my need to cough or sneeze, how controlled my burst of humor — a quiet laugh taking the place of an unlimited guffaw!

Immediate pain sets a limit, and the knowledge that more pain is to follow gives strength to the power of control. The freedom to cough, sneeze, and laugh becomes too luxurious a freedom, the cost is too great to indulge in it, except with firm limits! This is something of an illustration. We do set ourselves limits in a variety of things, even in areas that seem spontaneous. Say to yourselves, teach your children, "There are some things that are too costly to say, some things that are too great a luxury to use in sarcasm, some things that are too cleverly devastating to ever use in trying to get the better of someone. To win in the midst of saying that kind of thing, is to lose entirely. What rare and marvelous thing am I losing in order to win what little victory?"

There should be family discussion about the centrality of growing relationships being more important than individual points one wants to get across. Criticism of each other may be very necessary at times, but there must be encouraged sensitivity to the fact that the whole point of communication is to have a growing relationship come forth. If criticism is degenerating into simply a power struggle, one needs to stop short and ask, "What is more important, our relationship as a whole, or convincing him or her that I'm right?" There can be a change of subject, an introduction of a pleasant thing such as reading or music or just listening to the other, a game or puzzle, or listening to the news together. Every discussion in which two people are differing does not need to continue to the bitter end! This is where *time* and *balance* are again involved. Human relationships in marriage, the family, and on the wider scale require some person to realize that there is danger of throwing it all away in unfruitful unpleasantness. Children are quick to learn in early childhood how to clear the air by the introduction of a fresh subject, and they ought to be helped in this, not squashed. There should be open discussion as to how to use precious time together for everyone's benefit and to help the relationships, rather than to rush headlong into a quarrel.

There is a wide difference between *never* discussing serious subjects in which there is a difference of opinion and *always* discussing subjects which each person knows will end up in a quarrel of some dimension. I'm not suggesting a disregard of serious subjects. In our own family we have discussed serious subjects much of the time: philosophies, religions, true truth, the Bible, politics, art, music, literature, recent news, the current war, science, abortion, mercy killing, and so on. It isn't that serious subjects need to be put aside in order for relationships to grow — quite the contrary — but that does not rule out consideration and sensitivity in the midst of discussion. There must be sensitivity to the possibility of someone being shoved aside, run over as if with a truck, unable to express an opinion — so that the relationship between two people is being endangered, or the children are learning negative things about how to discuss. Perfection as the goal? No! But an awareness of what is taking place in this formation center for human relationships. The family is the place where loyalty, dependability, trustworthiness, compassion, sensitivity to others, thoughtfulness, and unselfishness are supposed to have their roots. Someone must take the initiative and use imagination to intentionally teach these things.

Human relationships are very different, under a much greater strain, in a "concentration camp." Children and adults react differently in emotional, spiritual, intellectual, and psychological areas when there is some special physical need. Not only does someone in the family have to be cognizant of this fact, but someone needs to take responsibility. What am I talking about? Blood-sugar level dropping, hunger pangs, fatigue, clothing, cleanliness, great heat or devastating cold, pleasant or unpleasant flavors, noise. "What a strange list of things!" (Is this your remark?)

David comes in from school, cold and cranky because his blood sugar is low, tired from the long day. This is not the time to say, "Go right over now and apologize to Mr. X. next door for the broken window. It was your ball game. I don't care if you threw it or not. And then get right back here and do your homework." Is not the impolite answer which David spits back partly due to his physical condition? Your understanding of the human frame ought to make you start out by saying, "Here, David, come and drink this hot chocolate [or vanilla eggnog or milk shake] along with some of my homemade brown bread and peanut butter. Isn't it good? Your pants and socks are wet from the snow [or rain]. Why don't you take a hot shower or bath, and get into these dry things right away." After David feels like a new person, full tummy, warm and dry, then the suggestion may be received with a different attitude, and the homework tackled with some feeling of being able to face it.

Your toddler and four-year-old are fussing and whining; nothing seems to suit them. Your understanding of the way bodies work should remind you that they, as well as adults, have lowered blood sugar when they get hungry. Not only is food needed, but something soothing and calming. Daddy will be home soon, and what disaster is about to happen (with scoldings and cryings imminent) as a bad beginning to an evening. What to do? Pop the two in a bath, a lovely, hot one if it has been a cold day, a cool one if it is a hot summer evening, some mild bubbles (if you believe in them) or a lovely-smelling bath oil, a few floating toys — a boat, a duck, a sponge, some bits of wood. They'll be in a different mood in a few minutes, and you can finish your last-minute preparations for supper. Take care of the hunger problem right then and there, unless you are certain that the supper table won't disintegrate into more squabbling. Put the four-year-old in bed with a tray, adorned with a few flowers, a candle in a stable little holder, or a fat one that stands on its own. Scrambled eggs, toast ("Cut in tiny fingers, dear, just like my mother used to cut for me."), yogurt or custard, or a bit of whatever you are making for yourselves. Feed the baby on your lap as the little one eats, or do the whole thing in

your kitchen. It can be varied at different times, but don't
have Daddy always meet his little ones at the very moment
when they are at their fussiest due to fatigue, hunger, plus
feeling too hot or too cold or too uncomfortable.

Adults who disintegrate into ogres yelling, "You must
obey me," to little people who don't know why they feel so
unable to get hold of themselves, and thus feel and act worse
and worse, ought to use common sense to think of the fact
that there are times when the basic needs of food, a freshen-
ing up with a bath, clean clothes, and a rest, are needed before the commands are even given. Seemingly mundane facts
about the physical body must also be taken into consideration
in the relationships between adults. It is ridiculous for a man
to come home and begin to deal with a very difficult problem with his wife when she is dead-tired, hot, disheveled,
and in need of some sort of break. Better to suggest, "Why
don't you take ten minutes for a bath and change before we
eat," and waiting to talk over serious problems until supper
is over and he has helped with the dishes, the children are
asleep, and there is a relaxed moment over a cup of coffee,
tea, orange juice, or ginger ale. Then, sitting before the
fire or in the cool of the garden, the problem can be discussed
very differently.

The same is true for the wife. If she has some request that
is going to be a shock financially, an announcement that a
new roof is needed, the news that moles are in the garden,
a bill that has come for the third time, a confession that she
has scorched his best shirt or spilled candle wax on the rug,
she ought to know that the time to talk is not just when he
has arrived, tired and hungry, cranky from low blood sugar,
nervous from a long, hard day filled with a diverse number
of problems. It doesn't matter whether he is a doctor, lawyer,
evangelist, painter, producer, president, plumber, electrician,
gardener, pastor, businessman, professor, wigmaker, congress-
man, mayor, grocery-store owner, fruit peddler, writer, boat-
man, ticket agent, or conductor. Whatever his work is, the

arrival moment is the time for some sort of comforting
fulfillment of a physical need — hot bath or shower, change
of clothing into pajamas and robe or blue jeans and shirt
(or fancy suit!). It does not matter *what,* but some sort of
putting off the day and putting on the home atmosphere,
then a glass of orange juice, tomato juice, and dinner as soon
as possible. It is when the physical needs have been cared for
that the time is ripe for talking over the disagreeable problem
or for proposing the new thing.

This is something that the family should be understanding
together as a very basic reality concerning human beings.
The preparation of a little tray, midmorning, midafternoon,
or midevening (for some other family member who is working on a project, recuperating from an illness, writing letters,
or studying) should be a thing children learn to do by example. Compassion and understanding of what *another* person needs comes through having been cared for. Anyone who
has had the comfort of a little pot of tea, some cookies or
toast, or a cup of coffee and some cheese and crackers, or a
glass of milk and some fruit — just when he was feeling
"down" in the midst of a project — then knows how to do
those same things for someone else. A family is the place
where this kind of care should be so frequently given that it
becomes natural to think of the needs of other people.

The idea of clothing having an effect on human relationships is not just a matter of getting out of hot, sticky things
in warm weather and thus becoming comfortable. How we
are dressed has an effect upon the way other people treat us.
People going to apply for jobs, going to meet the top boss,
going to meet their girl's parents, or getting ready for any
kind of meeting in which they want to make an impression,
spend some time preparing, as far as choosing what to wear
and making themselves what they consider to be presentable.
Why? Because people do form opinions from first impressions and connect how a person looks with what they are.
Opinions can change, of course, but no matter how long we
know each other, the matter of how we look and what we

wear affects other people's attitudes toward us, and has something to do with their treatment of us.

I don't think it is a superficial kind of thing to realize that if you have appeared in the same old thing day after day, it is adding a strain to other strains, and that as a wife you should change the balance of your use of time and set aside some time to get into a different kind of outfit altogether — before the evening meal or for lunch or for whatever time the family is going to be together. Don't think that it is only important to wear attractive things for your husband; it is also important to wear feminine things for your children — interesting new aprons with apples for pockets, even long dresses for dinner (cotton or wool, plaid skirts or denim). Children will behave differently towards an attractively dressed mother, just as a husband will. But, strangely enough, even though you are the mother, you will be more polite to your own children if you dress them attractively, just as you will look at yourself in the mirror with more respect if you splash cold water on your face, redo your hair, and put on something fresh. You can feel like a different person, as well as act like a different person, when you care and do something about your appearance.

I have always noticed that when one is traveling with children, if they are dressed alike in neat, navy-and-white-striped jerseys and crisp overalls or skirts, and are carrying interesting dolls or cars or blocks in a bag, they are not as "annoying" to other people, but are looked at with sympathy and interest. People so easily get annoyed with straggly-looking children dressed in an assortment of unsuitable clothes when they are on a train or a boat or in a restaurant. However, it is also good to face the fact that the whole family will treat each other differently if they are dressed for the occasion, whatever that occasion may be. Children dressed in their best clothes are apt to eat with better manners, so I have noticed, than when dressed in their old playclothes. Somehow, clothes do have an effect on human beings' behavior, and this should be taken into account when teaching good manners — as well as the whole matter of growing relationships.

"Oh, Mommy, you look like a princess!" Becky said in awe when she was nine and her mother was dressed for dinner the second evening of the family reunion. The very fact of having occasions when the whole family sees each other with "sudden new eyes" is not just a surface kind of varnish covering day-by-day blemishes. It is real — this dressed-up person looking so charming is also the real person. This is Daddy, this is Mommy, this is David, this is Stephen, this is Patty. We need to be careful in the area of human relationships to give each other the opportunity to be the diverse people we are, and variety of clothing helps us to recognize some of each other's diversity we might have missed.

Love is one of the basic commands which the Bible gives us concerning human relationships. Husbands are to love their wives. Christians are to love each other. People who are in the Family of the Lord are to love their neighbors (representing the ones who are not believers). We are to love our enemies. Love is a basic ingredient of human relationships which is meant to be taught in the family. This is the formation center for knowing how to love, how to express love, and what love is all about. How? By memorizing verses from the Bible? Yes, that is a help. By discussing the real meaning during mealtimes? Yes, that will help, too. We should be expressing love for each other verbally, and not be too embarrassed to say, "I love you, Mother — I love you, Dad — I love you, Genie." Say, "I love you, Susan — I love you, Udo," so that your children grow up in a place where love is freely expressed, and becomes a perfectly normal thing to verbalize, just as "What a gorgeous sunset!" is normal to speak about. Yes, this is needed.

But day-by-day living in the midst of an outpouring of examples of love is needed through months and years, if love is to be a basic part of the "warp and woof" of a person. This is meant to take place in a family. "Oh, well, we might as well split then; we don't love each other that perfectly, and we can't live out a farce." Is this the excuse for breaking up the only real formation center for human relationships? Never forget that if you insist on "perfection or nothing" in the area of love or happiness or any part of human relationship, you will have *nothing!* The reality of love we are meant to strive for in our family life is made clear in 1 Corinthians 13:4–8, the biblical explanation of love. (The King James Version speaks of "charity" but *love* is implied.)

"Love suffereth long, and is kind" (*see* v. 4). *Love suffereth long?* There must be some circumstances during which love has to suffer a long time in order to be real love. That doesn't sound like roses and moonlight, perfume and soft music! What does it mean — "suffereth long?" I think this can be combined with "tribulation worketh patience" (*see* Romans 5:3), and must be understood as declaring that the circumstances which bring out the reality of love are not easy circumstances, but difficult ones. It is during the bearing of someone else's weaknesses and irritating qualities that love must suffer long, as well as in the bearing of the ups and downs of poor health, floods, fires and avalanches, poor cooking, and no jobs to be found! In the midst of circumstances which would not likely make romantic, airy, fairy emotions to fill a person's heart, real love suffers long and is kind. The children will long remember the long-suffering of Daddy when Mommy burned the soup and then dropped the cherry pie upside down on the floor. He said, "Never mind, we'll call it smoked asparagus soup and put some croutons in it. And the cherries didn't touch the floor, only the crust, so let's carefully pick them up and put them in this dish. I think there's some of that vanilla ice cream left over from last night, and we can put the cherries on a little bit of that for each of us." The kindness is a demonstrated act of caring that will last a lifetime, in showing that love can be a workable thing.

Nor will any family of children forget the long-suffering and kindness of Mommy when Daddy forgot to get the tickets for the circus, and it was "sold out" that day. "Never mind, we'll have a special picnic and I have a lovely game to take along to play in the grass, and a new book to read to us. Don't make Daddy feel badly; let's try to make him have a good time, too."

"Love envieth not, love vaunteth not itself, is not puffed up. Love doth not behave itself unseemly, seeketh not her own, is not easily provoked, thinketh no evil, rejoiceth not in iniquity, but rejoiceth in the truth" (*see* 1 Corinthians 13:4–6). What conversations and what demonstrations can take place about these possibilities of showing forth love, day after day, week after week. How often each one in the family will fail, yet how often a success in showing real love can be pointed out. Love isn't just a kind of soft feeling, a thrill of honeysuckle fragrance while being kissed on a June night. Love isn't just happiness in ideal situations with everything going according to daydreams of family life or married life or parent-child closeness and confidences. Love has *work* to do! Hard and self-sacrificial work — going on when it would be easy to be provoked and to think evil as the clock hands move, and the person hasn't yet come home. Love has to be preparing the atmosphere and words to make the twelve minutes left of lunchtime pleasant minutes for the whole family! Love takes imagination and the balance of putting first things first, to be taught to the young pupils in their formative years.

"Love beareth all things, believeth all things, hopeth all things, endureth all things. Love never faileth" (*see* vv. 7, 8). Husband-wife love, wife-husband love, and parent-child love — in times of weakness and failure, when forgiveness must be asked for and given, in times when suspicions have been right — love goes on. A child needs to grow up knowing that love never faileth, that not only will Dad and Mom stay together in spite of each of their weaknesses as well as strengths, but that the door will always be open, the "candle in the window" will never go out. Love doesn't say, "If you ever do that again, never come home." *Love never faileth.*

Love keeps that door open, the light waiting, and dinner in the oven — *for years*. This is the love a family demonstrates in its formation center.

Can human love be perfect? No, but it is meant to be worked at through the years, and it is meant to portray something, within the family, of the love of God for His Family of children. "The Lord hath appeared of old unto me, saying, Yea, I have loved thee with an everlasting love: therefore with loving-kindness have I drawn thee" (Jeremiah 31:3). The loving-kindness of God toward us has been demonstrated *not* when we were being good, but in that, while we were yet sinners, Christ died for us. Then how can an earthly father or mother demonstrate love to children by saying such things as: "Unless you are good, I won't love you" — "If you sleep with a girl [marry that person, have a baby, get into drugs], the door is shut forever to you. Don't ever darken my door again!'"?

"A new commandment I give unto you, That ye love one another; as I have loved you, that ye also love one another. By this shall all men know that ye are my disciples, if ye have love one to another" (John 13:34, 35).

Yes, this was to be the mark of the Christians, that men should see them really carrying out love (the long-suffering, the kindness, the lack of envy, the not putting self first, the refusal to listen to the gossip's evil tales, the believing of the good things, the bearing of slights and snubs among the "all things," the *never failing*). Outsiders, people not in the family of born-again believers, were supposed to know them by these demonstrations of love.

But what about Christian families? What about grandmothers and grandfathers, mothers and fathers, children, sisters and brothers, aunts and uncles, nephews and nieces? The mark of Christian families should be the demonstration of love in the day-by-day, mundane circumstances of life, in the many moments of opportunity to show that love suffereth long. The "never failing" cannot have an eternity behind it,

as each of us has a short history and will die before too many
years (unless Jesus comes first), but the "never failing" is
meant to go on during our time in the land of the living.
This is what is meant to be learned in *your* formation center
for human relationships — and in *mine*.

What is a family? A formation center for human relationships — worth fighting for, worth calling a career, worth the
dignity of hard work.

# 5

---

# A Shelter in the Time
# of Storm

The storms of life which hit rich and poor alike, young and
old, brilliant and dull, are the winds and rains, thunders and
lightnings of sudden fevers, aches and pains, accidents, splitting headaches, broken bones, torn ligaments, viruses, can-
cer, pneumonia, burst appendix, infections, and death. There
is no insurance against a change from health one moment to
feverish illness in the next. There is no insurance against
stepping happily down a street one moment and the next
being plunged by accident into a state of pain and disability.
A person's first accident can take place at birth when, if not
enough oxygen gets into the system, brain cells die, and all
is not in order in the impulses going to the rest of the body.
The first serious illness can take place when a baby has not
yet left the hospital, and long, careful nursing is required
before the child can have a life without illness. Young people can spend years in a bed or wheelchair, and old people
can face the problem of having to learn to walk again with
a walker. A teenager can suddenly become blind and need
to learn Braille, and a middle-aged person can become deaf
and have to learn to communicate in new ways. Short illnesses such as flu or measles can cause physical misery and
loneliness because of neglect. There is scarcely anyone who
has not experienced some degree of physical misery, and

there are some people who have known one illness after another, with scarcely any well days in between.

For some people the memory of illness carries with it the memory of loving care, cool hands stroking the forehead, sponge baths in bed, clean sheets under a hot chin, lovely-flavored drinks, alcohol back rubs, medicine given methodically by the clock, flowers near the bed, curtains drawn when fever is hurting the eyes, soft singing of a mother's or father's voice during a sleepless night. Convalescence brings other memories, but some people remember care of this sort during times when fever was high, and pain ripped through some part of the body, and the changing of perspiration-soaked pajamas for crisp, dry ones brought and indescribable relief for a few moments, as did the crushed ice to suck, wrapped in a linen handkerchief or clean facecloth.

We are told in the Book of Matthew that there will come a day when the Son of man will say, "Come, ye blessed of my Father, inherit the kingdom prepared for you from the foundation of the world" (see 25:34). There are some amazingly sharp descriptions given as to what will be counted as things which have been done directly for Him. Among them are: "I was thirsty, and ye gave me drink . . . I was sick, and ye visited me" (see vv. 35, 36). And when asked, "When saw we thee thirsty, and gave thee drink? When saw we thee sick, and came unto thee?" (see vv. 37, 38), "And the King shall answer and say unto them, Verily I say unto you, Inasmuch as ye have done it unto one of the least of these my brethren, ye have done it unto me" (v. 40).

Surely these admonitions mean that we are to care for the thirsty and sick strangers and the poor people. Aren't we being told to care for needy people outside our home? Yes, we are, but we are carefully told: "But if any provide not for his own, and specially for those of his own house, he hath denied the faith, and is worse than an infidel" (1 Timothy 5:8). Perhaps you have always connected this admonition or command with meaning financial responsibility for people related to you. It does mean that Christians are responsible before God for the needs of people related to them, but we can relate the strong and clear commands to care for the needs of the sick and thirsty (as well as for the needy in other spheres of material needs) to what is expected of us within our own family.

What is a family? A family is a well-regulated hospital, a nursing home, a shelter in time of physical need, a place where a sick person is greeted as a sick *human being* and not as a machine that has a loose bolt, or a mechanical doll that no longer works — to be shoved aside because it is no more fun, nor is it useful! A family should be a training place for growing human beings to know how to care for a great variety of sicknesses and for people who have just had accidents or operations, because each one has received both knowledgeable and loving care and has watched it being given to others. The knowledge of what is necessary for basic care (and what is added thoughtfulness to make the time more bearable) should be absorbed through years of living in a family. If, however, a person has not been brought up with the kind of care that has given pleasant moments in the middle of misery, assurance of love in the midst of fear, or the mingling of gratefulness with pain, then one needs to be told. If a person has never had good, old-fashioned, motherly nursing, nor heard any details of what can be done other than giving the medicine, then how can he or she know what is *not* being done and what the children, husband, wife, or grandparents are missing?

When illness hits we should remember that this period of time is part of the whole of life. This is not just a non-time to be shoved aside, but a portion of time that counts. It is part of the well person's life, as well as part of the sick person's life. "In sickness and in health" is a promise made, it seems to me, to recognize that the time which sickness takes is part of the married life, part of the family life; and the time which health takes is another part of the married lifetime and the family lifetime. There is an importance attached to the use of the whole span of time which means that crea-

tivity, imagination, work, appropriate contribution, blending of talents, and pitching in to do whatever needs to be
done, applies to periods of sickness as well as periods of
health — periods of tragedy as well as periods of special happiness. We are to recognize that to waste this time is as much
a loss as wasting a time we might think of as the height of
productivity. Jesus tells us, ". . . he that loseth his life for my
sake shall find it" (Matthew 10:39). He is the One who also
points out that when we have cared for the very least of the
sick ones or thirsty ones, we have cared directly for Him.
How better could we use our time than caring for Jesus? If
we 'are losing time (which we had set aside for something
we thought very important) in order to care for a sick person's comfort, we are promised we will find something amazing one day when Jesus thanks us for caring for Him!

The opportunity to do something practical about making
your family remember their sicknesses with a feeling that
yours was the "best hospital in the world," is very real, and
becomes a challenge that gives purpose to some of the drudg-
ery of changing beds, struggling with bedpans, cleaning up
the sickroom floor, or thinking up something comforting to
do. It is a time when each of us can have the chance to be
practical about the command in Matthew 7:12: "Therefore all
things whatsoever ye would that men should do to you, do
ye even so to them: for this is the law and the prophets." What
other kind of circumstance would be more suited to carrying out this command? Couple with this that Jesus said we
are "to wash one another's feet" as He washed the disciples'
feet (see John 13:12–14). During sicknesses we can both
literally and figuratively "wash feet," as we do the messy jobs
that someone has to do, and then say, "Thank You, Lord,
for giving me a glimpse of what it is all about."

When a person has a fever, whether it is a two-year-old or
a twenty-two-year-old or an eighty-two-year-old, he needs a
few basic chores of nursing to be made as comfortable as
possible. The nicest thing is to have clean sheets at least once
a day. If this horrifies you as an impossibility, the next best

thing is taking off the bottom sheet, transferring the top to the bottom, turning it upside down, putting what was at the head at the foot, and then putting on a fresh top sheet and pillowcase. Again, if you don't have another sheet, and you have to wash sheets and put them back on the same day, then at least make the bed, brushing out any crumbs, getting rid of the wrinkles, and fixing a fresh place for the sick person, with at least a clean pillowcase. The time of day for making the bed should also be the time for a bed bath (or a bath in the tub if the doctor has said it is all right) or at least a washing of hands and face, feet and legs. How? Well, do the washing of the patient before the bed is made. For a bed bath or sponge bath, bring warm water (or cool water if this is a case of trying to bring down a dangerously high fever) in a basin, a plastic bowl, a pail, one of your cooking pots, or whatever you have — although a nice-looking bowl helps you to feel as if it is an official nursing job, as well as making the patient feel cared for. Be sure you spread a bit of oilcloth, a Turkish towel, or a dishtowel on a chair or small table, to protect it from water. Place on this protected surface your bowl of water, a soap dish with a bit of mild soap, some medicated lotion or alcohol, powder, ointment or whatever you are putting on diaper rash or bedsores (if it is a diapered baby or old person or a patient who has had a long illness). Bring at least two other Turkish towels (three will be more of a help) and stick an extra washcloth in your apron pocket to wipe up spills of any nature! Now you feel official, and the other person starts to feel cared for before anything happens. It is a break in the monotony of the day, even if appreciation is not forthcoming in the way of a shout of joy! Never mind the growls of a cranky patient; just go on. It is nice if you can do this portion of care at the same time each day, but not absolutely essential; the important thing is to fit it in at some time.

Now take off the nightgown, bed shirt or top of the pj's and cover the naked part with a dry towel, so that there won't be a feeling of chill. Then wash the face, gently now, with a little soap (and make it feel like *more* rather than less), then rinse, and pat dry with another towel. Now for the arms and chest: "Roll over on your side a bit. That's it. We can get the other side of the shoulder and under the arm." Gently wash, rinse, pat dry, then cover with the other towel. A towel should also be tucked under the portion being washed, to keep the bed dry. Yes, it's an art, and one to be learned for many years of use. Now for the other side –– the tummy and then the back. If the patient is really very ill, you figure out which will be the less tiring and take the order as your common sense tells you is best. With an extra blanket or clean pajama top on the upper portion of the anatomy, now comes the lower — and piece by piece the body is washed, the feet given a massage along with the calves of the legs, never forgetting the final back rub with medicated lotion, rubbing alcohol (perhaps the camphorated kind), or witch hazel. The smells now filling the air — as well as the tingling sensations of cool, slight stings, gentle massage, or brisk rubbing of feet — all mingle together to feel and smell like BEING CARED FOR with capital letters! If you don't remember such smells and sensations from your childhood, make sure someone else is going to have these memories in your family or your adopted family. Uncared-for sick people surround us. Don't ever say, "I would never have anyone to look after like that."

With clean sheets or freshly made bed, clean pajamas or nightgown, and the drowsiness after the exercise of being moved around, the person is ready for the next dose of medicine or the next little meal, a story, some music, or just plain sleep.

When the doctor says, "Give a cool tub bath to bring down the temperature," do be sure there are no drafts in the bathroom, that a little extra heat is added to prevent a miserable, chilled feeling. Make the water just body temperature or slightly cooler, and have a big bath towel which will cover the person completely as you wrap him immediately after the bath. It is good to get a special bath towel for such occasions, if you don't use them normally. If you have a big beach towel or you use big bath towels, that's fine. Otherwise buy some Turkish toweling by the yard, in the widest width possible. Wait for a sale if you want to, hem it or fringe it, but have it ready for wrapping up a sick person — after a standing-up sponge bath, one in bed, or a tub bath to bring down fever. It can be something to look forward to when fever follows fever in childhood, in an adult's series of illnesses, or for an old person after a stroke. Anyway, the care of sick family members is easier if you have a little supply ready, in the same way you have first-aid supplies ready.

It goes without saying that there should be a first-aid kit (or shoe box or shelf) always supplied with some sort of antiseptic (two kinds are better — a cream and a liquid, or also a powder — just for variety), Band-Aids, real bandages, sterile gauze squares, something to wash out dirty wounds, and so on. This isn't a medical book, but just a chapter on considering the important preparedness of a family in case of accidents. Children love the attention of a little bandage, even when the cut or burn is minor, and should not be pushed aside and told, "It doesn't hurt." This is the way *compassion* is learned. If you want little people to care about your headache, bring you a cold facecloth with compassion, and keep quiet "because Mummy's head hurts," then you need to treat their hurts, little and big, with a measure of compassion. A tiny bandage is a very small price to pay for the investment in teaching compassion. A little milk-of-magnesia tablet to chew or a bit of peppermint tea is a small attention to provide, even if you think that "My tummy hurts; I feel sick" is only a cry for some notice. The psychological help being given far outweighs the bit of time and trouble taken to treat with seriousness the request for help. Yes, you are to be ready to give the help which is very much needed physically, but you can't be sure when the seemingly unimportant request is the most important psychological help that can be given for the person's development as a secure person. It's all part of carrying out God's wise command: "Do unto others as you would have them do unto you," which brings far-reaching results. Aren't there times when *you* need someone's attention for more than the immediate physical need? Haven't you seen a child feel "important" with a bandage around his or her head, a big patch on a wounded knee, a piece of ice in a clean cloth to hold against a bleeding mouth where a tooth has just come out or a fall has cut the lips? Haven't you sensed that the good things taking place *inside* that child, because of suddenly becoming the center of attention, are far outweighing the physical hurt? Don't waste the opportunities to teach compassion and at the same time give the psychological help needed in building up secure and cared-for feelings. "Somebody cares" has to be demonstrated. So nobody has cared for you? Well, you can begin to start a long line of people caring for people. Isn't this a worthy piece of your career?

Back to the person in bed with an illness — the period of fever and lying down in a listless state needs special feeding. Use imagination about getting down liquids. Bring a variety of things prepared with some sort of imagination. If the liquids are to be fruit juices, have a pink one, followed by a purple one — cranberry juice, grape juice, orange juice, grapefruit juice, lemonade, limeade, apricot juice, tomato juice, V-8 juice, and so forth. Make your own combinations according to the person's taste. Use a different kind of glass each time, up to the limit of your variety. Put in ice. Nothing is lovelier if you feel hot and feverish than a tinkle of ice as a sound coming through the door. "Somebody cares about me." Stand or kneel beside the child or adult if he is really very ill, hold the glass, tip it just right, put the straw in the mouth. Make a sherbet of the fruit juices, if they won't go down another way, and spoon it into the mouth. Tell a story, making the straw a part of the story.

I remember when Pris had good old-fashioned measles with a fever of 104° and liquid was badly needed. Using clear straws, I urged, "Suck a little more now; the straw needs to be pink. It's a Maypole and you have to wind the pink ribbon around it. There it goes, good!" But you think of your own stories. If the liquid is to be milk, make eggnogs, milk shakes, Ovaltine frappes, strawberry milk. Try to make it tempting, but don't fall into the trap of becoming irritated when it isn't appreciated, for this will defeat the whole purpose! Just give it to a child who is well or put it in the fridge for later.

Convalescence is another thing. Then trays are to be made fun and interesting as the person sits up in bed to eat. A tiny eggcup or juice glass filled with whatever flowers you can pick, or a few leaves or a twig of pine, or if you live by the sea, a shell or two with bits of greenery, or just a colored rock. If you can find nothing outdoorish, then display a tiny doll or a wee toy dog — something to decorate the tray. I think a candle is a must but, of course, unless it is a responsible person, you should stay in the room while the little one is eating. Cut the toast in triangles, tiny fingers (four or five strips to a piece of bread), or in the shape of a gingerbread man. It doesn't take much time. Design a little man out of an olive and carrot sticks, lying on the plate next to the scrambled eggs. Use your imagination to make the tray a surprise. Bring a pitcher of ice water to put by the bed with a glass, or a healthy punch made of grapefruit and orange and lemon juice, and put in a bit of dextrose or sugar to bring it to just the right tart-sweetness. "Now you are a little princess [or king] with all that lovely drink at your elbow. What next?" Franky still remembers his six weeks of having hepatitis as one of the best periods of his life, with the great succession of pitchers of iced fruit juices and special drinks prepared to be taken every two hours. Not only did following the nutrition program I had chosen make a difference in recovery, but the way of being waited on became fun. When it is not necessary for the patient to lie down, if it is warm weather, a canvas deck chair can be substituted for the bed, and the kind of rest ordered by the doctor will be almost the same.

Of course, staying to read a story is part of the treatment that must be mixed in with the rest. If the appetite needs coaxing, you read as long as he or she is eating. You slip in to read midafternoon or at any point when things are disintegrating in the area of amusements, but your promise, "I'll read in another hour," must be kept as close to the promised time as it is humanly possible. The happiest memories of childhood can be the tucked-in, cared-for feeling that came when you were eating a poached egg on toast, orange juice, had just had a bath and clean pajamas and sheets, and Mother was reading you one of your favorite books. It turns past sickness into happy memories.

Occupation for convalescents at home can be made much less a time of stirring up frustrations and irritations if the things you provide give a possibility of keeping some sort of order in the bed. Bring a tray or a board for the lap, to provide a surface for coloring books, puzzles, magazines to be cut out. Put things in little drawstring bags to help keep them where they can be found — one bag for paste and scissors for making a scrapbook of cut-out pictures and cloth, another bag for crayons (when the scissors and paste are put away and shoved aside in their findable place), a box for the sewing cards and wool with the big needle, or for the embroidery threads and towel being embroidered by an older child. Add a shoe box for little blocks and wooden animals, also for the jigsaw puzzle if its own box is breaking. Nothing can be more frustrating to the half-well person of any age, than to have in bed a piled-up mess of things that are half "lost." Of course, if you have time to come in and out, that is different, for one thing can be handed to the person at a time, but the little bags and boxes and a nearby wastebasket will give you a longer break before you hear, "Mommmeee! Mommmeee!" yelled again. Remember that the ill adult or child can't or shouldn't "do it all himself."

We had my husband's mother with us for seven years before she died. Is it possible to fit in the care of a person who has had a stroke, needs daily attention, and later has a broken hip, a month of hospital care, and then a year and a half of care in the hospital bed brought home?

We must say to ourselves and to our children, "There is never a series of little packages of time given to you in life labeled: TIME FOR AN ILLNESS, TIME FOR A WEDDING, TIME FOR A DEATH, TIME FOR A BROKEN LEG, TIME FOR CRUSHED RIB MUSCLES, TIME FOR POLIO, TIME FOR RHEUMATIC FEVER, TIME FOR MUMPS, TIME FOR THREE CHILDREN WITH MEASLES ALL AT ONCE, TIME FOR THE HOUSE TO BURN DOWN, TIME FOR A DISAPPOINTMENT." You can't face the sickness, the operations, the broken arms and legs, the serious diseases, the disasters, or even the headaches, unless you realize there is *never* a convenient time set aside for joy or sorrow, protected by neat little walls so that the two things will not mingle and spoil each other.

This is a two-way understanding. We need to remember, as finite, limited human beings, that we cannot care perfectly for others' needs, nor can others care perfectly for our needs, even when we or they want to. Life has to go on, and we can only do the best we can in the mélange, the mixed-up nature of what there is to be done. There are no protected, neat little boxes of time which will not be invaded by a mixture of demands upon us. Life is not like that. It is another case of the danger of demanding "perfection or nothing" and ending up with nothing. Comfort yourself by saying, "I am limited, I am finite, I can only do one thing at a time. I know what would be the perfect care for this person, but I can't do it all. I'll give as much of the ideal care as possible." Certainly, as a Christian you can also pray for God's wisdom in the choices to be made and God's strength to be made perfect in your weakness, even while you drag off perspiration-drenched sheets and pajamas and stick them in the washer at three A.M. because your husband's fever from a strep throat has made it impossible for him to sleep, and you think a dry situation might help. Sure, the Lord hears and gives you the strength to go on, even though you feel like dropping. However, the need is still there to remember that you have limits, and those "limits" are not neatly boxed up and labeled so that you can put your strength and attention into one thing without interruption.

I remember that once Fran was speaking in Italy, and I was just down the hill in another chalet at a Workers' meeting when Franky ran down to get me: "Grandmother fell coming out of the bathroom, and I picked her up as carefully as I could and put her on the bed, but I think she is really hurt. Come quickly." I ran, saw her, phoned the doctor, and soon was on my way on one of those little seats in the ambulance, holding Grandmother's hand and trying to reassure *her*, while Franky looked back from the front seat where he sat near the driver, to reassure *me* from time to time. "Broken hip, operation needed right away," was the verdict of the surgeon after the X rays, and eighty-eight-year-old Grandmother, not knowing a word of French, began her month in a tiny French-speaking hospital, needing somebody she knew and trusted to stay with her most of the time. It was a period when being a family meant pitching in to do many things there was little time to do. I stayed day and night the first few days, Franky took one night shift, others helped out. Birdie came and took some hours, and others from *L'Abri* helped, but essentially it was a matter of family sharing. There were hours of Grandmother's having hallucinations, and she needed a voice she recognized, to help her come back to reality. There were things to be done to bring comfort which nurses had no time to do, and translations to take place because of language misunderstandings. And there were times when Udo, visiting me at midnight to have tea and break the long hours of watching, brought unforgettable moments of lifesaving for myself.

Various family members came at various times to visit Grandmother, to bring flowers or some fruit, or to help the person who was staying for the whole day or night to have a little time off. Yet life did not simply stop or revolve completely around the hospital. *L'Abri* was having days of prayer — my joining in was right there by the bed, with smells and noises of the hospital all around me, and the realization that this was my opportunity to have the reality of showing God that I loved Him and trusted Him. Is healing the greatest victory? No, so often the victory that is harder and more important, is having a reality of victory in the midst of 'he unchanging circumstances. But spreading out my Bible, studying and praying — then answering letters and piling up the stack to be taken to the post office — were not the only continuity with regular life that took place in that hospital room. Franky and Genie's wedding was to be taking place before Grandmother would be taken back up to the mountain chalet. Dresses had to be made for all the little nieces who would be in the wedding party, carrying the train, scattering flowers, bringing the ring up the church aisle. True, Kathie, a L'Abri Worker, had offered to cut and stitch them, and was valiantly doing her part in the chalet, but I had said I would do all the handwork. And there in the midst of the smell of medicine and antiseptics, with whiffs of ether, the sounds of beds being rolled down the hall to the operating room, and crutches on the tiles as someone learned to walk again, I sat midst clouds of fresh turquoise-and-white-striped cotton, sewing on yards of eyelet-embroidered ruffles around square necks and sleeves, and outlining the waistlines of little girls' dresses (long to the floor to delight them and all the wedding guests). Nurses came in with tired dull looks of duty on their faces, only to have them light up with interest and questions, and soon the wedding was something of "a bringing in another part of life" to the hospital for others, as well as my continuing with what needed to be done — one part of life merged with another.

The wedding day brought another time of mixing the realities of life in strange but important and realistic combinations. After the lovely organ music had finished, and the village children had been thrown their caramels (a Swiss custom), and the guests had all shaken hands and remarked on how lovely it was — after the last deep breath of wonder over the beauty of the bride (with daisies in her hair and

in her arms), and car motors were beginning to fill the air
with their noisy rumbles, and the fragrance of flowers was
being mixed with exhaust fumes — the bridal party, including the whole family, moved *not* towards the place
where the reception would be held, but onto the road to Aigle
Hospital. Yes, the bride and groom, little bridesmaids, parents, grandparents, children, and great-grandchildren were to
make a strange little parade down the sterile hospital hall to
visit the great-grandmother and let her be part of the wedding
day. She was to have a piece of cake later, and many pictures
taken, including the ones by her bed with the bride and
groom and her own son there beside her. Worth the trouble?
A million times *yes,* not just for her and all that this would
mean to her in the midst of the reality and unreality floating
around her like a fog, but for each of the other generations.
Continuity in the midst of sickness is as important as continuity in the times of health. Old age is important to youth,
as well as youth important to old age. There is meant to be
a mix in many kinds of situations.

But continuity cannot have a temporary substitute. In the
midst of wedding joys or hospital tragedy, the split and
shattered bits of divorced families cannot be expected to
suddenly merge into a false togetherness. Nor can compassion be mixed with concern, nor love and delight be mixed
with careful preparation and shared deeply for "one day
only." Everyone knows this is like trying to repair a Ming
vase with homemade glue, pretending it has been broken
"just temporarily," when everyone knows it will fall apart
again.

A price for the "real thing" has to be paid constantly
throughout life. The search for "happiness" has to be recognized as shallow and hollow somewhere along the line.
We learn our lessons at different times and in different ways,
but those who do learn that all the work and discouragement
and the moments of despair and depression are worth living
through, find that staying together through years of being

a family has no substitute. Unhappily, time moves forwards — not backwards. It is important to find this out.

It was in the middle of the sermon one Sunday that Giandy got restless and went outside of the Huémoz Chapel to find some other children who had slipped out into the flower-filled field to play with the big dog tied to the apple tree. Giandy, age four, for some reason thought it would be interesting to wrap the dog's rope around his own little leg, and carefully proceeded to do so. The sudden sighting of someone the dog knew caused him to leap up into the air! Giandy was thrown up and down with a swiftness that left him dizzy, and fierce pain burned through his body, stemming from that portion between the knee and hip. Some hours later — after a disappointing ride in an ambulance which didn't have the siren blown, even for this forlorn little passenger — the verdict was given. "Badly broken bone shoved three-quarters of an inch apart; traction for at least a month. He'll have to be in the small children's ward, no visitors allowed except for one hour, three days a week." After two weeks, special permission would be given for a one-hour visit per day. The nurses spoke French for the most part. And a four-year-old active boy was flat on his back in traction with that poor little leg stretched up at an angle, with weights on it, and no family to sit and read to him! How inhumane it seemed to anyone who had experienced "rooming in" with children in hospitals, or the twenty-four-hour visiting privileges common in many countries. What to do? Was there a perfect solution? *No*. But the whole family pitched in to think and do what each one decided might be a help. Notice that other things in each person's schedule had to be shoved aside, choices had to be made as to what to put first.

Fierce family loyalty is something the Bible points out as a mark of the Family of the Lord. When one part of the body hurts or is affected by something, the whole body is affected. This is the way it is meant to be in "the body of

Christ" which is the Lord's Family made up of believers, those who have been born into the Lord's Family through Christ. Thus, the "visiting of the sick" and the concern to be shown to those who are in need are meant to be very broad concepts — and we are to pitch in and help where help is needed. People living in the same apartment house ought to know when someone needs a bowl of soup, a pitcher of orange juice, a friend to go out and get the medicine or to stay with the baby while Daddy is taking Mommy to the hospital. The larger Family of the Lord is meant to take care of each other with a feeling for each other's hurts. This is what "bearing each other's burdens" is all about. This is what the "community" of a church family is all about.

However, the first lessons of this idea should be learned because the family has been brought up in a well-regulated home hospital which has been a shelter in the time of storm! The first demonstrations of what it means to take care of each other should be experienced in the smaller combination which is within reach. That first hospital night of Giandy's, Franky sat up all night, putting all the children's records of stories and songs that he could collect, onto tapes to be play- ed on a cassette recorder. By morning the job was complete, and off to the hospital went a pile of cassettes, the recorder, and big earphones. This was to be a lifesaver for the lonely hours ahead. Pris and John added cassette records of their own making — talking to Giandy, letting him hear some of the home sounds they recorded at suppertime, and reading his favorite stories in their own voices, since they could not stay to read to him. Were there no tears? Did it all become fun and no agony? Not at all, but Udo (Giandy's uncle and pastor) found he could visit as a pastor. So the children made a variety of things for Giandy. Natasha trotted off to the florist in Villars with her matchbox full of treasured little coins, and chose three yellow roses for him (more than the price of her little coins, but kindly given to her for their value by an understanding Madame Matzinger). Did the feeling that everyone was both suffering and doing something to help become very real to Giandy? Yes, to a certain degree, but more for Pris and John for whom the whole situation was even worse, and for Becky and Elizabee, the sisters.

Nony's "big stocking" was as much a help to the others as to Giandy, because it gave a positive thing to look forward to. Because I am Nony (Italian for "grandmother"), it was as much of a help to me, since it gave *me* a feeling of doing something. I took a large piece of quilted red material I had had in my "piece box" for years, cut it into a huge stocking, about four and a half feet long, with a width of about twenty inches — and an enormous foot. This I stitched with a ruffle of eyelet embroidery (still in my bits-and-pieces drawer as a leftover from the wedding dresses made years before) and outlined the whole stocking. Then I made a flat "boy" head and body, arms and legs attached separately, from leftover pieces of the red quilted material, and embroidered big blue eyes, a smiling mouth, and gave him yellow-wool hair. He had pockets made from the tops of one old leather glove (good use for the glove you didn't lose) and a tiny purse in the pocket. The "boy" was to go daily with the stocking to leave a gift from the stocking, but since he was flat, he became a good thing to leave behind — a flat little boy to keep Giandy company in the hospital bed. The stocking was filled with gifts — one for each day. These were things which could be done lying flat on the back, puzzles of a simple sort in a frame, a flashlight, some clay, pictures wrapped separately in sets for his View-Master, a Jack-in-the-box, and so on. It took a lot of thinking, and Fran went with me to the shop, giving his precious day off to do this shopping instead of hiking.

Later, when Jessica had to go for a double-hernia operation, her big stocking was a pink one, with a little pink "girl" doll, but she had to be there only ten days and could move around. It isn't just making the child feel cared for, filling up the child's time, trying to foresee psychological upsets and prevent them, but it is also the building of a solid family togetherness which cannot take place without living through the sharing of the "downs," the sharing of the sicknesses, the sharing of the "worses" in this work of building a family continuity through the years.

One of the important preparations of a child for the hospital, the dentist, or the doctor is proper explanation ahead of time of the variety of things which they might meet. However, there are many books for children about such "visits," so that needn't take much space here. A well-prepared child some-times startles the nurses with questions and interest, taking their own slides, ("Put a little blood here for me!") to be looked at through their own microscopes. A mother and father with understanding and love for their own child have imagination enough to discuss the event on a sensible level and alleviate fears, instead of adding to them with hor-rible hints likening a doctor to a "bogeyman."

This isn't a book about the problem of suffering (since that would make a book in itself), but it must be said here that children in a Christian family, sharing illnesses and ac-cidents, operations, and sudden death, need to be taught day by day that it is an abnormal world. People need to know that we live in an abnormal world which became that way when sin entered as Adam and Eve chose to believe Satan, rather than God — and that Jesus' suffering was necessary in order to do something about it. The tremendous suffering of the Second Person of the Trinity was necessary to make it possible for sickness and death to be done away with someday — forever. It took the death of Christ to bring *victory* over death. We know Jesus wept at the tomb of Lazarus, and that Jesus was angry because of death. "The last enemy that shall be destroyed is death" (1 Corinthians 15:26), and one day sickness, pain, all the abnormalities, and death itself will be destroyed. One day our bodies will be perfect, when Jesus comes back to complete the victory He came to accomplish. It is wrong for a child who is sick to think that he has done something he is being punished for, and it is terrible for a child to be afraid that God is punishing some sin because Daddy or Grandmother died. Yes, the abnormality in the world is a result of sin, but Jesus Himself said that sickness, blindness, lameness, and death are not by any means always a result of some sin in that person, nor is it because of a lack of faith. God hates the abnormality. It was His perfect Creation that was made abnormal by Satan's hideous subtlety.

Not only are we told to "weep with those who weep," making it very clear that God expects His children to have reasons for weeping, but we are told that we are to comfort others with the comfort which God gives to us. God comforts us in our troubles, pain, sorrows, sicknesses, and in our agony over the illnesses of others. We are to find comfort in His Word as we read it, and we are to find comfort in communicating with Him in prayer, but one of the purposes of our being comforted is that we can comfort others. Therefore, others need our comfort.

On a human level, children are meant to learn how to comfort others with the same kind of comfort they have received in their own pain, sicknesses, and deep troubles. Children are meant to understand compassion and comfort because they have received compassion and comfort — and this should be in the family setting. A family should be a place where comfort is experienced and understood, so that the people are prepared to give comfort to others. Comfort should be related to the word *family*.

Before finishing this chapter on this important aspect of what a family should be, we must consider the special needs of handicapped people. In many families someone is born with a handicap — cerebral palsy, blindness, absence of a limb, a body that is too tall or too short, deafness, a mental problem, or some disfiguring mark. Many others have an illness which suddenly paralyzes some part of their bodies, or a disease which leaves them deaf, blind, or unable to use their hands. Accidents change children as well as adults, in a moment's time, from perfectly active people into wheelchair cases or those limited by braces or crutches. Therefore, there are many families with one or more members who have some kind of severe handicap.

In this shelter-and-hospital chapter, the question "What is a family?" should bring forth the answer that the family should be the very most understanding and loving collection of people to surround a handicapped person. All of us have some defects, yet some handicaps are harder to get along with than others, and human beings as a whole can be very cruel to other human beings, and very full of pride. This is where the shelter and understanding of a family should mean that the handicap can be freely and completely discussed over and over again, whenever the child feels like asking questions or discussing the related problems. Imagination should be used in suggesting what might help in day-by-day situations. Occupational therapy should not just be a subject studied as career preparation for one who is going to help handicapped people find ways of overcoming some of their limitations. A family with a handicapped child should be full of fresh ideas of the occupational-therapy sort — figuring out, for example, how a person without hands might play checkers, put in the jigsaw-puzzle pieces, or learn to use a typewriter. Originality and creativity should be a matter of open discussion, and no feeling of embarrassment should be passed on to the child because the parent feels embarrassed. A balance, however, must be maintained to give other children — who do not have special handicaps — sufficient time and attention in the midst of the therapy or extra time which is spent with the one who needs more help.

Everyone who has had a long series of illnesses, a handicapping illness, a tragic accident, or a great disappointment in some physical area should consider the truth that the devil would like to make us feel rebellious against God, cry out against Him, say something like, "Why should this happen to me!" Our victory in the midst of the unchanging series of hardships is a victory against the devil, if we simply trust God and love Him even without a shred of understanding why. A second just-as-important factor is that God can use us *because* of the difficulty, sickness, handicap, tragedy — not *in spite* of it — to do something which He has for us to do, and which we otherwise could not have done.

We will meet certain people and be capable of understanding other people *because* of being brought together in the hospital, therapy center, or through the mutual needs of people who need our help. And the comfort with which God has consoled us is the solace which will comfort *through us* other people who have had the same kind of difficulties. As a parent you are going to be a help to other parents because of your handicapped child, not in spite of that factor. And the child will have certain sensitivities and understandings develop more deeply and fully because of having gone through the difficulties, not in spite of them.

Marry Berg-Meester married Hans Berg with stars in her eyes and dreams in her heart of having a home in South America where a big job was waiting for her husband as an engineer, and where they felt their home could be open for young people to listen to tapes from *L'Abri* and discuss them. She also looked forward to making a delightfully artistic home for this wonderful, sensitive, and strong Christian Dutchman who had gone through concentration camp in his childhood days and had seen his mother being beaten to death and his father shot, when Hans was only eight years old. What a special "making up" — for all that had been lost of home and family — was deep in Marry's desires as she began to do her creative homemaking. Hans's first job was in Holland where lovely little Jaapjan was born and began to grow with all the advantages of an imaginative and loving mother and father.

Then Steven was born, and a tragic mistake had been made in giving Marry a blood transfusion at a time when it made all the difference to the baby. The Rh factor was present — and it had been the wrong kind of blood. Steven was born beautiful to look at every way, but with brain cells destroyed to the extent that he would never walk or use his hands, nor would he ever hear. A complete change of plans had to take place and Hans took a job in Basel where little Steven could have the proper therapy. Marry's life consisted of giving Steven six hours of therapy a day, in addition to caring for little Jaapjan and the home. Hans was a wonderful father and husband in his patient help and love for both children, and his understanding of the importance of talking a great deal about the Second Coming of Christ when all believers shall be changed in the twinkling of an eye — "And Steven will be able to walk and run and sing with you, Jaapjan." The second thing Hans insisted on for the whole family was to really enjoy and appreciate the little things of every day. As they took walks, with Steven in his special wheelchair and Jaapjan running along beside them, leaves, butterflies, birds, tiny plants, ferns, and all the other beautiful little things were examined, talked about, and appreciated, as were the sunsets and the new moon. The table at mealtime was never without flowers or some Japanese type of flower or branch arrangement, and candles were used daily. A supper or a small biscuit and a cup of coffee was always a kind of important time to appreciate food in a beautiful atmosphere. It isn't that heartache was not present, nor that there was a romantic, unrealistic attitude about life, but Marry and Hans were very real in their belief of true truth, and with the Lord's help lived in an atmosphere of loving each other and of loving the Lord, without complaining about their troubles. There in Basel, instead of contacting South American students, they were helping other parents with children who needed the same kind of therapy, and a Bible class was started among them.

The time came when a five-day-a-week boarding school was discovered for Steven in Holland, where his bright mind could be trained — as equipment was available and skilled teachers who could teach him to "match cards" and "match letters" in preparation for reading and writing. Steven has proved to be exceptionally bright, and he is learning to choose the right cards every time, using a pointer fastened to his chin and cards which appear on a screen near his face. He will learn to type with something fastened to his chin, too.

Hans Berg found a job about 200 kilometers from this school, and 800 kilometers would be driven every weekend to bring Steven home, where the family communicated with him in ways they had learned to do. Bible study was a special part of each day, and Hans never left for work without a half hour of prayer before going. Their relationship was a deep and special one, and one night Marry awakened after a vivid dream, so vivid that she wakened Hans to ask him to talk to her about it. She had dreamt that Hans and Steven were walking and running together in a most beautiful field of flowers surrounded by wonderful woods. The place was vivid in its loveliness, and Steven looked so happy and well — he was running, jumping, and laughing as his father caught him and played with him. "Hans, it frightens me a bit. What can it mean? It was so very real!" — "Perhaps, Marry dear, the Lord is preparing us for Steven's death. Perhaps Steven is to be taken, and you have been shown what it will be like for him in the new heavens and the new earth." They spent the rest of the night talking, Marry has told me since, and their conversation was about death and heaven and the wonder of the resurrection and the marvel of the resurrected bodies.

A few days later the family went to a little woodsy cabin for a short vacation. It was a Monday morning, a week after the dream, when Hans kissed Marry good-bye, expecting to come back at the end of the week. He was going to work, and they were to have a little rest there in the woods, where he would join them for a second weekend. It was a rainy day and the roads were slippery. An hour after Hans had left Marry, a truck coming toward him made a wrong turn of the steering wheel, and plowed straight into the driver's seat, and Hans was immediately absent from his body and present with the Lord! His mangled body was left to be gathered up and put in a box and taken home. Marry did not find out about the accident until very late in the day, because she wasn't in their own home. She had to care for all the details, she had to get the things out of the twisted car, she had to see Hans's blood spilled over the street. And she had his body brought to their house in the coffin. Why? Because she didn't want the artificial step of a funeral home; she wanted the reality of being alone to cry and pray in privacy, with the physical remains of Hans there beside her. She wanted the aloneness of their own home in which to talk to Jaapjan about the things his father had taught him so well. Prepared? Yes, the Lord had given Marry a special preparation, a gentle way of talking to Hans which helped her when he himself was the one to die. Easy? No, no! But possible. Marry has been experiencing not ease, but *strength* given from the Lord to move to another apartment nearer Steven's school, and to continue to make a family for her boys.

Has she not wept? Oh, yes, many hours. But Marry was watering her flowers three days later. And when Marry moved to the new apartment, when day came after a night of weeping over the "impossibility of going on alone," she awakened with a determination to go out and buy paint for the walls, to bring some beauty in the midst of the starkness of four whitewashed square walls. Out came her copper and brasses and a fresh determination to make a *home* for Jaapjan, Steven, and herself. There is no box labeled TIME FOR GRIEF or TIME FOR A DEATH which gives protection against all the responsibilities of life. Life goes on, and the days right now are important for little Jaapjan and Steven, as well as for Marry herself. It isn't necessary to waste them. Then the date of Marry and Hans's wedding anniversary arrived and Marry said, "I made a cake and a nice supper and bought a new candle and a flower. I told the boys we were sad that Daddy was away from us, but could thank God for our wedding day because now we had each other to be with. I read them a funny story then, because I felt they needed to laugh." Jaapjan compliments Marry on her nice dress, "Because Daddy used to tell you how nice you looked;

I will do it now," and Marry is reading the stories which Daddy used to read. The family life is going on. There is a continuity, so important for Jaapjan and Steven, and Marry says, "God is strong, He is so wonderful, He helps me so much, and Hans helped me to know God so well." You see, Hans had a mother and father. Killed? Yes, before his eyes in a concentration camp, but they taught him that the Lord is God indeed and that when Jesus is your Saviour nothing can separate you from His love! "We may be killed, Hans, but we will go to be with Jesus, and you will meet us when He comes back." That was a separation, but not as destructive as some separations.

The will-o'-the-wisp, end-of-the-rainbow, daydream idea of happiness, of happy marriages, happy families, happy people, and "having a right to happiness" doesn't touch upon reality.

What is a family? A family is a blending of people for whom a career of making a shelter in the time of storm is worth a lifetime! A Christian family is meant to be different because of its knowledge that human beings are significant in this life and through eternity. A Christian family has been given enough in God's verbalized Word to know that when one part of the body hurts, the rest of the body is affected and does something to help. The rest of the body doesn't just "give up," but goes on. Because we have a handicap or broken ribs, a foot in a cast, dizziness or headache, we don't come to a DEAD STOP with the rest of our bodies — we go on in the best way we can.

As our family stood around Grandmother's grave on the day of her funeral — realizing the reality of the separation, but thinking also of the reality of the resurrection — the three generations, each in its own sphere of understanding, turned away with an expectancy of the return of Jesus taking place in future history. But we didn't cease to wash dishes that night, put them away, and consider the preciousness of our next few hours together. The continuity of the Lord's

Family bridges the centuries and is not meant to be represented by splintered, shattered, broken human counterparts. Togetherness in sickness and in health is to be "till death do us part."

The togetherness will not have been perfect, the care will not have been flawless, and mistakes will have been made, but sitting together after the dishes were done, each one could be thankful that while Grandmother was in the land of the living — "I sang to her every night those last three weeks. Whether or not she recognized her favorite hymns, I don't know." — "I brought her favorite flowers from the woods." — "I stood and spooned in the orange juice when it didn't seem she could swallow." — "I'm glad even the little children could bring flowers after she had gone, and come to understand something of how the *person* is in heaven, and the body is waiting for the resurrection." — "I'm so glad that I had that talk with her months ago, just to make sure that she really understood that she had accepted Christ as her Saviour. I always had a little fear, and I am glad I spoke then, because her response was so real."

Yes, it is while we are in the land of the living that the family is meant to care for each other, and to be a real shelter — from birth to old age.

# 6

## A Perpetual Relay of Truth

What is a family? It is a perpetual relay of truth! Watch the children as you organize a relay race, a running contest in which two lines of children wait as one from each line runs a distance and returns to hand the flag to a team member. Back and forth they run and pass the flag. If one drops it, there is a forfeit of returning to the starting place. What excitement is generated, as those finished (or waiting for their turn) watch to see how soon the flag will come back, groan when it is dropped, cheer when someone falls and skins a knee and then pops up bravely to run on again. This is a relay race in which it matters whether one person gets there, because if the flag is not handed on, the next person can't start on his or her part of the course.

Listen carefully as we come to Hebrews 12:1, 2:

Wherefore seeing we also are compassed about with so great a cloud of witnesses, let us lay aside every weight, and the sin which doth so easily beset us, and let us run with patience the race that is set before us, Looking unto Jesus the author and finisher of our faith; who for the joy that was set before him endured the cross, despising the shame, and is set down at the right hand of the throne of God.

We who are believers — who are in the Lord's Family —
are in a race, each of us as an individual. It is a race that is
constantly hindered by sin, by falling down and skinning
our knees, by weights which we are unnecessarily carrying
along like a rucksack full of heavy nonessentials. We are
urged to put these aside in ways which other portions of
Scripture help us to know. It is a race in which we *do* fall,
and we are told that two are better than one in this life,
because when one falls the other can lift up the fallen one
(Ecclesiastes 4:9, 10). This is true in walking down the
sidewalk — or in the spiritual walk. There is meant to be
help given in the race, from one to another, as we are placed
in different combinations together. But in this particular
understanding of the *race* spoken of in Hebrews, there are
three aspects to be thought about seriously. First, it is a
race in which others have already taken part and are now
finished. Jesus Himself finished His race, and His was the
supreme one of continuing to the cross in spite of the shame
and suffering of it all, to finally sit down at the right hand
of God. Had Jesus not completed His race, none of us would
be in it at all, neither those who looked forward to the
Messiah, nor those who have accepted Him as Saviour since
He came in the flesh. However, others have also run and have
finished — Abraham, Isaac, Jacob, Moses, Isaiah, Jonah,
Joel, Amos, Peter, Paul, John and the people in the generations of the last two thousand years. These are the "cloud
of witnesses" who are watching to see what will happen as
new generations "pick up the flag" and run on, as some fall
and get up and rub their knees, keeping ahead in spite of
an ankle swelling out of all proportion to its normal size,
running in spite of pain and difficulty, even when nasty people
throw stones from the sidelines. There are clouds of witnesses who have gone ahead and are waiting for the final results,
and Jesus is among them. Jesus intercedes, prays for the ones
now running, one by one, hour by hour. We are told that
He is praying and cares about anyone coming along in the
race.

Second, in the understanding of these verses, we need to recognize the fact that we have special help ready for the asking. Not only is Jesus watching and already interceding for us, but we are to "look unto Jesus," not with eyes that see His physical form, but with the reality of communication by reading His Word in the Bible. There is this help to be had in the race in a very practical area.

Third, I think we can see the whole race as one in which true truth is to be handed over like the flag in a relay race, from generation to generation. The cloud of witnesses is concerned not just with us as individuals (although we are significant as individuals — to others, as well as to the Lord Himself), but with the next in line. We are responsible for "handing on the flag" and for being very careful not to drop it — or to drop out — because of our responsibility to the next generation.

The primary place for the flag of truth to be handed on is in the family. The truth was meant to be given from generation to generation. If those who knew God and who had so very much to tell about Him had always been faithful, and had always stuck to the commands or the rules of the relay, there would have been no gaps. Each generation would have learned from the one before. Fathers and mothers were to tell sons and daughters. There was supposed to be a perpetual relay of truth without a break. The gaps in the world's history and in geographic generations of families came because of the refusal to pass on the truth — as a flag in the race. The first family which suffered was Cain's family, as he belligerently brought his destructive piece of creative art and called it the right manner of worshiping God. What Cain handed to his children was *false!* You can picture Cain as the one who first dropped the flag and opted out of the true race, picking up something false to pass on, running away from, rather than toward the goal! And a long line of children followed him. We live not unto ourselves; we affect other people. Cain did. Rebellious Israelites did, when they followed the gods of the Canaanites. Other people did when they spit at Jesus and screamed against Him just when He was finishing His race — or when they threw the early Christians to the lions. The people who did the throwing had children, too, but they were passing the wrong flag and leading their children in the wrong direction. Jesus cautions against false prophets, telling us that even some who do miracles in "the name of the Lord" are not true but false (*see* Matthew 7:22; 24:11), just as were those who put "the name of Jehovah" on the golden calf and brought their children out to dance around in an orgy of false worship. Just the name *God,* or the name *Jesus* is not enough. The name can be printed on a false flag, and the race can be running off at an angle, completely in the wrong direction.

Foolish fathers and mothers! Cruel families — who did not hand down true truth, but who handed down the opposite and led their children away from God. Look in your imaginations at the long lines waiting for their turn to run, grabbing the wrong flag, speeding in the wrong direction — in country after country and generation after generation. Listen to what God says to the children of Israel:

> Only take heed to thyself, and keep thy soul diligently, lest thou forget the things which thine eyes have seen, and lest they depart from thy heart all the days of thy life: but teach them thy sons, and thy sons' sons . . . when the Lord said unto me, Gather me the people together, and I will make them hear my words, that they may learn to fear me all the days that they shall live upon the earth, and that they may teach their children.
>
> Deuteronomy 4:9, 10

How clear it is. The truth of the existence and the character of God is to be made known to the children and the children's children. We are responsible for our children and for our grandchildren, for our nieces and nephews and our grand-nieces and grandnephews. That they may know *what?* The wonder of who God is, what God has done, what God has said, and what He has meant to those doing the telling. There must be some reality to relate, some true understanding of God to pass down. But does it mean that the first thing to teach is *fear?* Oh, don't let anyone make that ignorant mistake. The "fear of the Lord" is a thing that makes it possible for us *never* to be afraid of Him. "The fear of the Lord is the beginning of wisdom: a good understanding have all they that do his commandments: his praise endureth for ever" (Psalms 111:10). It is clear that whatever the "fear of the Lord" is, it is something to be understood and taught and which will bring praise as a result. But this same Psalm says; "He hath made his wonderful works to be remembered: the Lord is gracious and full of compassion" (v. 4). This One is marvelous and He is compassionate. This is the God of love, and "love suffereth long and is kind." This God is perfect in His gentleness, and is the One who says He will never fail His children nor forsake them. To fear Him means to fall flat on our faces in adoration. His greatness and love are beyond anything a human being can really understand, and we need to have for Him a feeling beyond that which we have for any human being, a feeling that makes us want to worship and be respectful. This One who is the Creator is to be marveled at, and as we walk and talk with our children, the wonders of His Creation should be pointed out.

"Look, dear, at that wonderful magnolia tree coming out with creamy, perfect blossoms. Only God could make such a growing thing. Just imagine; it once was a tiny little tree, and it grew into a big one. God can make things that grow, and then seeds that start new trees of the same kind. Isn't He wonderful?"

"Did you hear that bird's song? Listen to it! Imagine God's creating birds that could sing like that! He would have those sounds in His mind first, just like a music composer has sounds go through his head when he is writing music for a violin or a whole orchestra. How great God is."

"I see the first star; can you find it? Did you know that there are so many stars that no one can count them? But God

knows, because He made them and He made all the complicated things of the whole universe to fit together perfectly.
You'll never get to the end of discovering the amazing things
of God's Creation."

"Let's play a game about who made what!" — "I see
Patty's dress. Mommy made it." — "Good for Mommy. She
chose the stuff out of lots of material, and chose a pattern and
imagined in her head what it would look like on Patty. Good
choice, don't you think?"

"I see a building; an architect made it." — "Well, actually
a lot of men did different parts of it, didn't they, Mommy? I
saw it when it was all orange steel in funny shapes. It looks
better now." — "I wonder how many people had ideas and
put them together in that building? Just think: every single
tiny part was in somebody's head as an idea first. Wow!"

"Ohhhh, I see lights coming on along the bay. What a sight.
Some man thought up how to use electricity, didn't he? And
another designed those shapes for the lamps?" — "Amazing!
You can see the sunset in the water at the same time. Imagine
people thinking there was *no person there* to design the sun
and the water and the reflection on all those ripples!"

Come back to Deuteronomy:

> Hear, O Israel: The Lord our God is one Lord: And
> thou shalt love the Lord thy God with all thine heart,
> and with all thy soul, and with all thy might. And these
> words, which I command thee this day shall be in thine
> heart: And thou shalt teach them diligently unto thy
> children, and shalt talk of them when thou sittest in
> thine house, and when thou walkest by the way, and
> when thou liest down, and when thou risest up.
>
> Deuteronomy 6:4–7

These are parents being spoken to, and family life and family
conversation are being underlined as basically important in
teaching true truth. In other words, "Ye [the parents] shall
not go after other gods, of the gods of the people which are

round about you" (v. 14). You see, it is a handing down of *truth* from generation to generation, and people are being warned of their responsibility for the next generation.

When are you to "talk and teach" day after day? Well, there is no fuzziness about the words. It is ridiculous to say you can't understand the ancient English. It is clear that you are to talk and teach when you are sitting down in the house, walking together, about to go to sleep, and when you get up. You can't talk if you aren't together at some of these times, and you can't discuss if you aren't together. What does *talk* mean? It is a verbalized communication which gives some amount of *understanding* to the person listening. Is it only a speech or a lecture? I think it is a two-way communication of questions and answers. Is that just an opinion? No, continue in Deuteronomy: "And when thy son asketh thee in time to come, saying, What mean the testimonies, and the statutes, and the judgments which the Lord our God hath commanded you?" (v. 20). That is an honest question asking for information. Is the father or mother to reply, "Never mind, just obey the statutes and believe the testimonies and don't ask any questions"? No, the reply which God's Word gives is that the parent is to be fair and give an intelligent answer: "Then thou shalt say unto thy son, We were Pharaoh's bondmen in Egypt; and the Lord brought us out of Egypt with a mighty hand: And the Lord shewed signs and wonders, great and sore, upon Egypt, upon Pharaoh, and upon all his household before our eyes: And he brought us out from thence, that he might bring us in, to give us the land which he sware unto our fathers" (vv. 21–25).

The answer was to be one going back in *history* and telling what God did. It was to show the marvel of God's work, but also the fact that He kept His promises to His people. We are to answer our children's questions from the history of the Bible, but should also have something real to say concerning the wonder of God's work in history since the first-century church, and even in our own lives. We should have some answered prayer, some experience of His strength in our weakness, His grace having been sufficient for us in a time of terrible disappointment.

"Look, Steve, the great Paul had so many troubles you can't imagine how terrible they were; let's read them in Second Corinthians 11:22–30. Then turn to chapter 12:4–10, and let's read that together, Steve. Isn't that amazing? Paul says he has all those troubles, and then he felt the absolute last straw was the thorn in the flesh, but when he prayed for God to take it away . . . ."

"What was it?"

"We're not told, but apparently it was something physical. Anyway, his prayer was not answered, but God said that His grace was sufficient for Paul, and that His strength was made perfect in weakness. I just want to tell you that when Mommy broke her leg, and you got measles at the same time, and I had to get a leave of absence, and I was afraid our money wasn't going to cover it all — I had a very real experience of His grace being sufficient for me. No, the measles didn't get healed any faster, and the broken leg went into a cast, but day by day I discovered that God brought little things, just enough to go on for that day, and in the end we had enough for the doctor bills, even some flowers for Mom on top of the groceries. Nothing spectacular, maybe, but it seemed spectacular to me — because I know I am just not like that. I am a worrier, really. It is hard for me to be quiet and to trust. I know it was something God gave me, just as He gave Paul."

"Know therefore that the Lord thy God, he is God, the faithful God, which keepeth covenant and mercy with them that love him and keep his commandments to a thousand generations" (Deuteronomy 7:9).

"Dad."

"Yes, Steve."

"What's it mean to keep His commandments? We can't be perfect, and Jesus says that if you get really angry it is already killing in your heart."

"Well, Steve, in the Old Testament times they had to come bringing a little lamb to sacrifice, to atone for their sins and look forward to the Messiah. We now can know that we have forgiveness through Christ the Messiah, the One who died as a lamb, *the* Lamb, in our place, so that we can come to God. Jesus kept the commandments in our place, as well as dying for us."

"When did you really believe, Dad? Did you ever have doubts?"

Questions, answers, conversations while walking, natural discussions about great varieties of things, an atmosphere of reality; an atmosphere of honesty. The family — a place where true truth is to be discussed, taught, lived, and passed down. Taught? How? By example, as well as by stating facts or rules. When Jesus washed the disciples' feet He said, "If I then, your Lord and Master, have washed your feet; ye also ought to wash one another's feet. For I have given you an example, that ye should do as I have done to you" (John 13:14, 15). Who is washing whose feet as an example? Jesus, King of kings, and Lord of lords, Master of the universe, is washing the feet of created human beings — finite, sinful, limited, imperfect in every way. He is washing their feet, He who is the Bridegroom. *What?* The people whose feet He is washing are likened to the feminine; these are to be the bride of Christ, as all believers are. "Husbands, love your wives, even as Christ also loved the church, and gave himself for it. . . .So ought men to love their wives as their own bodies. . ." (Ephesians 5:25, 28): Jesus the Bridegroom, giving Christian husbands an example of what it means to be in the place of the husband loving his wife — it means, among other things, washing her feet. What an example!

Are wives not to obey their husbands? Yes, this is also there and full of reality, but it is in the same way as we are to be subject to the Lord as we follow His plan and will in our lives. Does He force His will upon us? Is it not a matter of our willingness to do His will, and His unfolding it before us, and our having minute-by-minute communication with Him? Yet, He is perfect, and in our human relationships this perfection is missing. Admonition has to be given, so that the parents — in handing down the "flag of true truth" to the children — do not hand down a flag which is a travesty of the truth.

"Let all bitterness, and wrath, and anger, and clamour, and evil speaking, be put away from you, with all malice. And be ye kind one to another, tenderhearted, forgiving one another, even as God for Christ's sake hath forgiven you (Ephesians 4:31, 32). Here is another example given to us. Jesus does not need to be forgiven as the Heavenly Bridegroom, but in our families, as we give examples of what is to be right, we are to forgive one another. Father is to forgive Mother, and she is to forgive Father; Steve is to forgive his parents when they ask forgiveness for having done something wrong to him; Father and Mother are to forgive Jessica when she has done something wrong to them. The forgiveness is to be real and not just something mumbled the way some people mumble the Lord's Prayer — as if it were some sort of set of magic words. It is an impossible thing we are asked to do — to forgive one another "as God for Christ's sake hath forgiven you." God forgives perfectly and "will remember their sin no more" (see Jeremiah 31:34). "As far as the east is from the west, so far hath he removed our transgressions from us" (Psalms 103:12). That is the extent of His forgiveness. But that admonition is not to be kicked under the rug just because it is impossible to follow perfectly. We are to be an example to our children, and in our relationship with them, of what God's forgiveness means — in some small way. We also are to be kind and tenderhearted. These are things to teach by example, so that children can understand something of the meaning and truth of the Bible. The word *father* is meant to have some of the content of faithfulness, gentleness, forgiveness, kindness, compassion, long-suffering, which will make the very word a sound that brings comfort and security.

This I recall to my mind, therefore have I hope. It is of the Lord's mercies that we are not consumed, because his compassions fail not. [Oh, my dear daughter and son, if God treated us as we deserved, we would be really consumed. But He is compassionate.] They are new every morning: great is thy faithfulness.

Lamentations 3:21–23

As a father, as a mother, as a parent, what lovely things do you have in mind to make the mornings and the days full of expectancy? How is your faithfulness being demonstrated; how is your example of faithfulness being shown? Have you ever spent time and imagination thinking up ways to snow this? A little child is meant to be able to have some understanding of this description of God the Father, because of what that child has experienced in an earthly relationship. "The Lord is my portion, saith my soul; therefore will I hope in him" (Lamentations 3:24). Thus when your child waits expectantly, sitting on the step, feet kicking the dirt, looking up the street — what sort of a response does he or she get? How much reality is there in the goodness you demonstrate? And when the little one patiently climbs the stairs, dragging a toy behind him or her, *seeking* you, really seeking you, wanting communication of some sort — what is the reception? What kind of an example are you of God's promise that "Him that cometh to me I will in no wise cast out" (*see* John 6:37).

"Thou drewest near in the day that I called upon thee: thou saidst, Fear not. O Lord, thou has pleaded the causes of my soul; thou has redeemed my life" (Lamentations 3:57). How do you teach the love of God, the tenderness of God, the compassion of God? We can't begin to do it perfectly, but we need to be conscious of our responsibility to try. Where do people get their warped and twisted ideas of God? From someone who has gotten hold of a wrong "flag" and is running off at an angle. In this relay race, the race that is the true one, the flag handed down from generation to generation

is to be the truth of the original complete Word of God.
Thank God that He did not only leave the handing down of
truth to people by word of mouth. (None of us would have
it straight by this time!) He had it written in verbalized form,
so that the truth could be preserved, and people who had parents with wrong ideas of God could still seek and find Him
— whom to know is life eternal!

"I love you, Daddy; I love you, Mommy. You are so kind
to plan this lovely day off together so we could have a picnic,
and even go to the zoo. Thank you for explaining about the
animals, and wasn't it fun to read about Noah's Ark while
we were in the zoo after our picnic? Oh, I love you."

"Do you know, Billy and Jane, that the Lord is so good
to us that we can't possibly imagine the things He has planned
for us. He says that eyes have not seen, nor ears heard, nor
the heart of man imagined the things He is preparing for us
in the future. We're going to see things much more astonish-
ing than this zoo — fantastic beauty — as well as find out a
lot of answers we don't know yet. What a terrific God we do
have. Daddy and Mommy make so many mistakes, but I'm
glad we do understand each other and love each other so that
we can know something of God's love."

Stilted conversation? Perhaps you'll think I've made it so,
but it isn't so far off. You'll have your own ideas of weaving
in truth. While we are walking through the zoo, putting children to bed, sitting and eating meals on the grass, in the
kitchen, or by the fireplace, conversation is meant to have
some connection with the reality of day-by-day life. Explaining the things of the Bible, of God's love, and of future pro-
phecy is not meant to be something separated into a cubby-
hole of "religious instruction" or "family prayer." As children
grow older there is to be a flowing unity in talking about history, present world news, science, which has its seeds in the
beginning days of the first understanding of sentences, the
first questions. Children's questions must be taken seriously
at the ages of two and three, or they won't be continuing to
ask you at twelve and twenty-three. The importance of being

given answers and being treated as a significant human being begins as soon as answers are asked for. An honest answer must be given, or you must say, "I'll try to find out."

In a Christian family there is a real discussion of when the first most important question might be asked. It would be a very different time in different families and in different children's lives, but I can remember being as worried about my children's doubts, and answering them as carefully at five years of age or even four or three, as I would be over the questions of a teenager. One never knows which answer, which explanation, which attitude, which time of treating the child as a person (as important as anyone else being talked to) is going to be the *most important time*. It is a great mistake to put off an answer, unless you say something like, "I'm so sorry, but right now I really have to finish cooking this meal, because everyone needs it on time tonight — but just as soon as I can, we'll go to your room and talk." Then keep the promise, as faithfully as a date with an adult.

The Book of Psalms is so very strong in emphasizing exactly what I have tried to illustrate with the example of the relay race. The admonition to the parents to "hand down the right flag" all those centuries ago should be really titanic to us in this century, when some people are saying that they think not only the family but Christianity is about to become extinct.

> I will open my mouth in a parable: I will utter dark sayings of old: Which we have heard and known, and our fathers have told us. We will not hide them from their children, shewing to the generation to come the praises of the Lord, and his strength, and his wonderful works that he hath done. For he established a testimony in Jacob, and appointed a law in Israel, which he commanded our fathers, that they should make them known to their children: That the generation to come might know them, even the children which should be born; who should arise and declare them to their children: That they might set their hope

in God, and not forget the works of God, but keep
his commandments.

Psalms 78:2–7

Then the Psalm goes on and tells of all the amazing things
God did in dividing the Red Sea, bringing water out of a rock,
sending the manna down daily for food, and sending meat in
the form of edible fowl.

The plea of God is to *keep* handing down the true truth —
don't miss a generation. He wants people to *know;* it is to
continue to be known. In Psalms 81:13, 16 we have the compassionate Words of God which remind us of Jesus weeping
over Jerusalem because the people turned away: "Oh that
my people had hearkened unto me, and Israel had walked in
my ways . . . . He should have fed them also with the finest
of the wheat: and with honey out of the rock should I have
satisfied thee."

God's direct Word comes to us — consider your place in
the family as central, not just in this moment of history, but
as part of the "relay." Don't let a gap come because of *you.*
Don't take the beauty of the family life — and the reality of
being able to hand down true truth to one more generation
— as a light thing. It is one of the central commands of God.
It is direct disobedience to God to *not* make known His truth,
to *not* make known the truth of Himself, and to *not* make
known the wonderful works that He has done. It is not a
responsibility to be handed over to the church and Sunday
school. In fact, in many churches and Sunday schools there
is a false flag being handed to the children, and a wrong path
being pointed out. The Word of God has been ignored by
some, and so the blind are leading the blind. Yes, finding a
true church for your family is important, but it can't take the
place of the teaching by example and speaking, when going
to bed, getting up, eating meals, and walking together. This
is a *family* task and pleasure, and one of the basic "together-
nesses" commanded by God since the beginning.

We live in a day of real desolation as far as breakdown goes. In many universities, high schools, primary schools, and even kindergartens, such a thing as the *existence of truth* is laughed at. If a child writes CREATION as the way the world began, the answer is marked wrong, because according to many textbooks and teachers there is no Creator-God. The teaching is of an impersonal, chance universe, in which there not only is no God, but no real meaning to human personalities and therefore no real significance to an individual human being and no reason to have any morals. What a black outlook! No wonder our children are handed drugs by people who couldn't care less how many lives they destroy — because they don't really believe life has any value. "What difference does it make," thinks some intellectual, "whether we live or die. There is no meaning to life." It follows naturally that someone else thinks he might as well earn a living smuggling drugs as selling milk — what difference does it make? We are told that God sent word to Joel: "Tell ye your children of it, and let your children tell their children, and their children another generation" (Joel 1:3). Tell them what? That a desolate time is upon them, and that they need to do something about it. How is the time described? "The vine is dried up, and the fig tree languisheth; the pomegranate tree, the palm tree also, and the apple tree, even all the trees of the field, are withered: because joy is withered away from the sons of men" (v. 12).

*Joy withered away!* What a description of much of today. The experiments in drugs, free living, open marriages, multiple divorces, and bisexual life have brought a withered joy. Man without God is truly like withered fruit, and "withered joy" is a great description of it. But a further verse calls for a time of prayer: "Sanctify ye a fast, call a solemn assembly together, gather the elders and all the inhabitants of the land into the house of the Lord your God, and cry unto the Lord" (v. 14). There *is* something to do about the devastating problem of living in a time when not only is joy withering away, but papers are full of horrors and fresh stories of man's cruelties to man, of twisted views of families and human relationships and their results. The "something to do" is made vivid in the next chapter of Joel: "And rend your heart, and not your garments, and turn unto the Lord your God: for he is gracious and merciful . . ." (2:13). It is a picture of the reality of coming to God, seeking Him and seeking His truth with a desire to repent of having *not* been close to Him, of having turned to run away with a false flag on another path — but it is also a picture of prayer. This prayer portrays a seriousness which puts aside food for time to concentrate on the prayer and includes whole families, children, and babies in arms coming to the Lord (v. 16). The answer coming in the future is going to affect the children and the babies in arms. It is their future. Whether or not the adults of families lead in a true seeking of God and true prayer is going to affect the history of not only their own lives but of future generations. What did God have Joel write of the future answer?

> And I will restore to you the years that the locust hath eaten, the cankerworm, and the caterpiller, and the palmerworm, my great army which I sent among you. And ye shall eat in plenty, and be satisfied, and praise the name of the Lord your God, that hath dealt wondrously with you: and my people shall never be ashamed. And ye shall know that I am in the midst of Israel, and that I am the Lord your God, and none else: and my people shall never be ashamed.
>
> Joel 2:25–27

The prophecies of the Bible will come true literally in the future, even as the prophecies of the First Coming of Jesus came true literally two thousand years ago. There will indeed be famines and pestilences and wars and rumors of wars — until Jesus comes back again — but the families that truly seek the Living God now and hand the correct flag of truth to their children now, do not need to be a part of the spiritual famine that is spreading across the earth. The casting away of the Bible continues to take place in subtle and open ways. The placing of biblical truth into the boiling pot of relativity, and watching it melt and merge into all the other relative teachings, is what is happening in the very middle of religious teachings on every side. How is the next generation going to have any possibility of making a choice as to what true truth is? The responsibility of teaching by words and by example *is* in the family as much as it has ever been. God meant the relay of true truth to continue throughout all the generations until the return of Jesus and the "time of the end."

> And he spake unto the children of Israel, saying, When your children shall ask their fathers in time to come, saying, What mean these stones? Then ye shall let your children know, saying, Israel came over this Jordan on dry land. For the Lord your God dried up the waters of Jordan from before you, until ye were passed over, as the Lord your God did to the Red sea, which he dried up from before us, until we were gone over: That all the people of the earth might know the hand of the Lord, that it is mighty: that ye might fear the Lord your God for ever.
>
> Joshua 4:21–24

God meant each generation to have honest answers and explanations, so that they could know what He had done to make it clear that He is the Living God indeed. It was to be made known to sons who trusted their fathers to be speaking truth in all earnestness. Before Joshua died there was already a turning away to false gods. How quickly people shirk their day-by-day responsibilities, and how quickly their eyes turn away from the path where the true race is being run. Zen Buddhism, Yoga, Transcendental Meditation — "Let's try this a bit; what difference will it make?" Shortcuts to some kind of "spiritual feeling" can be a snare on every side in a variety of forms. In Joshua's day it was no different, and people turned to the shortcuts of what was around them in false religions and handed the wrong flag to their children and their children's children. Joshua spoke to them in the midst of their turning to false religions: "Now therefore fear the Lord, and serve him in *sincerity* and in *truth*: and put away the gods which your fathers served on the other side of the flood, and in Egypt; and serve ye the Lord. And if it seem evil unto you to serve the Lord, *choose you this day whom ye will serve;* whether the gods which your fathers served that were on the other side of the flood, or the gods of the Amorites, in whose land ye dwell: but as for me and my house, we will serve the Lord" (24:14, 15; *italics* added).

Perhaps your own parents turned away from God into atheism, agnosticism, coldness of a neutral sort, or some false religion. The people Joshua talked to that day were a mixture, some of whom had faithful fathers and mothers and some of whom did not. The reality of God's readiness to accept us, as we come to Him through what Christ did in His death in our place, is a continual thing. A new family grasping the right flag, so to speak, and determining that from "this generation on" the children are going to have a continuity of true knowledge of God's Word to hand down, will have God's help in being faithful as long as they *ask* Him. They could say it centuries ago and we can say it now, "As for me and my house, we will serve the Lord."

And if you haven't any new family, and your father and mother have split, and there isn't any continuity that you can see? Then there is a promise which David knew to be true as he sang, "When my father and mother forsake me, then the Lord will take me up" (Psalms 27:10). The Lord is *family* indeed and in the midst of writing about the relay it is important to include the importance of the closeness to the Lord of a single person who is cut off from human family. The Lord puts it this way: "Can a woman forget her sucking child, that she should not have compassion on the son of her womb? yea, they may forget, yet will I not forget thee"

(Isaiah 49:15). But one who is alone with the Lord as his family needs to be aware that there are children who have no one to hand them the flag, and needs to spend time communicating with his Father in heaven about whom to hand it to!

There is no easy, push-button method of teaching your children the truth about God, and there is no romantic, smooth, undisturbed section of time in which to do it! Just as life is not made up of neat little packages of time for other things, so this matter of having good intentions, but always being disturbed in scheduling the "right time" for Bible reading, prayer, discussion, reading Bible storybooks, or answering questions, can go on so long that the precious years are gone! What God put in Deuteronomy cannot be improved upon as to "when" — and that is when you are together eating, getting ready for bed, walking, and so on. This means time is meant to be spent together. Something is wrong if a person, even a pastor and his wife, have so many meetings to attend that the family, the children, can never have time for questions or the togetherness which brings natural questions and answers.

A child must know that time spent together for answering his or her questions and for explaining the Bible, reading Bible stories, or studying in some way together is considered by you as important as any of the other things you do. "Sorry, Mrs. Jones, but we can't come over this evening; this is the evening that we read *Everybody Can Know* with the children, around the fireplace right after dinner. We eat dessert in there by the fire, or rather *they do* while I read, and I get the things ready for us to do together during the reading. It is our unbreakable date of the week, every Tuesday night."

"Sorry, Bill, I can't do that from six to seven because that is the hour that I keep, five days a week, for the kids. We are reading an adventure story together and we give a block of time for that. Then we're doing a study of a book of the Bible, and the kids each bring a question — you ought to

see the six-year-old's wobbly writing in her notebook. She's
got some stumpers sometimes; keeps me thinking. After
seven, maybe."

"No, I can't come to the phone right now; this is Natasha's
story time. I read her a story — we're doing *Treasures in the
Snow* right now, then a few poems out of her *Flower Fairy*
book, and then she reads the Bible. She can read it without
asking help on many of the words. Usually some questions
come out of that, and then we pray together. Tell whoever it
is to call back in about an hour."

If you have family prayers at the table, the reading should
be fairly short, and the prayer time very real. If it is to be
prayer, it should not be superficial, but actual praying for
needs of the family, for people the children ask prayer for
— or whose needs you share with them. When children pray
at night, they shouldn't be forced to pray, but you should
pray with them if they don't want to pray. "Oh, you don't
want to pray tonight? That's all right. You can talk to God
alone after I've left the room, if you want to. He doesn't go
out, but He's always here with you, and always has time to
listen. I'll pray, though, for Fiona and Margaret and Kirsty
and Ranald." And you pray for cousins or playmates, people
the child knows, and you don't make it some sort of a pattern for them to follow, but real for *you*. Many a time my
children have fallen to sleep as I've knelt by their beds
praying for the very real needs of the moment.

A little child should be sung to before he or she is old
enough to know the words — but gradually such words as
"Jesus loves me! this I know — " and "When He cometh,
when He cometh to make up His jewels, All His jewels, precious jewels, His loved and His own — " will be familiar,
happy words, connected with his mother's and daddy's certainty that the words are true. It is also a special incentive
to the mother to keep on praying for Johnny after his first
"following along" takes place and the sweet soprano chimes
in — "Like the stars of the morning, His bright crown
adorning, [Jesus loves little children] His loved and His own."

The singing of hymns, choruses, and psalms, songs with hand
motions should be joyous times, around a piano if you have
one, banging on triangles for little ones — and by recorders
or violins if you have budding musicians. Music played on
your record player should be taking place along with the
reading of the words, so that there can be discussion about
the great words based on the Bible's truth. Marching around
while banging on little drums or cymbals, little children
should be singing, "Dare to be a Daniel, Dare to stand alone!"
They will be enjoying it like mad, but also, as time goes on,
learning that standing alone like Daniel can be very real in
their *own* lives, and the life of the family.

Do you have a rocking chair? A sleepy child, a feverish
child, a sad child, a child full of fears? A child needing some
special closeness can't have anything quite like a parent rocking him or her with a quilt thrown around both people, rock-
rock, rock-rock, and the song — never mind the voice or the
ability to keep a tune —

> Great is thy faithfulness,
> Great is thy faithfulness,
> Morning by morning new mercies I see;
> All I have needed thy hand hath provided —
> Great is thy faithfulness, Lord unto me!
>> THOMAS O. CHISHOLM

There is something you can give your child in hearing the
marvelous words of God's promises sung along with your
faithfulness and love being demonstrated — rock-rock, rock-
rock. You are handing the flag to the next generation. You
are doing what God told you to do in Deuteronomy!

What should the Scripture-centered home — trying to hand
the flag to the next generation in the relay of truth — do about
discipline? What does the Bible have to say? The first thing
to be said is that the Bible is the Word of God, and God's
Word is fantastically *balanced*. Human beings are very unbalanced and prone to go off on tangents in every area of
life — with too great emphasis on one thing, leaving out

another important thing altogether. None of us will ever be perfectly balanced in our spiritual lives, our intellectual lives, our emotional lives, our family lives, in relationship with other human beings, or in our business lives. *But we are challenged to try, with the help of God.* We are meant to live in the Scriptures. Parents who want to follow what God teaches need to have blazoned in their minds, if not tacked up on a bulletin board: "This book of the law [the Scriptures as a whole] shall not depart out of thy mouth; but thou shalt meditate therein day and night, that thou mayest observe to do according to all that is written therein: for then thou shalt make thy way prosperous, and then thou shalt have good success" (Joshua 1:8).

It is impossible to meditate on the *whole* Bible if it is not being read privately as well as being taught to the children. As we come up against: "Be ye therefore perfect, even as your Father which is in heaven is perfect" (Matthew 5:48), we gasp, "How can I be perfect as a wife, husband, father, mother — in my discipline and in my love and obedience as a wife — in my loving as Christ loves, as a husband. How can I be *perfect?*" And then we read on and find that this verse (which is what we would need to do if we were to get to heaven by our own goodness) is balanced by: "If we say that we have no sin, we deceive ourselves, and the truth is not in us. If we confess our sins, he is faithful and just to forgive us our sins, and to cleanse us from all unrighteousness. If we say that we have not sinned, we make him a liar, and his word is not in us" (1 John 1:8–10). Our wonderful God, who has told us that He remembers that we are but dust and that He knows our weaknesses, reminds us over and over again that we cannot be perfect — until Jesus comes back again — but that there is forgiveness in the blood of Christ and there is day-by-day help as we ask Him.

With this as a start, yes, the Bible does say that there is to be a balanced structure in the family. The Book of Proverbs says, "My son, hear the instruction of thy father, and forsake not the law of thy mother" (1:8) and, "My son, keep thy father's commandment, and forsake not the law of thy mother" (6:20). Both parents are involved and both parents are to have some very firm rules and regulations. There *must* be some way of teaching that although there is a difference between the absolute unchangeable law of God and the rules of your household, there have to be firm rules which you agree upon. The headship of the father means that there are not to be two divergent, confusing sets of rules, but it does not mean that the mother is a non-person with no intelligent ideas in the area of good firm rules for children to obey. We can see this confirmed in Proverbs. What are the punishments to be? This needs imagination and an understanding of the individual. You will never have two children alike. A child who may respond to a spanking may have a brother who needs to be sat in a chair and told to keep still for a half hour. One kind of offense which calls for something like the removal of a dessert is quite different from another which needs an even number of whacks on the bottom. There should be an attempt to be fair and to have the child know why he or she is being punished. There should also be times when the parent says, "I was angry when I hit you, and I was wrong. I'm sorry. You were being very annoying, but it wasn't really that bad." A child is happier within the firm walls of some regular discipline, rather than living with permissiveness, but every child is not alike, and every parent is not alike. Therefore, it would be impossible to make a how-to-do-it list that would fit every situation and every person.

Children, obey your parents in the Lord: for this is right. Honour thy father and mother; which is the first commandment with promise: That it may be well with thee, and thou mayest live long on the earth. [This is quickly followed by just as strong a command in the next verse:] And, ye fathers, provoke not your children to wrath: but bring them up in the nurture and admonition of the Lord.

Ephesians 6:1–4

In Colossians 3:21 are added these words: "Fathers, provoke not your children to anger, lest they be discouraged." So the punishment by fathers and mothers is something for which God is going to hold them responsible in this direction, too — whether they are being so *unfair* in their treatment of the children that it is not helping to bring them up in the "nurture and admonition of the Lord." In other words, it is discouraging them in many ways. It seems to me that the way indicated here would be "turning them off" as far as Christianity goes.

Timothy was very obviously not "turned off" from the loving of the Lord and from following truth in His early training. Paul writes with deep feeling, "When I call to remembrance the unfeigned faith that is in thee, which dwelt first in thy grandmother Lois, and thy mother Eunice; and I am persuaded that in thee also" (2 Timothy 1:5). Terrific statement. Both the grandmother and mother had an influence on little Timothy — which produced the man Timothy. What a responsibility grandmothers and mothers have in handing the flag of truth to the next generation, and what a well-commended job these two did! Yes, fathers are warned not to discourage with what God calls "provoking your children to wrath" — and this must not be disregarded. It is well for us as fathers and mothers to remember that we are imperfect, and we are not God. We need constantly to pray for help in our treatment of our children, and to tell the Lord as we pray that we are glad we have Him as our Father (and not ourselves as our "father"), because He is so forgiving and gentle as to say that when we confess our sins He immediately forgives us and cleanses us from all unrighteousness. In the balance in our training — firm rules, punishing, forgiving, teaching — would it be possible for Paul to say to our children (as God gave Paul the words) what he said to Timothy? — "But continue thou in the things which thou hast learned and hast been assured of, knowing of whom thou hast learned them; And that from a child thou hast known the holy scriptures, which are able to make thee wise unto salvation through faith which is in Christ Jesus" (2 Timothy 3:14, 15).

At this point I literally stopped to telephone Priscilla and was told that when asked, "What would you say makes a happy family?" five-year-old Giandy, rolling his blue eyes angelically, said, "Tell them to spank them enough when they are bad, 'cause then you don't fight, and that is happier." So you have the evidence that I'm not putting forth a romantic picture of all sweetness and light and no need for spankings!

For children to grow up with a respect for Scripture, we feel strongly that it must be consistently treated with respect and reverenced as God's Word, different from all other books. Meaning what? Meaning that if a passage is used in a Sunday-school lesson or at family prayers or preached about at one time — and then the same passage is paraphrased another time as a joke at a party or a dinner — it is impossible to feel that the joking, laughing people *really* feel this is seriously the Word of the Creator of the universe, the Holy God. Jokes using Bible passages, jokes about heaven or about baptism, misuse of verses to make puns giving double meaning to try to be funny — all of these dishonor God's Word and disregard His holiness, both while they are going on and in the growing question which forms in children's minds if they are thinking, sensitive people. There are enough other books to quote from if one wants to make puns or be funny. The Bible should be protected as truly the Word of God, to be used with deep respect, excitement, joy, hope, searching, wonder. Listen to Paul as he continues in Second Timothy: "All scripture is given by inspiration of God, and is profitable for doctrine, for reproof, for correction, for instruction in righteousness: That the man of God may be perfect, throughly furnished unto all good works" (3:16, 17). *All Scripture* — read it over again — has its specific purpose, is inspired by God, and will bring about a result in the *man of God* who will come forth as Timothy did, having been brought up not only knowing it, but having it given to him consistently in its true meaning.

Another area which is important in passing the flag of truth to the next generation is being careful to always tell the truth (in as far as you are able) about everything you are asked. "Let's pretend!" should be a wonderful development of imagination, and "pretend" fairies, "pretend" people who live under the furniture, "pretend" animals that talk, can be encouraged, and talked about. Fairy stories are a wonderful part of childhood, but with the understanding that "this is just pretend." When it comes to "Santa Claus bringing the gifts," it is important that this not be given in a confusing way: "Oh, yes, it is true," when you are later going to say, "No, it wasn't really true all those years." We'll talk about special traditions in another chapter, but right here there is the need to realize that a child needs to be able to really depend upon you to tell the truth and to differentiate between pretending, kidding for a short moment, and declaring something is true, only to say later that it is not. A child should be able to be sure that when Mother or Daddy say, "We're going out and we'll be back at ten," that this will actually take place, or that you will call up to say it is going to be longer. To disappear and say nothing (unless it is a small baby who is asleep) can start a lack of trust. It is confusing to say, "Santa Claus is real — Jonah really was a true man — And Jesus was born as a little baby in a stable; but He had lived forever and forever before, as the Second Person of the Trinity — An Easter Bunny put this on the table for you — Jesus rose from the dead in a real body, and ate fish with His disciples by the seaside." It can sow the seeds of doubt in a dismal way to later "unmix the mix" and say, "This was true truth, and that was just for fun," when you have gone on for years mixing it all up in one dish. Truth must be given in answers about sex, about how babies are born — and about how steel is made! As much as is possible you must give correct answers and understanding answers about Creation and the true truth of Genesis!

One final thing about Christian families which is different from any other kind of family — as soon as a child is born into the Lord's Family, whether at five or fifteen, twenty or forty, a *double* relationship commences. There is still a father-child, mother-child relationship, but there is immediately a brother-and-sister-in-Christ relationship! Husband and wife are also brother and sister in the Lord, in the Lord's Family. Child and parent have the brother-and-sister-in-the-Lord relationship, and the whole family is "one in the Lord." This is very exciting and a special thing, but it brings with it some specific realities of choices which face each individual at times in life. The small child, of course, is told to obey parents. The parents are to be careful to ask the Lord for guidance. The child is also to be taught that "prayer changes history," and that they *do* have access directly to the Lord in all kinds of things. Prayer with and for a child, prayer as a family together, should not take the place of the child feeling that he or she can come privately to the Lord and talk to Him and bring problems to Him and ask Him about things. A child should be able to feel, for example, that God could bring about a change of the school he or she is attending, by putting it into Daddy's mind that another school would be better. Even at an early age, a child should *not* feel that there is no direct appeal to the Lord in the area of problems, even with the need to obey the parent.

The hard choices come when parents (as a child grows to adulthood) come between the leading of the Lord to the child and give opposite commands. Matthew 10:37 says, "He that loveth father or mother more than me is not worthy of me: and he that loveth son or daugther more than me is not worthy of me." And in Luke the admonition is made very strong by saying, "If any man come to me, and hate not his father, and mother, and wife, and children, and brethren, and sisters, yea, and his own life also, he cannot be my disciple" (14:26). What does it all mean? Aren't we to love one another? This is not contradiction, but simply strong, forceful language showing that our love for the Lord, our consideration of Him *first* is to be so great, that any other love would seem like hate by contrast. It is telling us that we are to really put the Lord — our love for Him, our doing of His will — before all else, even before our own lives. This speaks not only to those facing martyrdom right now in many parts of the world, but it speaks to people who are in the dilemma of whether to put parents' commands first, or the clear leading of the Lord first. A parent (when that parent is a Christian) should declare to the Lord, "This child is Yours, and I will never hinder him or her from doing Your will, even if it is against my desires or my ambitions or my hopes for his or her life." This is what the parent is meant to do, and if this is adhered to there should be no great tearing, searing breaks in a Christian family — simply much praying on the part of parents that the children will really want God's will and recognize His day-by-day leading. The decision of a child to do the Lord's will should be a joy to the parents. Unhappily, this is not always the case, and when a choice has to be made between the two, the Bible is clear — each individual's responsibility before the Lord is to obey Him and Him only!

In a case where only one parent is Christian (or when only one person — a child in the family — is a believer), then great division can result. Jesus has specifically said, "Think not that I am come to send peace on earth: I came not to send peace, but a sword" (Matthew 10:34). He is talking about this very thing as He continues in Matthew — it can be that "a man's foes are those of his own household" (see v. 36). This has happened time after time in history, as family members have become "spies" and handed· over someone to be burned at the stake, eaten by lions, or buried alive, and it is taking place today in certain countries.

Martyrdom is not the result in all families who are "split" by Christianity, as often it simply means that a wife or a daughter or a father or a son is to show great love and patience and to demonstrate the reality of the truth in very mundane, everyday, unglamorous, undramatic ways. It may mean a lonely walk within an unchanging circumstance, and part of "putting the Lord first" may mean much "foot wash-

ing" or doing the hardest dirty work there is around the farm
or house.

One person in one family in one village in one county in
one nation can, even *alone,* be the one to start the beginning
of a new line of believers, as that one begins to really pray
for specific individuals, to talk when the moment opens up,
and to lead a few others one by one to know true truth. Suddenly a nation which has seemed completely shut off by the
laws of a religion such as Islam can have springing up in it
a beginning "line" in the relay of truth. Truth *will* be relayed
— in every period of history — by some. This we know from
the Word of God.

Can't you imagine them now? Throughout all centuries,
all geographic locations — some from every tribe and nation
and kindred and tongue and people — being faithful, handing the flag of true truth, not dropping out, starting new
family lines — right up to the moment when Jesus comes
back again! Let's say with Joshua with a shout (inside our
heads if we don't want anyone else to think we're being too
dramatic), "As for me and my house, we will serve the Lord!"
in this twentieth century.

# 7

## An Economic Unit

What is a "good" standard of living? How much is "too much," how little is "too little"? What are the necessities of life? What are the luxuries? What are the things of harmful affluence? What degree of poverty is crushing? Where should money be saved and where should it be spent? Who is right in "pinching pennies" at one place, and being "extravagant" in another area, when someone else does the very opposite by economizing in the second area and being sure that the right place to spend is where the other person is "too stingy"? How much does a family need to have for a "good family life," and how many people need to contribute how much work to bring in that amount? Do both mother and father have to work full time to provide? To provide *what?* What is most needed — the "things" and the abundance of TV easy-to-fix dinners to eat in front of the numerous TVs, or the real home atmosphere which someone needs time to work at, and the home cooking which someone needs to have time to do? How can a family be a family economically, rather than being torn apart by the frantic acquiring of money which will bring in an acquired number of things or pile up a bank account? There has been a lot of serious thinking and praying (for Christians) to do in the area of *balance* in economic life in every period of history, and perhaps especially at any time "depression" is prophesied.

We knew a family in Lausanne some twenty years ago, a mother with a son and daughter who sometimes lived with her at the then-temporary apartment and went to a day school — or sometimes went to boarding school. Father was an importer-exporter who traveled most of the time around and around the world. When the teenage girl asked, "Why, Dad, can't you ever be home? Why can't you do less and have some time together with us?" The reply was, "I have to earn enough to have enough to leave for you and your mother and the boy — so that if I die you'll have enough." This is not exaggerated. It is a true situation — that family lived in a "temporary" situation for years, getting ready for a future which, when it came, would leave only part of the family there to pay the goverment taxes on inherited income, and they would be without a father. *When* did that man picture a family life being "normal" — when was the temporary portion going to end?

We all know examples of homes where both father and mother work "until we get another car" or "until we pay for this house" or "until we buy a summer cottage" or "until we get the furniture we need" or "until we get more electric timesaving devices" or "until we save up for Johnny to go to college." Months go by, years go by — Johnny and Jody are out of the nursery they had been dropped in daily and are now in school. More time goes by and they can have a key worn around their necks instead of a baby-sitter to be there when they get home from school. Never will these two in my imaginary family know what it is like to have Mother open the front door or the kitchen door and say, "Hi! How was your day? Smell the bread baking? I'm making orange rolls. Want some dough to make into a 'man'? Come on in and have a glass of milk." *Never*.

Some human beings remember a day nursery, a school, a strange succession of people who yelled at them or gave a mixed blur of teaching, a key around their necks, more schools, a college, a job, a succession of jobs, an apartment or a house with a wife or a husband who also worked and whom they met at times in the evening, a hospital, a nursing home, an old-folks' home — *finis!*

What is important to *provide* with the "work" that is being done? Let's go back to the beginning of things to take a look from this viewpoint of economics. God said unto Adam: "In the sweat of thy face shalt thou eat bread, till thou return unto the ground . . ." (Genesis 3:19). Yes, thorns and thistles and all the other results of the Fall were being unfolded as the result of sin and of believing Satan's lies, but part of the result was that *work* would be necessary for human beings to be able to eat. The hard work was being handed to Adam as his part of the responsibility for providing bread. Now without thinking of any other aspects at all, please let's think first of all of the terrific *change* taking place. Before this, Adam had had the joyous and fulfilling creative work of naming the animals, having dominion over the earth, caring for the garden, communicating with God as well as with Eve, having ideas of a variety of sorts, and the opportunity to do things as a result of his ideas, with the only restriction being: "Don't eat of the fruit of this one tree." Eve shared the freedom and scope of possibility with Adam.

What is different now? Not only is a pure democracy no longer possible because of sin, and man is named as head of the home, but man is given a command which is part of the curse — he must work to produce food and the necessities of life. Eve is told that the multiplied possibility of conceiving children is part of her "sorrow." It won't be the perfect spacing, whatever that was meant to be before the Fall, and there is to be a relationship which will not be as perfect with Adam as it was before. But the economic responsibility was not a joyous one, and there began the long process (which continues through the centuries) of some kind of work being needed to provide the necessities of life: food, drink, shelter, and clothing — differing greatly from century to century and from geographic location to geographic location as to what is considered "necessary."

Now God in His gentleness has caused the sun to shine on believers and unbelievers alike — so that people can grow crops well whether they are atheists or children of the Living God through belief. The acquiring of the necessities, and the luxuries of life has not been limited to people who believe in God. In fact, the Bible clearly shows that often the ones who have much in this life are going to be the ones who will have *nothing* in the next life. In the whole scope of the "curse," God has allowed men to find things to alleviate the pain and suffering and the hard work, too. For example: wheels, fire, instruments of metal (first spoken of in Cain's family), right on down to modern washing machines. It is not necessary for us to live in a log cabin and do our washing in the river, never take vitamins, and refuse to have our appendix out in order to live directly before the Lord. But there is a need of serious discussion and family prayer together in considering the area of economic things. There should be a family togetherness in this.

It is imperative to say that there *is* real poverty in every country, including the United States, and worse poverty in many other countries of the world. People needing definite outside help and seeking ways to survive hard times, must never leave out the importance of sharing with those who are in tragic need. Before going on to speak of family oneness in economic survival, it is a realistic thing of balance to turn to the Bible and see what God says about economics: "Jesus said unto him, If thou wilt be perfect, go and sell that thou hast, and give to the poor, and thou shalt have treasure in heaven: and come and follow me" (Matthew 19:21). Now this was to the rich young ruler who thought he was *perfect* and who had said he had kept all the law — to him Jesus says in effect, "You have no idea of what perfection is. If you were to be perfect you wouldn't love your riches so much; you would demonstrate that you loved God with all your heart and soul and mind in this way." Jesus is also speaking very naturally of "treasures in heaven," indicating that there is a "bank account" there being filled with what human beings *give away*.

Matthew 6:19–21 speaks to the whole family with a lesson on economics:

> Lay not up for yourselves treasures upon earth, where moth and rust doth corrupt, and where thieves break through and steal: But lay up for yourselves treasures in heaven, where neither moth nor rust doth corrupt, and where thieves do not break through nor steal: For where your treasure is, there will your heart be also.

Whatever is to be said about family economics, a small child earning its first money should have the attitude and excitement bred into him or her from early talking about how to share the family money. A tenth or other portion will naturally be put aside into another matchbox — or a different little bag, a wee purse — something to distinguish it as "treasure" which the Lord has commanded us to save. That really is the only "saving" which the Lord has commanded, but I don't believe He has commanded *against* having a portion in the barn or bank or storehouse here. It is like the matter of loving the Lord *more* than father and mother and children, wife and husband and sister and brother — being made emphatic. We are strongly told we are to love each other with a reality that is to be carefully demonstrated. Because we love the Lord *more,* we will not love each other less — because we give to those with whom the Lord would have us share economically, we will not have less in the end!

Come now to "family economics." Is not the making or building of a home one of the primary necessities of having a place and an atmosphere for family life? Read aloud together Laura Ingalls Wilder's books *The Little House in the Big Woods* and others, and your children will be wishing Daddy could build the log cabin himself, shoot the meat, capture wild turkeys, smoke bacon, and clear land to plant while Mother spins and weaves, makes bread and a zillion other things along with churning butter. The pioneer days were days in the United States of young wives and husbands carving out a life in the wilderness with much struggle and sorrow, but also with some people having the kind of memory which Laura Ingalls Wilder had of a family life which many could envy today. There is a need of sharing the work to provide food, shelter, drink, clothing. There is something very special about father digging the garden, making a chicken coop, examining the profitability of keeping rabbits, working in a way that three-year-olds can watch and copy, with realistic demonstration before their eyes of just what their father is providing. There is something that can't have any substitute for having the mother be an expert in making a tremendous variety of bread (brown, oatmeal, whole wheat, honey and butter), rolls, gingerbread men, apple pies, and homemade ice cream. Smelling, watching, helping, tasting, and feeling have no counterpart in growing up with the security of tangible evidence of the needs being provided.

There are interesting jobs and areas of creativity in work itself, but to put the *home* on one side and a *career* on the other as two opposite things — one mundane and only a matter of washing floors, dishes, and ironing clothes, the other fascinating and fulfilling — is to be just plain *bankrupt* in the area of knowing what life is all about, and particularly, as a married person, what *family life* is all about. In the process of providing all the economic needs of the family, if the family itself is being wiped out entirely, it all becomes a sad farce. How many people today are rationalizing the fact that they are neglecting to make any kind of a home at all and failing to spend any time with their children — because they are "providing more" or "being fulfilled" or proving they are not "downtrodden slaves to a house" or "doing good works"! It is possible to destroy the family, your own and others', because your home has fallen apart in the name of "doing good works." There is a great need for *stopping* as a family together, praying for a whole evening, for a whole day off together, discussing, praying, asking God, "Please show us before it is too late; what balance are we to have in our family in order to have time together before it is too late?" What is worth putting first?

I have a personal advantage in having lived for sixty years, having been married for forty years, having had four children and now four children's marriages and families to observe and be a part of, and twelve grandchildren. I can say positively that the years fly past like a mist in the night! Time disappears more quickly than smoke! It is not possible to go backwards. The "now" is important if there is ever to be any family life. Steve Turner, a young English poet, has lines in his poem "Ageing" which I would like to quote from the book *Tonight We Will Fake Love*:

> "At some point in his life
> there came a shortage
> of future."

Apply to the family life Steve's capturing of truth concerning time. Economic shortages can never compare with "a shortage of future." How long do we have in this mixture, in this blend, and what can be our list of priorities as we think of this shortage? Perhaps you have had narrow escapes. John and Pris were driving home late at night, coming back from a time with John's parents, when a truck loomed into sight, wedged across the highway without any parking lights on. There was no time to stop, except as the brief moment before the crash gave a moment for less speed, and the engine of their little car wedged a fraction of an inch before the windshield was smashed. Had the engine not been that *exact height* and had become wedged under at that spot — or the truck a bit higher — the whole family would have been wiped out. It gave a great deal to think about for John and Pris and the children. What is important? What is the best use of money and of time?

Naturally, as Christians, the first important thing is to know that the family is in the Lord's Family and will in the future be together eternally. Nothing can compare with that importance. But for a Christian family the reality of having a family *life* is an important fulfillment of what God made families to be, as well as an example. And the snare Satan dangles before us — to "put off" until some future date the reality of togetherness —is a snare that robs people of day after day of the "now." Marry and Hans Berg only had ten years of days, but they were full of living in the "now" of putting the Lord first (and each other and the family life also first, in the sense that this is a part of putting the Lord first) and the economic supply *after* that!

How can a family be a completely independent economic unit? Of course, one can find hundreds of examples of farmers — those who have fruit orchards, ranches, egg farms, fish hatcheries, and those who grow poinsettias or orchids, raise dogs, breed horses, and so on. There are great varieties of things that can be done on a piece of land, including raising enough vegetables to eat, enough animals to provide meat, enough fruit and berries for the year's needs, to say nothing of making one's own jam, pickles, and other preserves. I well remember our years in Grove City, Pennsylvania, when Fran was a pastor there, not only of having our own garden and canning great varieties of things, but being shown proudly by wives of farmers their rows and rows of artistically arranged fruits and vegetables in shining glass jars. "I did up five hundred quarts in all this year, not counting the pickles and jams, and, of course, the honey from our bees." This was before freezers had been invented for home use, and the year-round canned supply of food from the land was complete for many families. Crops which yielded "too much" were shared with town friends.

Whether on farms or ranches or plantations, growing products for sale or caring for a piece of land for one family's needs, the beauty of this sort of economic provision is that the whole family shares in all kinds of work together. Not that one should only imagine rosy-cheeked, smiling, happy children and parents, never tired or cross or hungry, bringing in crops in garland-decked baskets! Of course, there is blood and sweat and tears, but there is a possibility of survival even when the world's economic system collapses, and there is also a possibility of working together and putting imaginations and ideas together to figure out what can be done to meet one's needs.

What about sudden loss of jobs and the bleak reality of *not* living on a farm? Are there any family-together ways of meeting sudden economic depression or the special needs because of illness or accident on the part of the wage earner? At the time of the Russian Revolution a lovely Russian family, aristocratic, cultured, well educated, well-off, were vacationing in Biarritz when the announcement came that the borders were closed. It would be impossible to return home, and they were fortunate to be out with their lives. They were cut off from money supply forever, from all their possessions except the few things in suitcases in the way of clothing, with only enough with them for the vacation, as far as cash went. Of course, there was no way ever to draw from the bank in Russia again, and they were faced with the brute, hard facts of life: money to live on must be earned. The father was a gentlemen who had great knowledge of skiing, sailing, swimming, horseback riding, and such things, but who had never had the need to earn a living and no preparation for any specific job. The mother had a skill in doing fine sewing and embroidery. They put their thoughts together and decided that Madame would make children's clothing — exquisite hand-embroidered, smocked, hand-hemmed, and marvelously Parisian-correct children's clothing — which would sell in good shops. Father could learn to cook and would make beds, do dishes, and help the children with their homework. They settled into years of life in Switzerland, putting the two little girls through school, and then university and special graduate work — one of the little girls was our first doctor when we came to Switzerland. Dr. K. and her sister taught philosophy at the university. A stranded family with no formal "work" — but becoming an economically self-supporting unit because of really sharing what could be contributed by each one.

It isn't a bad thing to think together of possibilities. "Mom, you make great apple pies. We could have a special catering thing: APPLE PIES FOR SPECIAL DINNERS, or maybe we could bake bread, too, and deliver it and different kinds of pies. People would get used to it, and when their company tasted it, we'd get new customers. Let's try, Mom!" — "Dad, let's start a lawn-cutting service, since you lost your job. We could get another lawn mower, and go do it together when I'm not in school. Then with cutting shears and studying up on plants and things, maybe we'd get kind of expert on horticulture. It's good, healthy, outdoor work and probably better for your health than the office anyway. Why not?"

Bea and Eddie started a candle business in their own barn, and it has grown into a wholesale supply place, as well as an attractive gift shop. Candles are still made in the basement where they first started. Their five children have not only helped to unmold candles, to pour, to paint special decorations on some, but to wait on the store, or to "get supper ready while Mom and Dad are finishing this pour." This family working together to support the family does the opposite thing from scattering to different directions for jobs — although even in this kind of economic freedom from being fired there are problems. Not the least of the problems is being sure to keep a "balance" — how big to let the company get. How much time should be used in the work, and how much used for being together, *really?* When is the scale tipped into working only for a future, rather than living in the "now," even in this? When do you shut the doors to go to church or off on a picnic or have an "early closing" for a family reading time together?

Whether you are pushed into the need of studying how to economize because of depression, or whether you decide as a wife to give up your job and do more creative and interesting things in stretching food and clothing, it is good to think of some of the things that can be done to make life more interesting, as well as to develop creative talents in the framework of the family. Making your own clothing costs less than buying ready-made things, especially if you buy your material at sales, or at factory-outlet cloth stores. One step even less expensive than this is taking clothing that is old, but with still good material, ripping out the seams, washing and pressing the pieces, and figuring out what you can make for the children out of the shapes. I remember that my mother (who did not learn to do dressmaking until she was in her forties — after she had returned from China as a missionary) made us the most amazing clothes out of other people's hand-me-downs. She once ripped out a gray linen suit with a gored skirt into many thin, strange-shaped pieces. Washed and ironed, these bits presented an amazing "impossibility" as material suitable for the straight, shapeless, short dresses of the twenties — for my oldest sister who was going to college. Mother got an enormous piece of brown paper and cut it into a kimono-sleeved straight shape just the right size and kind of dress Janet wanted. Then she took the gray linen and figured out — as with a jigsaw puzzle and geometry problem combined — what size pieces she could get, and how to fit them together to form a really lovely design. The pieces were cut with enough for a hem, painstakingly, pressed under a damp cloth with crisply folded-in hems, and the pieces were ironed again after hemming. Then the pieces were basted to the brown paper with about one-eighth inch left bare. I remember being full of awe as an eight-year-old kneeling on the floor watching the whole process. How on earth would all this make anything? I felt sorry for Janet. Then my mother got gray embroidery thread the same shade as the linen, and the fagoting started. Do you know what the fagoting stitch looks like? It is like a cross-stitch, but with a twist in it, done by holding two pieces of cloth together, with a thin rim of space showing that there *are* two pieces, giving the same effect as hemstitching. Out came a very expensive-looking dress that looked as if it could have come from a shop on Rue St. Honoré or Fifth Avenue. I remember that Mother was criticized for "dressing her children too well — tsk, tsk — a missionary, too!" Not only "new" clothing can be made from ripped-out clothes, but quilts, as the early American settlers discovered, or quilted materials can make skirts. If depression hits, or if you decide that kneeling on the floor and figuring out creative ways to cut clothes is more fun than working in an office, remember that your imagination can be stretched to see what you can make out of "nothing," not forgetting the woolly toys out of sweaters with moth holes in them — skip the holes or embroider them with flowers!

Which do you think a child would prefer — quantities of clothing bought at stores (with no Mommy around to be with, no Mommy to talk to, cook with, ask questions of, or watch being creative) or even imperfectly made things which the excited child watched being made, while sewing doll clothes out of the leftover bits? When there is no money to buy toys, they can be made by an imaginative father out of wood, and out of cloth, wool, cotton, oilcloth, or all sorts of things by a mother. The wealth of ideas as to what can be made out of shoe boxes is endless — a shoe-box garden with grass and bits of mirror for lakes and tiny pipe-cleaner dogs; or a shoe-box doll's bed, all complete with matching blankets and pillows; a shoe-box "room" with others to be added, when dollhouses cannot be bought, and with beds made out of cardboard and empty cotton spools, even a shoe-box baby carriage with a string to pull it along the floor. Depression times can take away the money for toys, but not the ideas for original and more-fun things because Daddy or Mommy made them.

There are times when there is no job for the father and one turns up for the mother. If the family is close together and they have prayed about work turning up, of course Daddy can cook (Maybe he is a better chef, anyway!) and bathe the baby, fix the bottle, wash the diapers, clean the house, and so on — while Mommy works. There are periods in life when a sharing is needed. A husband who is in graduate school (and whose wife is earning to help him go on through) ought to cook if he gets home first, and wash and iron in the evenings, too, until he can get to his studies — and the wife can go on marking papers, if she is teaching. I've lived through seminary days and during depression times when there were no jobs. Not only did we make our own furniture out of junk (And we loved it, too, and have the leather-covered nail keg still in our bedroom — it wore well!), but I did dressmaking for the seminary professors' wives and designed and made leather belts and buttons and sold them in sets. The leather was a leftover from making our furniture, and we had bought it for twenty-five cents a pound at a factory outlet. (This was early thirties, if you wonder!) True, it was a minimal amount of money, and I had to do the other part of stretching food and making my own clothing out of mill ends, but we didn't starve. Fran helped to clean the house, to swish the sheets up and down in the bathtub (and poke at them with a contraption on the end of a stick which was supposed to be suction to get out the dirt better than a machine)! Fran was the "machine part" on the other end of the stick. There are all kinds of ways to pitch in when needed — to become a team.

Pris and Debby had positions quite different from mine when their husbands were in seminary, as they taught French in good private schools in Saint Louis. However, the husbands' sharing of housework during the days of the girls' earning the money was the same. Udo was a good cook and even baked cakes. John couldn't boil water, but valiantly did other things with much energy! In *L'Abri* they still share in these ways. That is, the men help with children and house and a variety of jobs. Who said a woman couldn't share and contribute and add to the exchequer? Certainly not the Bible. Read Proverbs 31 which describes the *virtuous woman*. This woman is pointed out as especially righteous. Perhaps she discourages you with all her talents and all her opportunities to use them, but there are certain things to be considered carefully in the atmosphere of her adding to the material "wealth" of the home. Read from verses 11 to 31, and although it would be possible to write many pages on this, we do need to condense a few things to fit into our understanding of the biblical view. She seeks wool and flax in order to spin thread. Later we see that she weaves tapestry and that she makes scarlet clothing for her household, as well as silk and purple clothing for herself. She isn't afraid of the winter, because she has been looking ahead with these preparations, so that she will be ready for the first storm. She not only weaves cloth for her household, but she makes girdles and fine linen to *sell* as she delivers them to the merchants (v. 24). She is involved in real estate as she looks at a field with knowledge and understanding sufficient to make a decision to buy it and to plan a vineyard which she plants (v. 16). She has the knowledge that such a decision would take concerning the land's suitability for that crop, landscaping, and planting, but also she evidently has the *freedom* to do it. She is obviously doing some sort of social work for other people, so she is allowed to share with the poor. This woman has freedom to give a portion of their goods to help poor people, as well as time to spend doing something for others outside the household. Her children have enough of her time, however, and know her well enough and are happy enough with her as their mother to "arise up, and call her blessed," so this speaks of a family life of some very definite kind, as well as a good relationship with her husband who "praiseth her" (v. 28). She is specifically a woman who is a believer, and is said to be one who fears the Lord, so she has a balance in the spiritual portion of life — some reality which the Lord says is worthy of praise (v. 30).

As we think of this whole matter of the family as an economic unit, I would think that this chapter of Proverbs gives us two vitally important points to remember. First, her husbands trusts her in these material, economic realms: "The heart of her husband doth safely trust in her, so that he shall have no need of spoil. She will do him good and not evil all the days of her life" (vv. 11, 12). There need to be specific and real areas — things that count — where such a trust is demonstrated! If a husband earns the actual money, and the wife does the multitudinous number of things we have been talking about in creative areas (chef, gardener, nurse, dressmaker, interior decorator, spiritual teacher, educational guide, caring for the living artwork — the day-by-day mobile of the family), then not only should there be a togetherness in the total of the family life in all the other parts when there is time to be together, but a certain portion of the *money* should be in the wife's hands to spend. How? As a household account for food, seeds for the garden, plants, tickets for a concert, anything she can make out of it because of being very resourceful — baking her own bread, stretching a chicken to feed ten people, and so on! If a woman has ability to be a good manager, she ought to have some scope in which to show forth this ability and have it be a practical help to the family. Always remember that trust needs a very real place to be demonstrated, and ability needs an opportunity to develop. Second, there is no competition with the husband. "Her husband is known in the gates, when he sitteth among the elders of the land" (v. 23). Whatever this wife, this virtuous woman, does, it enhances her husband's leadership and his place "in the gates and among the elders of the land." She does not compete with him. She does not put her work before his and cause his place to be diminished.

Two people with two separate careers and living in one house, but infrequently together — with children who are more frequently cared for by other people than by their parents — have really not formed a family, and the economic things have become a kind of people-eating monster taking all the humanness out of the relationships. What a cold thing is a check for the poor little rich child, if that is the only thing that either parent has ever "made" for him or her. A boarding school — with a check for Christmas and DO WHAT YOU WANT WITH IT attached! Lots of "economic" and no "family" and no "unit" in any sense of these words. Exaggerated? There are many in this situation, as well as many in rags on the streets of India. Two extremes — but the oneness that can come in sharing the material needs — by each one contributing in a way that enhances family life, rather than tearing it apart — is something to be sought for in a moment of history when not only the ravages of depression and the fears of losing everything face some people, but when the ravages of divorce and breakup of the family also face others. What can money do to replace the oneness which can result even in the economic area when people work out a planned togetherness of sharing things, instead of stubbornly driving ahead like a truck plowing through a flower garden? If affluence is the *goal* — no matter what — it can be the only result, with the family completely *lost*.

"We'll get along somehow; I can plant a garden of vegetables in a rented plot if we don't have space, and I can make amazing things out of old clothes." — "We'll get along, I can learn to make bread, and I'll start a little nursery school for the neighbors' children, three days a week." — "We'll make it if we get rid of the car, and use bicycles." — "We'll sleep in a tent this vacation and have just as much fun!" — "Let's stick together and work it out."

If economic matters are pushing you apart, rather than drawing you together, spend some time thinking and praying about it. "For the *love* of money is the root of all evil" (*see* 1 Timothy 6:10), not the money itself, but the lack of balance in what is put first. The family can be an economic unit, a "company" of its own, a oneness of loving-each-other people who say, "That might sound like a great opportunity, but if it takes us away from each other I'd rather have less." There is a really crazy idea which comes forth in a conversation which makes a contrast of importance like this: "Do you work or have a career?" — "No, I'm *only* a mother and a housewife." Or, "What do you do?" — "Oh, I support our family with a better salary than my husband; I have a career as a buyer." *This* type of contrast seems to make the "mother and housewife" inferior in some way, and also puts forth the supposition that she is doing nothing to help out economically to raise the standard of living for her family — and that she has no "career."

It would make a good mathematical game some evening for the whole family to sit around a table and figure out what would have to be paid in hard, cold cash for what "only a housewife and mother" is doing day by day. How many days has she been a nurse for sick children? What would you have to pay for her baking, her cooking, her canning and freezing of vegetables? What about the slipcovers she made for the couches and chairs? What about the sweaters she knit for her husband, the boys and girls, and herself? How much would that crocheted afghan on the bed cost if it had been bought? How about the curtains in the living room or dining room? What do embroidered cushions like those cost? Count in the homemade toys and the fudge and the thousands of cookies and the popcorn, while you are doing it. As recreational director, party planner, and organizer of picnics, what would she be paid an hour? What about the letters she typed for Dad? What would a taxi driver be paid for all the driving she has done to take the kids to school? Who could pay for the loving child care with baths and rocking, singing and reading aloud, teaching and answering questions honestly? Now that she is doing dressmaking and she has started to learn to tailor vests and jackets, the price of a tailor must be added in! What about the vegetable garden, the flower garden, the window boxes, or even the pots of chives and cress on the kitchen windowsill? Maybe she has grown her own bean sprouts for Chinese dinners; so add that as a contribution! Maybe she tutors the children in math or teaches them piano.

The list would be much longer for many housewives and mothers. The point to be underlined and put in capital letters in that there is always a double contribution to the economic situation in every family. To think of "wage earning" as the only financial contribution is to be utterly blind and without imagination. A family with a father farming the land or earning money to buy the necessities in other ways — and a mother who is free to contribute all that her vivid imagination, talents, and constantly developing new skills can contribute — is rich indeed in warmth and variety and inspiration. It is not long before children are adding their contribution, too, whether as window washers, grass cutters, or kitchen helpers. If an allowance is given to children it should be pointed out that it was earned, and that other things have been contributed that haven't been paid for — "Because we are a family, and we do things to help in which we all share. See? Think of how much we all enjoy the fire that Franky cut the wood for, while he enjoys it, too! And think of how we all drink the milk that David got at the store, while David drinks it, too!" — "Thanks for planting the tulips we'll all be excited about in the spring."

The reality of the family being an *economic unit* is important, whether it is some very drastic moment of having to change the standard of living (and each one is being asked to help in new ways and not to growl about doing without some things they used to have), or whether it is simply being aware of exactly what the balance of contributions is made up of — day by day and week by week in the changing years of family life, as a part of practical oneness. The material situation can change — up or down — but the pleasure of contributing something which makes more vivid the feeling that "we're facing this together" is so important that family life is not complete without it. The man who shelters his wife and children from any painful moments of being "broke" (and just borrows to go on as if nothing had happened) is not only entering a dangerous path himself, but actually depriving his family of a situation in which they could pull together instead of apart. Not only may he head for a nervous breakdown, but it is not "better for them." It is decidedly worse, for a wall is building up which nothing can prevent from harming the openness of communication. There is an opportunity for the contribution of something very real, which children as well as mother are deprived of making, if the need for sudden economizing is not shared.

In Christian families the moments of material need are also opportunities for taking seriously the reality of prayer. "Call upon *Me* and I will answer you," says the Lord in every kind of situation. To only tighten one's belt, do with less, use ingenuity and imagination, figure out ways of saving, ways of making things at home, ways of earning, and not to recognize that we are meant to ask for help from the Lord, is to fail to demonstrate the existence of God to any who are watching us. If we believe that God hears and cares about us, then we need to be interested in seeing what His solutions will be as we pray for His help. We need to pray "believing that He *is,* and that He is a *rewarder* of those who diligently seek Him" (*see* Hebrews 11:6), as we ask Him to show us what to do about paying the rent, mortgage, taxes, back bills, and for the food for today. Children need reality in prayer if they are to grow up knowing the reality of the existence of God and realizing that their parents' faith is practical and woven into the warp and woof of the fabric of everyday life, rather than separated into a Sunday-church kind of thing. A family needs to consider together that God has said, "But seek ye first the kingdom of God . . . and all these things shall be added unto you" (Matthew 6:33). This means the things which would fall into the category of material needs, the things which wages supply. In being told that God will provide the things He knows we have need of, if we honestly want to do His will first (rather than putting the accumulation of "things" first), this portion of Matthew goes on to tell us, "Ask, and it shall be given you. . . . what man is there of you, whom if his son ask bread, will he give him a stone? . . . If ye then, being evil, know how to give good gifts unto your children, how much more shall your Father which is in heaven give good things to them that ask him?" (7:7, 9, 11). Read together Matthew 6:19–34, and 7:7–11. Then go on to read this: ". . . ye have not, because ye ask not. Ye ask, and receive not, because ye ask amiss, that ye may consume it upon your lusts" (James 4:2, 3).

Is this economics? I do believe so. "Give us this day our daily bread" should not be just a recited prayer in church services or military chapels or on other formal occasions. *We are meant as families to pray in times of real need,* and not just to ask for bread when we know where it is coming from. It is when money is lost, the job is gone, the house has burned down, or some other calamity has hit financially, that the entire family together should gather together to *pray.* In asking for work, for ideas as to how to earn money, or in asking for the Lord to send money in some special way for the immediate need, it is important for each person to search his or her own heart as to the honesty in asking, "Are we each really wanting the Lord's will for us as a family?" Are we wanting His kind of work for us, His use of our lives, or have we put up limits and are we asking God to supply some work within those limits? Are we asking for what the Lord says in Matthew He knows we need? Or are we asking for far more than we need? Often He gives us far more than we need, but in seeking our motives and our willingness for what the Lord wants, it is easy to fall into asking amiss. The reality of living together as a Christian family unit before the face of God in such a time of special need cannot be counterfeited by just saying these things as a "devotion" when no material need is present. It need not be a desperate need — of starvation or losing the home — the family should pray together about the Lord's provision for vacations, clothing, a pair of roller skates, or a new car when the old one is broken. Children should be brought up not to consider praying for material things as a last resort, but as a natural part of life. When saying, "Thank You for this food," there should be a true ring to the words, with a realization that answered prayer is being thanked for.

What is a family? A family is an economic unit — willing to live in conditions "better and worse" in different times of life, expecting to have ideas and a pioneering spirit of approach at times, but also having a deep understanding together that the family is not floating alone in an impersonal universe with no one to appeal to. We understand that God is there, and that the family members can, together as a unified group, come to Him and say with honest belief and expectation, "Please, God, do a new thing for us as a family, such as You speak of in Isaiah — *make a way in the wilderness for us, and rivers in this desert"* (*see* Isaiah 43:19).

# 8

## An Educational Control

We need to understand the meaning of the word *control* in the sense in which it implies a careful supervision of some important factor. For instance, the blood pressure is "controlled" by frequent notation of its rise or fall, to be sure it is not going out of the normal range for someone who has the possibility of a sudden change precipitating some serious attack. If you walk through today's hospitals, you may pass at some point an electrocardiogram being flashed in constant jagged or straight lines on a TV screen, as an interne is making a control for a patient in intensive care. A red light and a beeping sound remind the interne, if he or she is not watching every second, that something dangerous has taken place, and medical personnel then run to the patient's side. A *control* is a matter of constant attention to some kind of dangerous deviation in one direction or another, in some area of physical, psychological, or material part of life. The grocery store, bread store, or milk store (if you live where things are still sold in specialized stores) runs a control of whether your bill has been paid, and the telephone company has a very effective way of controlling —by shutting off the phone when the bills have not been paid. People who know each other very well realize the danger signals of overtiredness or nervousness and have strong understanding as to when an hour of relaxation or a week of rest suddenly becomes a "must." Then the loving friend, husband, wife, sister, brother, father, mother, child, or grandparent does something about the warning signal and goes to the assistance of the one in need, even as the interne does in the hospital.

It seems to me that one answer to the question "What is a family?" which cannot be left out is "A family is an educational *control*." A family has a strong responsibility for the education of its children, who are the next generation and who are going to influence not only their own generation but the one after. When we are told in Proverbs 22:6 to "Train up a child in the way he should go: and when he is old, he will not depart from it," it is not an admonition to simply "whack" the child to make him or her obey, nor is it just an admonition to teach that child Scripture as a separate subject. I believe strongly it is a command to train the whole person — intellectually, spiritually, culturally, emotionally — in things of creativity, in understanding the whole of history, in relationships with other people, and in seeing something of the tremendous scope of the universe from the viewpoint that God exists, God is the Creator, and that He has made us with the capacities we have in His image, to think and act and feel and create on a finite level. As our children are being educated, they are being taught to think and act and feel and to be creative — and we need very much, as parents, to be *aware* of what is taking place, as much as we are able. We are very much put in the place of responsibility and can either simply go out and have a milk shake and let the TV electrocardiogram ring its bell and blink its red light with no one caring — or we can ask God to help us to watch and recognize the educational danger signals day by day.

Among other things, we need to discuss with each other or some other members of our families or close friends, the interesting subject of how much school hinders the real education of our children and where it is a help. To simply assume that school is an education is rather naive in this day and age, it seems to me. *Real education* can be given in school and *is* in some schools, but can also be twisted so that it prevents and "turns off" any curiosity in the basic areas of the search for real knowledge. To assume that we send our children off to school, and that is IT, is shirking the responsibility of being a control, which no one else is going to take, and which God has handed directly to us as Christian parents. The Bible doesn't say anything about educational systems, but does speak of teaching our children, as we have seen in the Deuteronomy passages and by Timothy being taught the Scriptures by his grandmother and mother. The "teaching" certainly includes being taught to read and being taught to relate the words to true life, and also includes the answering of questions. All this is very clearly seen. Children's questions cover a large range of related and unrelated subjects — when they begin at one point they often end up miles away. You may be sure the children in Old Testament times and Timothy in his childhood were not "dumber" or less curious (about life and creation, animals, nature, the conduct of people, and all sorts of "Why?" questions) than your children. Responsibility is basically the family's, as far as the framework and cross-relationship of all learning being established. Established once and for all? How? With an injection at the age of two? Of course not. Like any control it is a day-by-day matter of conversation, sensitivity, sorting out, praying with and for certain trends which seem twisted to us — not barging in with a loud shout, but quietly looking up books that might help, taking time to walk and talk and study in the woods and fields, museums, and libraries, and keeping an atmosphere of open discussion.

What is an education? I believe that one important thing about an educated person is the realization that learning never comes to an end in this life, and probably goes on throughout all eternity. We will never be infinite and we will never come to the end of all that God knows and all that He has created in His infinite knowledge, wisdom, and marvelous sensitivity, both in the machinelike precision of the universe, and the gentle sensitivity of all the beauty of sound and sight, smell, taste, and feeling. It boggles the mind to think of how much there is to discover and learn and understand. There is much ahead. An education for a child is giving that child some tools with which to work — the speaking of first one, and then perhaps two or three or even more languages, and the reading of one or two or more languages. The child also needs tools with which to do some sort of mathematical problems, the understanding that there is much more beyond, and tools with which to communicate by writing in Braille, script, printing, typing — the more mediums the better. There is then needed the opportunity to have as broad a base as possible and to have a discipline of mind and concentration to continue thinking, talking, reading, and writing for a long enough time to finish something — a subject, a book, a project — without starting and stopping everything that is touched. A child must have the understanding of where one can look for information which is not in the immediate book at hand, and the realization that there are other people who have studied longer and know more and can be consulted. There should be the constant questioning of any teacher (without being rude), particularly keeping the constant base of the biblical absolute as a control. In other words, as you exercise your control in the area of education yourselves, there is a need of teaching a child to suspend making a decision until there is *time* for this control. An educated Christian is not too easily tossed by the wind and blown in different directions. Too many Christians are like that today — out on the sea with a tiny windblown boat, swept by every wind of false teaching concerning the Word of God. The Christian's control is God, and He has given us His verbal Word by which to compare things. If we don't see how it all fits together, we reserve judgment until all the facts are in.

Children should approach education in this framework, knowing that teachers make mistakes and that many do not even believe that God exists. A child should know that a teacher can teach them to read and write and do arithmetic, but that there will be all kinds of bias that will come in with the whole gamut of subjects, and as time goes on that there will need to be a mental resistance and a decision to talk that over at home. Naturally, respect of teachers (as far as manners and polite answers go) must be insisted upon and the reasons given: "We feel seriously about *true* truth, and we want the teacher someday to come to understand, too. It won't help the teacher to want to get to know you or visit our home or be interested in any book we might give him or her to read, if you are rude and the most difficult child in the class. It is good to have these discussions at home, look up things in books together, and try to find out how all this fits in with history, but you can't go and try to teach the teacher!"

"But I send my child to a *Christian* school, so I don't have any need to do anything further." Is that your situation? There are no perfect people and no perfect Christians, and a Christian teacher, too, can be turning off your child because of harshness or simply a personality that clashes or by actually giving wrong teaching. After all, Christian teachers are also "mixed-up" at times, and the need for the home conversation control of "What did you learn today? What did your teacher say about these theories?" is just as important. There can be a lack of both cultural understanding and exciting teaching of literature, history, music, philosophy, and so forth — even in a Christian school. A child can find his or her own longings so unfulfilled for the things that are of interest that he finds it fulfilled elsewhere and begins to make the wrong comparison: "All Christians are people who are not interested in culture and intellectual conversations, people who have never read Shakespeare, the old poets, and historical novels — and are so dull to talk to that I can't believe it." Children can make this adverse comparison because of having been put into the hands of a few people who have given them this false idea of *all* Christians. Just as other children, they may study under unimaginative, dull teachers lacking in any creativity or original ideas, and conclude that this is synonymous with Christianity, and that all excitingly creative and original people interested in culture and fascinating discussion are non-Christians.

There is no perfect school in every respect, and there is no mother or father who can shrug off the responsibility to have the home be a part of the education of their child, and also a place where some sort of sensitive control is going on in spot-checking attitudes as well as the facts being learned.

What to do about it? Debby and I were talking about this whole subject as we sped along the lake on the train to Lausanne. Sun was streaming through the window and the lake was a blue-green, one of the rare moments when Lac Léman looks like the Mediterranean. "I personally think the important thing, Mother, is *compensating* for what is not in the school. For instance, the Swiss schools are so very disciplined and strict that I feel freedom in doing creative things is what is needed at home after the homework is done."

True, there can be no specific thing needed at home which would fit the need for every combination of things influencing children outside of the home, or to make up for a lack outside of the home. There are the really far-out schools which have no set program, and in which the children never do what they don't want to do. For children in this kind of a school the home should have some very specific tasks or studies which must be done "from four to five" or whatever the time might be. You could get a set of reading books from another school system, set your own kind of arithmetic problems, or use an old-fashioned writing system of making a line of *eeeee*s and *oooooo*s, and so forth — not as a punishment, but for definite variety. Or you could set jobs to be done to fulfill the need for meeting a thing head-on, being told to do something that has to be done whether you like it or not. One poem a week could be memorized, for example.

The Swiss schools and most other European schools have old schoolbooks. Natasha is learning to read from the same book her mother, Debby, had twenty-six years ago! There is a continuity about this which is pretty terrific! If people learned to read well and do mathematics well twenty years ago, why change? The discipline includes long lines of letters, then long lines of written words (and longer lines for a punishment for talking in class!), and arithmetic in both the writing of sums and learning mental adding and subtraction. The children are called upon to hurry with an answer to numbers called out by the teachers. Homework is given from first grade on. *Dicté* consists of a little paragraph, even in first grade, read out like a dictation, and written by the children. This is instead of just lines of spelling, but the mother is meant to drill the child at home in the *dicté* for the next day. There are poems to be memorized at home, with the mother or father drilling the child the last thing before going to sleep. John or Pris will stand by Becky's bed, listening and correcting and getting the poem fixed in her mind for the next day! If you telephone Debby at a certain time in the early evening, your conversation is punctuated by the reading of the *dicté*: "*La petite chat . . .*" — "I can hear what you're saying, Mother, go ahead."

In addition to the old strict form of basic tools being given, little girls are taught to knit from first grade on, and also to sew. By the time children are ten or eleven they are knitting sweaters and making quite nice aprons or blouses and doing such work as embroidered table mats. What is needed at home is some freedom to finger-paint, paint with brushes, go sledding, make a garden in the summer, make original things out of paper or cardboard (little scenes, shoe-box gardens), dress up in mother's discarded clothes with high-heeled shoes and put on plays, make puppets for a show, and so on. The spontaneous, creative things which are not in the child's school are needed at home.

The compensation for what is not in the schools would include continually some additional cultural interest, both during term and at vacation times. Wherever you live, books can be bought or brought home from a library. There should be a great variety of books read aloud or given to the children to to read. *National Geographic* should be in the home, with doors of interest being opened to a great variety of

countries and nature studies, including animal and under-
water life. Items in newspapers, *Newsweek,* or *Time* — on
pages concerning medical research, scientific reports, the situation in various parts of the world — should be brought to
the table and read or discussed, so that the family together
keeps up with what is going on, rather than just bolting
food and running, or sitting in front of the TV and eating
silently. If there are really educational programs on TV, they
should also be discussed after they are watched, and an
attempt should be made to put things into the framework
of true truth. Since so many things in the twentieth century are
screened through a sieve of Hegelian relativistic thinking —
that everything is relative and truth does not exist; that there
is really no right and no wrong — then it is important to
have discussion about articles or news items in which the
children at even ten or twelve begin to spot what is wrong
(and begin to put a "red light and beep" in their own minds),
rather than being brainwashed.

If you live in a city where there are museums, you should
visit art museums together and buy some art books and study
something about the great artists, with some discussion at
mealtimes. Visits can be made to a natural-history museum,
but with the "red light ready to flash," since evolution is
taught as a *fact* rather than a *theory* in most such museums.
The whole humanistic brainwashing of teaching about the
history of man is so strong in books, documentary files, and
museums, that you need to know how to offset it — and if
you don't, then *study* to find a way of offsetting it. The family is the place where control must be early established as a
perfectly natural thing: "You see, we are among the few in
the world who believe that God really exists; believe that He
really created the world and created Adam and Eve in His
own image, and believe that all knowledge does *not* come
from man starting with himself and trying to discover everything. We believe that God spoke — and God told us what
took place before man was even made, and told us what
turned this into an abnormal universe, rather than a normal

one. *God* has given us the knowledge of who man is, and why he is important and significant — and unhappily a lot of these brilliant men don't know all this, because they don't know God. The statement God gives: 'The fear of the Lord is the beginning of wisdom' [*see* Psalms 111:10] fits in here. These men don't believe God is there to fear, to worship, to adore, to admire, to love — and so they don't have the beginning of wisdom. They have a lot of knowledge, and a lot of them are brilliant, but they don't have the key to wisdom, which is the fear of the Lord. We can't talk to anybody if we don't know what makes him tick, so we need to understand what is behind the mix-up in people's mind. People can find out fantastic things which prove the Bible, but they don't put it together in the right way, because they are trying to *dis*prove the Bible."

It is important in this educational-control idea not simply to criticize, but to see the marvel of what man — made in the image of God — has done, even unsaved man, because all men have been made in the image of God. An encyclopedia can be opened (if you have one) and you can talk about the early inventors, and the early scientists and point out that the early ones *did* believe in a universe made by God. You can read together and discuss together, and go to see whatever is of historic interest in your own area. So often people don't know or talk to their children about what took place "right here" two hundred years ago. The home is the place to spark curiosity and interest if the school is "too narrow" or "too free" or "too dull" or "too *nothing*." What kind of compensation is needed? Only you can know, but in order to know, you need to know your own children as well as the school — and that takes time.

It is a career — this monitoring system of control. Do you have any idea what the children are learning at school which is *not* in the curriculum? Drugs are coming in so very early. What preparation are you giving to offset the prevalent idea that "smoking pot is nothing"? How many teachers are on LSD weekends or smoking pot each night, and what slips out and is overheard in their conversations? What kind of propaganda is being handed down from older children to younger children, and what takes place at parties? How quickly can an innocent invitation to "explore some caves" or to "come listen to music" turn into a situation of smoking pot or a drunken party in which everyone ends up sleeping in a sad, destroyed-looking heap of limp bodies. How easily children can be made to feel as if they are not "with it" or are "just afraid"? The scorn and sarcasm of other contemporaries and the feeling of being shut out and ignored can pull a child into things he or she really has no wish to do, except for the desire of being accepted.

There should be discussion and reading of articles from secular papers (not "church papers," but simply the ordinary magazines or newspapers the children might accept as the opinions of a variety of people) which tell of the dangers of drugs and alcoholism. There should be a study of what happens to brain cells and what happens to the stomach walls and to the body in general — from drugs and from alcohol. A good healthy fear of results ought to be instilled in children by *facts,* as a protection against being completely taken over by false teaching in these areas. To wait until the whole thing becomes a problem is too late, and even though the early preparation may not be the protection you pray it will be, it is in the family that warning education should be given. If there are any young people who have gone through a drug problem and have come out of it, and could be a help in having dinner with you and giving some first-hand warning, that might be the most realistic kind of "proof." Of course, you need to know the individual and be sure that he or she will be helpful.

Along with other things discussed concerning drugs and their various dangers and effects (the frequent nonstop process of going from lighter drugs into heroin and other hard drugs) and concerning alcohol and the new fad for drinking parties, there should be a discussion of "Why?" Why do people do it? Of course, one reason is that people are like sheep! If you live in the country or can go where there are sheep just to watch them for a day, then you can let the children watch the amazing way the whole flock follows one sheep which turns in another direction. Fantastic — the sudden, stupid-looking change of direction, pushing and shoving all in a tight crowd, trying to eat the same grass. "All we like sheep have gone astray; we have turned every one to his own way . . ." (Isaiah 53:6) means more after you have watched sheep. But this illustration can be used to show that human beings are very like sheep in following each other rather aimlessly without thinking, just to be "in the crowd." In addition to this reason which might be a temptation for your child, point out that if there were no God, if there were no right and wrong, if people have no base, no absolute, no control to judge what is worthwhile doing and what is a waste of life — and if they have no reason they can think of for *not* doing any old thing with their time, health, bodies, brains, creative talents, brain cells — then they might answer, "Why not?" And they think their question has no answer!

The Bible tells us that people should not as Christians commit fornication because ". . . God hath both raised up the Lord, and will also raise up us by his own power" (1 Corinthians 6:14). I believe this gives a powerful reason for not living promiscuous lives: that our bodies have been a thing so precious to the Lord that He died that we might be raised again as He was raised. Our bodies are not *un*important; they are to be raised from the dead, and Christ paid a great price to make this possible. If He considers our bodies that important then we should consider what we do with our bodies. It seems to me that the destruction of brain cells — freaking out so that there is a danger of never getting the brain put together again, and starting down a road on which it may not be easy to turn around and find the way back — is deliberately denying that the body has any importance. A Christian parent should teach the children (not all in one lecture, of course, but gradually here and there as it comes in naturally with news items or articles in news magazines) that there is a need to regard our bodies, our brain cells, our health and creative talents, and our energies as worth not only taking care of, but trying to make better, rather than taking chances of throwing it all away on some stupid "dare."

There are many children who never go to a school outside their home. Some diplomats' children, military people's children, oil men's children, missionaries' children, children living in far-away places where there are no nearby schools, have studied under the Calvert school system. In addition to those who are a distance from regular schools, there are ill or handicapped children who can't go out to school. This is another whole area of consideration, for if there is no one else to come in and be the teacher, one of the parents needs to become a teacher. The need to consider that the time will come when schools are more of a detriment than they are education is not simply a topic of conversation. It is a very present situation in some places. Often a school hinders education instead of educating the child. We should think about what alternatives are possible.

Susan was in bed with rheumatic fever for the better part of three years, from the age of thirteen to sixteen. She first had the Calvert course and then the University of Nebraska high-school correspondence course. Studying alone seemed to spark creativity in Susan instead of squashing it. She thought of an amazing number of things to add to her "courses" on her own, writing to the teachers and getting their ideas back in response, making relief maps with paper-mache hills, adding all sorts of charts and illustrations for what she was studying, and reading mountains of books on the side. She decided, without telling us, to add another course of study — and sent away for Braille *Jack and Jill* magazines, copies of which she already had in regular editions for sighted people. When the big packages came, she began to teach herself to read Braille painstakingly by comparing the feel of the Braille raised dots with the sighted copies. Eventually she did learn, after praying about how to do it, and having a most amazing dream in which a blind person came to her door and *saw* her feeling the dots in the wrong way and said, "No, do it with circular movement like this," and came to show her. When Sue awakened she quickly tried the new method and later found it was correct — and that it was no wonder it worked! Then she sent for a Braille writing board and the kind of "pen" one needs to make the dots, and began writing letters and stories for blind people with whom she had correspondence. Her sickroom was so full of projects and education that people who came to visit her to "cheer her up" left amazed at the interesting conversations into which they were plunged.

With Susan, as with all our children, there was the advantage of the education of a diversity of people with whom to talk. Franky, who had an insatiable curiosity and interest in every kind of thing, would somehow be able (from the age of six or seven) to get a brain surgeon started on telling him the details of an operation; Bob H. started telling him how he designed the 707, making diagrams on Franky's blackboard to illustrate; a nurse explained how one takes blood pressure, and all about her nursing in the African bush, with varieties of experiences; and a racing driver told him details of car motors and driving experiences. It is true that not only did the discussion of serious subjects — concerning widely divergent religions, philosophies, and explanations for any purpose in life, plus the many questions coming from science and history — take place at our dinner tables, but also our children had a chance to "pick the brains" and ask questions of people from many kinds of professions and backgrounds as well as from many countries.

The real education which takes place in personal questions and answers with people who are experts in some field could only be compared with seminars in universities or the one-to-one tutor system, in which personal discussion is possible with someone having a great store of knowledge in some area. You may say, "Where can I give my child any opportunity to have conversation or ask questions of anyone other than ourselves?" First, there are the older members of your family. Grandparents should have real contact with grandchildren, telling them all kinds of things from firsthand experiences. "What were you doing when Lindbergh first crossed the Atlantic, Grandmother? Did you get excited?" — "What were the first radios like? Did you have one?" — "Do you really remember going forty miles an hour in a car and it seemed *fast*? Was that really speeding?" — "What about the First World War? Oh, were you just a baby then?" — "What did you study in school, Grandfather?"

My own father just had his ninety-ninth birthday. A year ago Susan visited him and took along a tape recorder. She asked him all kinds of questions and recorded his answers — all about how he felt when he arrived in China at the turn of the century, his attitudes toward the Chinese, how long he studied the language, what his work was. Captured in his voice are amazing things for the great-grandchildren to hear, and which they will never forget. How their grandfather played football with his very big bush of curly hair "protecting my head; you see we didn't wear helmets," and how he studied Greek in high school and read classical Greek with the headmaster so he could skip first-year Greek in college. "You know, in those days we needed four years of Latin to get into college, and at least two years of Greek, but I was ahead of the others."

Children need grandparents in so very many ways, as a continuity with the past, as a comfort, and a feeling of the specialness of this being their mother's mother or father, or this being their father's father or mother. There is a security in having a grandparent say, "I used to do this with your mother," or "I read this story to your father." But in addition to all the other things that are helpful in having grandparents, there are the educational advantages. It is ridiculous to always have the feeling that "The children must run out and play; they'll be bored." Children should have a chance to hear grandparents tell about things they experienced — which are now taught in history books. Children should hear about things they are interested in about their grandparents' education. Uncles and aunts, and great-aunts and great-uncles should be drawn out in conversations alone with children, so that it is a direct communication, with time for questions and a carefulness in giving answers. Of course, not all old people have sharp minds and memories, but many do, and if your children have no living grandparents they should have an opportunity to "adopt" some older friends of that generation. If your church goes to sing at old-folks' homes, remember that just to walk in and sing and have a service and walk out again is not only very little real human contact with lonely people — but that there is a wealth of education locked up there in the minds of people in these homes. Some have been doctors, lawyers, teachers, professors, captains, sailors, have been in two wars, have seen all kinds of travel, have lived in the horse-and-buggy days, have made discoveries, and created inventions. Arrange visits to some of the old people, find out who really appeals to your children and with whom they can really communicate, and you will add a new dimension to "education" that is real.

Get the history book and read up on things to help the children hear about other things that happened in the time when their older friends were children or young people, so that they can have new questions to ask. The old people will be refreshed and given connection with today's generation in a way that will give some measure of understanding which they couldn't possibly gain by reading newspapers. It can be a two-way help which could belong in another chapter, but which I feel belongs in the chapter on education!

For my own children I always tried to remind them to take the opportunity to get all the information and interesting facts they could, in the midst of their own times in hospitals or dentists' chairs! "You may never have this chance again; find out all you can." Not only does it help to alleviate the fears and take minds off pain, but it is an honest fact that one may never have another chance to see certain things and to ask certain questions. "Now is your chance to find out all you can about a children's hospital." — "Now is your chance to see how a blood transfusion works." — "Now you can read on that bottle what is mixed in the liquid they are about to put into you instead of food." — "See if you can look at the X ray of that leg. Amazing the way a bone is apart! Think of what it must have been like before X rays were invented." Education is talking to an art-history professor when you are walking around an art museum, talking to the nurse at the dentist's to see how she mixes something, talking to the butcher to find out about what "hanging meat" means, getting a ride with the engineer of the train and finding out what his work is like, talking to an old fisherman about his catch and how he mends nets. Education is watching a sculptor, learning to grow silkworms, making a collection of stamps, or collecting rocks with bits of mineral in them. Education is so much wider than school and needs so much broader an influence than one school teacher, as well as the vigilance of constant control in being sure the little ship is sailing on an even keel.

The family may have another language in the not-too-distant background. Was Grandfather German? or French? or Italian? or Chinese? or Dutch? or Japanese? or Spanish? What language do you speak at home? Wouldn't it be good to try to learn at least a little bit of the language of the grandfather or great-grandfather, or grandmother or great-grandmother? It is possible to get grammar books and records with correct pronunciation, and to start at least a small bit of knowledge and speaking ability in another language at home. Have a supper that is typical of the country whose language you are studying, and try to have that meal using only that language. It may peter out very soon or it may be hilarious, but it will never be forgotten, and even the small beginnings may inspire language study to be dug into in a difffferent way than ever before. Get a record of a song performed in that language and play it during your German sauerkraut supper, your Italian pizza snack, your French meat-and-salad meal, your Chinese egg rolls and fried rice, your Japanese sukiyaki, your Dutch apple cake and coffee, or your Spanish rice.

The point (although maybe you have seen it long ago) is that you make your *home control* not a thing of anti-education in any sense of the word, but a richer education at every point, so that the contrast is all the other way. Your Christian home is one of living, exciting, real interest in studying, learning, discussing, finding out, discovering, reading, and comparing, but always in the framework of true truth. Your home is a place where people are considered important and are listened to — in the form of aunts and uncles and grandparents as well as people of the same age. The tapestry of history is a *living* one, rather than just a printed page. The narrow idea of school education broadens into one of finding out that the ability to have a wide cross-analyzing of subjects and periods of history, culture, and art, and to listen and contribute ideas and to be inspired toward fresh creativity or discoveries is what education is all about. It is also something to discover that finding a really fascinating, educated fisherman on some sandy shore or rocky coast can be a richer find than locating a new book.

*What are you?* "*Just* a mother and a housewife." — "*Just* a father and an office worker."

*What are you?* "We monitor an educational control for three new human beings." What a challenge in affecting the new generation! It is a battle that can be fought.

There is a lot of brainwashing in textbooks, in teaching, in newspapers, in all sorts of media. There is a need to fight for keeping truth alive and for seeing a connection between all subjects, rather than keeping the teaching of the Bible as something separate from everything else, and allowing our children to think there is a big wall between their education and their Christian faith. Who has the greatest knowledge? Who has created both music and the musicians? To whom and from whom was given the possibility of bringing forth poetry and prose? Who sees all history in the right perspective and knows the future also? Who speaks of praising Him with music, harp, psaltery, and all kinds of instruments and also the dance? Who has instructed people to make artworks to the praise of His name for His Temple? Who has spoken of making things of gold, silver, and precious stone and there-fore has given people the possibility of discovery in these realms as well as all others? Our God is the God of all Creation and all knowledge, and to act as if education is something that separates one from the *truth* is to miss altogether the understanding of the Word of God and God Himself.

"The fear of the Lord is the beginning of knowledge. . ." (Proverbs 1:7) — and we are told that one day ". . .the earth shall be filled with the knowledge of the glory of the Lord, as the waters cover the sea" (Habakkuk 2:14). That day there will be a blending of knowledge in the way it cannot be blended now. We don't know everything, and pieces are missing, but the day is coming when the knowledge of the Lord — not the knowledge of just His existence, but of all that He has made and has given us a capacity to be able to know — will be put together as it should be. It is the abnormal situation in which we live, the spoiled universe that has come from denying God, that has fractured knowledge and has caused men to think they can find, *apart* from God, the answers that will tie everything together. It has also caused others to think there are no answers and that nothing can ever be tied together!

We who are Christians should not let our children receive their education from a biased source on one hand, nor from an incomplete or mixed-up source on another hand. Are we perfect? Of course not. But we have a responsibility to pray in this area, too, and to ask the Lord that our homes and families may be places where some attempt is being made to keep things in perspective, and to let our children grow up knowing we believe truth is *so true* that real education cannot shake it. The winds will not upset the little boat of the man or woman who is asking wisdom of God by praying for help in the business of "educational control."

> If any of you lack wisdom, let him ask of God, that giveth to all men liberally, and upbraideth not; and it shall be given him. But let him ask in faith, nothing wavering. For he that wavereth is like a wave of the sea driven with the wind and tossed. For let not that man think that he shall receive any thing of the Lord.
>
> James 1:5–7

Coupled with this, as we think of asking for wisdom to control the education with some supply of what is missing, let us apply "...ye have not, because ye ask not" (James 4:2). Do we really ask for the help of the Lord in our communication in the area of our children's education? And then, "But be ye doers of the word, and not hearers only, deceiving your own selves" (James 1:22).

What strong language! If we are not asking for wisdom, asking for that which we have not, then we are not doers of the Word of God, because we are told to *ask!*

*Oh, God, help me as a mother, help us as parents, to be sensitive to the red light flashing on, to the beep-beep of warning when one or another of our children's "educational electrocardiograms" shows a dangerous condition. Whether it be in the area of science, history, literature, language, or the early ABCs — whether it be drugs or alcohol or a matter of wanting to break away and try everything — give us Your help, give us Your wisdom. As You have asked us to ask — we are asking. Help us to really have our family be a true educational control for the twentieth-century needs of our dear kids.*

# 9

# A Museum of Memories

Smoke curling up towards the autumn blue sky drifts to your nostrils, "Mmm. The burning of leaves always takes me back to when I was nine and used to shuffle through the maple leaves curling up in yellow and brown drifts on our lawn — Dad raking them, Mother helping — a warm, happy feeling of preparation for the winter. Mother saying, 'These ashes will be so wonderful for the rose beds,' and Dad asking, 'Did I hear you say not to forget to remind you to get the apple pie out of the oven? I think it's time now.' Just the *smell* of that smoke brings back the whole period of my childhood I loved best."

"Fresh coconut, mmm, what a lovely, wet, crisp taste. This flavor always brings back the beach at Alassio, where the one thing cheap enough for us to buy each day was the coconut cut in slices and carried by the beach vendors in bowls of water. I feel the sand, the spray of salt sea in my face, and remember the call, 'Come on in and jump these next waves!' — 'Soon as I finish my coconut!' What an amazing thing *taste* can do to you!"

"OOOwwwooo — listen to that deep-throated sound of the boat whistle — my favorite noise in the world. It brings back the whole feeling of the throb-throb of engines starting, of the bustle of a ship setting sail across the ocean, the sadness of leaving, the excitement of going, the curiosity of what the first dinner would be like, the unpacking to settle in for the period of suspended time between two continents — the feel of hot sun on the deck, the marvel of water splitting apart in white froth as the midnight moon lights up the wake and one feels alone in such a different way, hung out over the sea on the upper prow of the ship. Just the wwwOOOooo of the whistle brings it all back. Boat whistles! What a string of things that *noise* does to me."

"Satin, what a feeling between the fingers. I remember the satin binding of my first blanket. How old would that memory be? The feel of satin always brings back the contented sensation of being tucked in bed, of the satin binding under my chin and reassuringly felt between my fingers. The 'lovey' blanket of my childhood and strings of nights of security. Satin brings it all back." *Feels* are like that. The rough tongue of a cat brings back not just the ginger cat of our old Cape Cod cottage, but the whole summer we were there — the treks to the beach past the graveyard, the heaviness of pushing two two-year-olds in one pram, the picnics on the beach, and the mice running along the skirting boards. A cat's rough tongue, the feel of it! What an amazing thing is *feel!*

Music is incredible. Sudden strains of the wedding march, or the Handel played at other weddings you've been to, and the whole wedding comes back — the panic of the missing flowers, the disappointing color of the cake's icing, the beauty of the whole ceremony, the loveliness of the bride, and the depth of emotions. A few strains of music, just that particular music, and it all floods back. The first song your mother ever sang to you, the first symphony you ever went to, the popular song that everyone was humming when you were thirteen — it isn't just the music that you "put into a slot" timewise when you hear it, but it is the flood of related experiences that come back to be relived. Memories with a sudden searchlight of music focused into the present.

Memory! What a gift of God. And what a tragedy at times. Memory can be of horrible things one wants to forget, coming at times like a nightmare bringing trembling and horror, or memory can be of wonderful things one enjoys living and reliving. Memory can bring sudden understanding later in life when things suddenly fall into place and you realize what was happening, and memory can give courage to go on — just when it is needed. Memory can quiet one in time of turmoil or can transport one out of the danger of being plunged into something false. Memory can suddenly become so vivid as to stop a person from doing something wrong — because of the unmistakable contrast being flashed on the screen of the mind — and memory can cause someone to be compassionate to another in need, whose need would not have been noticed had it not been linked in the mind's picture with a deep experience in the past which prepared an understanding.

A museum has a selection of things worth preserving. There are art museums, natural-history museums, maritime museums, and those preserving documents of a variety of kinds. There are period-furniture museums, those with jewelry from different periods of history, or with rare Chinese pottery. Some cities are a museum in themselves, like Florence in Italy, where the buildings, gates, doors of churches, towers, and outdoor statues make walking at any time of the day or night a time of exclaiming over marble, intricate carvings, wonderful architecture, sudden vistas with a bridge showing up between angles of buildings, and the moon sliding around an ancient tower. Not as old, but still with as much history behind it, is Salem, Massachusetts, with not only a collection of museums, but houses furnished with the possessions of four generations, and old Chestnut Street with its Early American houses and lovely old trees preserving the flavor of another period of history. Had someone not had the idea of selecting and putting things together in some sort of order, much of past history would be lost as far as the vividness of reality given by the collections of things in museums.

What is a family meant to be? Among other things, I personally have always felt it is meant to be a *museum of memories* — collections of carefully preserved memories and a realization that day-by-day memories are being chosen for our museum. Someone in the family — one who is happily making it his or her career, or both parents, perhaps a grandparent or two, aunts and uncles, older brothers and sisters — at least one person needs to be conscious that memories are important, and that time can be made to have double value by recognizing that what is done today will be tomorrow's memory.

Memories (not all of them, but *some* of them) should be planned with the same careful kind of planning one would give to designing a museum. A family life in retrospect should be a museum of diverse and greatly varied memories, with a unity that makes the grouping of people involved share at least many if not all of the overlapping memories. Memories don't need to be just a thing of chance collection, but can have some measure of planning. Of course, no one can plan an hour, a day, a week, a month, or a year without saying and meaning that, "Lord willing," we will do thus and so. The Bible makes this very strong: "Go to now, ye that say, To day or to morrow we will go into such a city, and continue there a year, and buy and sell, and get gain: Whereas ye know not what shall be on the morrow. For what is your life? It is even a vapour, that appeareth for a little time, and then vanisheth away. For that ye ought to say, If the Lord will, we shall live, and do this, or that" (James 4:13–15).

This is a basic teaching of the Bible to those of us who are the people of God. We must always remember within ourselves and teach our children that in any plan we should not only *say*, "Lord willing," but mean it. We should believe and teach our children that *only* God can always keep His promises and make plans that cannot be broken or suddenly changed. We can say, "I will do that and go thus far and no farther." We can promise, "I will be there tomorrow and make such and such for you." But — we may be in a hospital by that time — or be forced to fly around the world to meet an emergency — or be interrupted or hindered in a thousand possible ways. As we go on to think of planned memories, it is with the need of always saying, "Lord willing," and actually praying, "Please show me, Lord, whether this is Your will or not."

With that being laid down as an accepted and understood condition, memories ought to be planned, memories ought to be chosen, memories ought to be put in the budget, memories ought to be recognized and given the proper amount of time, memories ought to be protected, memories ought not to be wasted, and memories ought to be passed down to the next generation.

How can memories be planned? First of all, as a new family starts, it is good to carry on *old* traditions and to start some *new* traditions of your own. What kind of traditions? Birthdays should be celebrated in some special way. Each family can have its own traditions woven into the remembering of a birthday. Perhaps everyone screams, "Happy Birthday!" first thing in the morning, or the birthday person is served breakfast in bed. Perhaps it is your tradition to wait and surprise the person later in the day with an afternoon party. Indoors or outdoors the party can be decorated with long streamers of crepe-paper festooning in loops from trees to the birthday person's chair (or indoors from the tops of the curtains or lamps to the chair). The birthday chair can be made into a traditional "throne" each year, with flowers tied to it or ribbons adorning it, and the gifts placed on the table before it. The celebration can be at mealtime or, in the case of children, with games and balloons and Pin the Tail on the Mouse (or Elephant) and Drop the Handkerchief. Of course, there can be a variety of surprises and changes, but it is a lovely thing to choose one or two things to become a family tradition, and whatever else is done, always do that special thing as well, year after year. A cake with the number of candles representing the years is the tradition of many families, and if this is yours, it is important to always have it — no matter how simple the cake, even if it is just with a cup of tea. In Switzerland there are "bombs" which have a fuse, and go "poof" when lighted, tossing little favors, paper hats, whistles, tiny balls to throw at each other (with burrs that stick) — and many people have a traditional "birthday bomb" at the party or supper. Perhaps you will want to have a traditional menu which is your birthday meal, or a special kind of ice cream which is "always the birthday ice cream," along with perhaps a chocolate cake with peppermint icing and dribbled with melted chocolate. If there is some tradition that goes with the birthday in *your* family, you'll find that the very preparing and serving and putting out the things of tradition will bring along the memories of past birthdays and give a strength to the feeling of belonging which comes as people remember your special day.

There is discussion among Christians as to how Christmas should be celebrated and what sort of traditions should be handed down. It seems to me that God makes this clear to us in Romans 14:5, 6 — which strongly says that there are some who place one day above another in importance, and that it is up to the individuals as to whether they regard certain days as special or not. There is room for individual differences, as long as we do what we do "unto the Lord" in the way we regard the day. If you think that Christmas should not be a family day of gift sharing and special feasting together, but a day of special worship and fasting, then that is up to you in *your* family setting. However, one thing is very important — if you are not going to make Christmas a special day for the family and the little children to grow up enjoying as one of special surprises, then you must choose another day of the year — let us say the sixth of June or the fourth of August or just any other day you choose — and you must have that be a day which is looked forward to all year long as the Family Day with all its wonderful traditions. One day a year should be this kind of carefully planned-for occasion.

I feel that the Lord is pleased with our giving each other gifts and having special feasts connected with the remembrance of the birth of the Messiah who came to save people from eternal separation from God — or eternal death. In the Old Testament, Esther was given the authority to call for a feast and the exchange of gifts to celebrate the salvation of the Jews from the death that Haman had planned for them. This was the feast of Purim, and was meant to be kept year after year as thanksgiving to God, but with the exchange of gifts among the people. It seems a lovely thing to connect the gifts with the thanksgiving of that special gift of God — the salvation from a general death — worse than Haman's planned massacre would have been.

Our traditions connected with Christmas are very special. Our four children and their families have their own careful Christmas traditions — some are the same ones we had and some are different ones. For all of our twenty-eight years in Switzerland we have had the five-o'clock Christmas Eve Service in Champéry, with over a hundred candles to be put in wooden candleholders made of rough logs, and also fastened on fresh green trees. The supper at home has always started with cream of tomato soup with salted whipped cream on top, and has had a main course of easy-to-serve ham and potato chips and salad with special trimmings and homemade rolls. The apple-mince pies with crisscross crusts (or pumpkin if you would rather) are also a traditional dessert. The Christmas tree has been trimmed the night before, during a traditional time of drinking iced ginger ale and eating homemade Christmas cookies spread out in lovely rows on a tray. The Christmas stockings, filled with all sorts of interesting but inexpensive things, are the old hand-knitted stockings our girls wore the first years in Switzerland. Full of holes, but still usable, they add much in the way of memories as they are pulled out one night and filled and then found on Christmas morning. There are always tangerines to be eaten as we come to them, and homemade Christmas bread, along with tea or hot vanilla eggnog to be enjoyed in the bedroom as we open the stockings. The traditional lunch of homemade rolls (filled with thin beef), tomato juice, olives and pickles, and either milk shakes or ginger-ale floats for dessert, is eaten whenever we feel hungry, sitting around the Christmas tree, opening gifts. There is the customary reading of Luke 2 and prayer together before eating. For dinner in the evening, there is a traditional tablecloth of lovely thin linen with appliquéd deer on it (bought at a sale in Philadelphia twenty years ago and used every Christmas since).

There is something about saying, "We *always* do this," which helps to keep the years together. Time is such an elusive thing that if we keep on meaning to do something interesting, but never doing it, year would follow year with no special thoughtfulness being expressed in making gifts, surprises, charming table settings, and familiar, favorite food. It is important to have certain times when you look at the calendar and say, "Oh, yes, time for the geranium plants to be put in the window box!" — "Oh, look at the date; we'd better get ready for our traditional treasure hunt." — "I've got a wow-ee idea for Christmas stocking tops this year — I'm going to make *Alice in Wonderland* people in felt on the back of these cheap mirrors and stick them in the tops. Then we'll read some *Alice in Wonderland* to go with them. Don't tell the others, but you can help me." There is something inspiring about having a tradition of making a surprise. This can be the "mother of invention," as creativity is sparked by coming to a date marked on a calendar as a time for some sort of celebration which follows a yearly tradition.

We never use flowers for the Thanksgiving table, but make some sort of an original arrangement of vegetables, sprays of leaves and bittersweet, or bits of pine or ivy. The tradition of using vegetables means that at least this one time a lovely, green, curly cabbage comes into a place of honor, along with smooth, beige-skinned onions, green peppers, red tomatoes, some mushrooms, carrots, turnips, ears of corn, a few gourds if you have any of them in your garden, and ivy leaves or whatever you can find as you scramble through the garden or woods. Children love to prepare the traditional May baskets — tiny wild flowers found in the grass and arranged in baskets made of paper by hand — to leave at someone's front door, even if they never had a part in a time-honored Maypole winding. Couples can establish the tradition of giving each other a rose to celebrate the day they met or became engaged — or some other outstanding date private to themselves. Children can be encouraged to start their own little traditions (perhaps allowing only a limited number). Grandparents can also have their traditions, such as a family reunion or special parties or occasions to which other members of the family are invited. Aunts and uncles can choose to do a definite and regular kind of thing, whether for the family or for friends — if they are living alone some distance from the family. And whether a person adopts children, adopts grandparents in the old-folks' home, or adopts someone in a hospital ward, no one needs to be without someone to care for on dates ticked off on the calendar as special for some reason.

How do you choose a memory? First there is the choice that involves *time,* but no money. You've gone to the doctor or the dentist or grocery shopping or to do a business errand some distance from home. You are together as a whole family — or you and your husband are alone or with one child or a sister of yours or a friend. The "efficient" thing to do is to take the first bus or train or subway back home — but actually there is an hour or two or three that you could choose to use in a different way. You could take the boat back from Lausanne, if you live in that part of the world. It would take longer, but you would have a lifetime memory of the sunset on the lake, a cup of tea in the tearoom on the boat, the feeling of being far away from everything, although you are actually a very short distance from the train rushing along the shore of the lake. What you have taken is three hours to cover a distance you could have covered in about a fifth of the time, because of schedules as well as the slower pace of the boat. Is it worth it? The same ticket is accepted on the boat as on the train. It is *time* we are talking about. Time not planned ahead, but decided upon on the spur of the moment. Shall we do this? Is it worth it to take two or three extra hours, when you could "get all that done at home" or "at the office"? Upon what basis is your decision? This is the crucial place of understanding where many people are blind. Are you actually choosing three hours having tea, walking together in the park, going to a zoo and taking a later train, going to the wharf to watch the ship unload, stopping to look into a museum together, parking the car by an historic or woodsy spot, going to Kew Gardens or Forest Park or whatever is a possible place or thing to do that occurs to you — are you actually choosing between that "luxury" or "foolish romantic idea," rather than keeping on with your scheduled duty for two more hours? Are you actually choosing between accomplishing something worthwhile and giving in to a temporary little "waste of time"? Remember that you are often choosing a memory. Many times you are not choosing what to do with the two or three hours for the immediate result, but you are choosing a memory (or choosing *not* to have that memory) for a lifetime. For years the ten-year-old and the three- and five-year-old will remember the bubbles of excitement that came when Mother and Daddy said, "We have finished the doctor's appointment and we could take the next train [or drive home on the expressway as fast as possible], but we have decided to turn off and go to the zoo [or the aquarium or the birdhouse in the park]. We didn't plan to do this, but we thought it would be fun for all of us." The bubble of excitement, the thrill that comes in being loved and considered important, the reality of discovering that our mother and father really like to be together with us, the high-lighted enjoyment of whatever it is you decide to do, will make it a stronger, longer-lasting and more vivid memory than even the planned days off could ever be. The memory multiplies the use of those hours into hundreds of hours!

When you choose a memory in this way, you are choosing to lose hours of time — in order to keep them! A family should have a whole museum of memories gathered through the years — of moments when the choice has been to go ahead and lose a couple of hours in order to save them. Perhaps you are on a vacation and realize that you could cut short one day on the farm, on the beach, at the lake, in the mountains, in a certain city, or wherever you are, in order to stop someplace and add another dimension to the whole

time. Living here in Switzerland, I think of when Debby and
Udo decided to go to Florence in their little old car, rather
than to stay at the Italian beach two days longer. But would
Natasha be old enough to appreciate the museums and even
Michelangelo's statues? Why not wait until she was older?
"We'll do it when she is at the right age," came the thought.
Then they decided: "No, let's give her this memory now
Who knows when we can ever have the opportunity again."
Natasha is seven now and she still remembers some of the
outstanding things there in Florence. When they all look at
an art book, Natasha will get excited about a certain painting
or statue and exclaim, "Oh, I remember that; I really remember that." The thing to note, however, is that there has never
yet been another opportunity to go to Florence together, and
no one knows when it will come again. If they never go to
Florence together again, the memory of being there at three
years of age will belong to Natasha for the rest of her life.
No one can take it away.

Our three girls, the year Franky was born, went off to
Florence with their daddy. I stayed with the new baby. My
husband methodically mapped out the things he felt they
needed to see and to remember. You can imagine the lectures
and explanations that went on, and the intensity of finding
out when each museum would be open and when it would be
closed — and trying to get to each spot at the right time. A
seven-year-old Debby, eleven-year-old Susan, and fifteen-year-
old Priscilla went rushing up and down the streets, stood in
awed wonder in front of Michelangelo's *David,* marveled over
the stairs in the courtyard of the Bargello, and sat for a long
time looking at Etruscan tomb paintings. What was missing
at that time was "meals" — Daddy felt that the finishing of
his plan for seeing a flow of everything in Florence, along
with some understanding, should take all precedence over
food, drink, and rest! Not until evening, when the museums
were closed, were they allowed to stop to eat. Blisters on their
feet and aching calves in their legs have long since been forgotten. The memories of Florence as a city they "mastered"

with Daddy has always remained and can never be taken away from them. The fact that I didn't go along on the vacation, but stayed where the baby could be properly cared for, doesn't loom up as any divisive thing in the family. The thankfulness that Fran was able to give the girls this once-in-a-lifetime experience was not only a reality at the time, but has remained an appreciation in memory ever since. It has *never* happened again — for the girls.

If you wait "until you are older" or "for a more convenient time," the time of life — which is like a river flowing under a bridge — will all be gone, and the "right time" will have passed under the bridge along with the rest of time! Memories must take time, and the *choice* of a memory always means that a negative choice is made not to use the time another way. We are finite, and in our finiteness and limitedness we can never choose to do something without choosing not to do something else. There is usually the need to put aside ten other things to do one special thing.

Whether you live in the Midwest of America, in a big city, in the south, in the east, whether you live in Scotland or England or Austria or Hong Kong, Nairobi, Bombay, or a farm out in the countryside of any part of the world, there will be decisions to make from time to time concerning choosing to go together to some ancient place of interest, to explore a cave with an underground lake, to look at a temporary exhibit. Something will be suddenly possible one day, and the choice will be between taking the hours to have a memory to add to the all-too-short family years together — or waiting for some other time. There must be some times of choosing memories very consciously or your family museum will be an empty, echoing building waiting for new acquisitions which you will never have time to acquire. This is because *people* are involved in the memories, and the togetherness only lasts a certain length of time. The together-as-a-family memories are limited as to "gathering time."

"How romantic! Children don't remember things all that early." Do I hear you objecting? People differ in the things they remember and as to the age they were when they started collecting memories. For example, I only lived in China until I was five years old, yet I have so very many strong memories — memories of being taught how to scoop the rice into my mouth and pack it with chopsticks at one side of my cheeks while tea could be sipped down the other side from the lovely cups without handles, not disturbing a grain of rice! I remember the anxious, loving faces of my dear Chinese friends teaching me this, and the children I had been playing with before, running in for that particular meal. I remember my lessons in bargaining with the vendors who came to the door, and the Chinese cook and gatekeeper of the compound who were so delighted not only because I spoke perfect Chinese, but knew how to get the price down! I remember the sad shock of the realities of human beings' ways of cheating and stealing — when my beautiful kite was flying high, but another kite cleverly maneuvered from the street side of the wall pulled down my kite and someone cut the string, so that I stood dismayed with my empty string, disillusioned for the first time! I have hundreds of memories which must have been collected before I was five.

Memories not chosen, but given day by day, are also being collected. Is a slap in the face the first memory? Or is it the memory of Mommy still being there when the early streaks of dawn starting to come in through the curtains startle you into seeing that "Mommy has been up all night because I had the croup. She didn't go to bed at all. Oh, Mommy!" You can't choose the first memory; you can't regulate what will be remembered and what will be forgotten. If there are enough lovely memories, and if there are apologies for making really wrong choices, then the museum will have a good balance and a nonromantic reality of what life is like.

Of course, there will also be memories of flare-ups in the family. "Daddy is awfully mad right now!" can be said by a four-year-old without any tragic results. "Mommy is in a bad humor; I'm going to stay in here till she feels better!" will not harm any child. The reality of the ups and downs of dispositions, of people's tempers or of their mistakes and actual sins, does not tear apart the museum of memories, nor does it have to tear up the home or split the family. A realistic facing of the imperfections, faults, weaknesses, blind spots, and sins of each other in the family, although it will never be a complete facing of the whole person, will be a measure of understanding the whole person which will give a preparation for the future. If every fault, weakness, imperfection, blind spot, or sin was able to be *hidden* from each other, the relationships and the reality of having lived together as a family would be a hypocritical farce! To succeed in hiding everything but the good things in the years of living together, would be like a married couple never undressing in front of each other, going to bed clothed, never seeing each other naked, as far as the physical "knowing" of each other goes. There were couples taught under Mid-Victorian asceticism who, although they produced children from their bodies, never saw each other without long-sleeved clothing during the whole of married life. It may sound impossible, but it took place! To never accept the fact that no one is perfect, while never allowing the family to remark upon our imperfections, is somewhat in the same direction — knowing a person only superficially.

In some ways a family ought to be a mutual-admiration society. That would be the title of another chapter if there were space. We need to give compliments, praise each other, point out the things we admire and love. Children need to be praised for doing as well as they can, even if their marks are not the highest. To teach parents to never praise, but always to set the goal higher, is to give children a horrible childhood of never feeling they have succeeded in pleasing anyone. Praise is needed badly, and the Bible sets forth the principle of kindness to each other in this area, too — praise and thankfulness and expression of appreciation are meant to be given to each other as well as to God. Therefore, before speaking of the fact that our memories will contain upsetting times which we lived through, it is important to set forth the strong fact of our need for reassurance time after time, and the pleading with each other not to "destroy" each other by constantly dwelling on the weaknesses (with a virtuous feeling of being honest or realistic or nonhypocritical). One can carry too far this pointing out or recognizing or talking about faults. That is called by a good old-fashioned word — *nagging*. A parent can nag a child, a child can nag a parent, a brother can nag a sister, a sister can nag a brother, a husband can nag a wife, a wife can nag a husband, and we could go on with the whole list of life's possible relationships. To recognize each other's good points and to have the family really admire each other is a basic source of stability in our lives. But to recognize each other's weaknesses and to speak of things that happened in the past which were a result of those weaknesses, is not harmful if kept in some sort of balance. The museum of memories will have memories not planned, not chosen, and some of them will be good ones — and some will be of flare-ups, arguments, disappointments, as well as of sicknesses, accidents, and tragedies.

Some family "skeletons," however, can be memories which will help in the next generation's married lives. THINGS TO AVOID also belong in a collection of helpful memories. My children will always remember my reaction to frustration or anger of a certain intensity. When my adrenaline flows, my reaction is to try to get more done in the next hours than any human being could do. My hands move faster, my whole body goes into high gear, and I speed up like a car passing the speed limits — the needle swerves and hits the highest point! What has set me off? Some criticism or disparaging remark: "Why haven't you done. . .?" — whatever it might be. "What have you been doing all this time?" Rather than sensibly pointing out what has taken my time (and what has been accomplished), I react (I could say react*ed,* but to be honest I don't suppose I have ever stopped) by zooming into high gear and for the next few hours doing ten times more than I should, whether it is washing windows, taking the curtains down to wash them, cleaning out cupboards, doing piles of washing and ironing, or whatever.

"Why aren't you keeping up?" is a question asked when I am walking slowly because I feel draggy, and it is enough (if I am suddenly unreasonably angry because of the question) to start my adrenaline flowing so thoroughly that I can out-walk, outrun, outhike the other person for miles. Is this good? No, undoubtedly not. But it is my weakness and becomes at times a family joke, and my children can remember moments of amazing accomplishments that had a very nonglorious or nonlogical beginning. I can't know just what all the ingredients are — it doesn't always happen, of course, nor can anyone else guard against ever reacting that way — but the lesson of what has been seen of this particular skeleton has not only been some tense memories, but memories of frank talking and figuring out by the children what to avoid in their own lives. Are they then *perfect?* Could three generations get rid of all the kinks in personalities and makeups of people? Of course not; this is not a sentimental romantic key to success in future personalities, but an attempt to show that our weaknesses, which could flow together into drastic occurrences, do not need to end in tearing up the whole family.

At times Fran's anger causes him to feel like throwing something. There was an ivy plant which came over from Champéry to Huémoz with us when we moved, and became the main plant on the coffee table (an old table found in a barn thirty-eight years before in Grove City — still part of our furniture). When a flare of temper would strike Fran like a cyclone, he'd lift up this red clay pot and heave the ivy on the floor. The floor was linoleum and the only damage done would be a scattered pile of dark brown earth mixed with bits of the clay-red pottery, and an ivy with its roots exposed lying somewhere on the floor. A broom, dustpan and brush, another pot brought up out of the woodshed, some extra dirt added to the old, maybe a shot of fertilizer, a pail of hot sudsy water and a cloth — and the room would be cleaner than before, the ivy repotted and back in its place! This ivy became a family joke. (For a few years it was not a joke to talk about in front of Daddy, but later he stopped being sensitive about it and it

became part of the family's shared experience and conversation.) "You know, that ivy is the best ivy plant in the world.
I guess that's because it gets repotted so often!" — "Hey, look
at the ivy! That's a bigger pot this time, and it's growing like
wildfire; must do it good to be thrown around!" — "What
happened? Oh, just the ivy again. Listen, there's that sack of
dirt I bought to put in the window boxes, some special kind
from Migros [supermarket]. Let's use some with the old dirt this
time." Yes, the ivy was thrown a number of times, but then
the day arrived when it graduated to a lovely bracket on the
wall. It had grown far too many long fronds to stay on the
table, and Fran carefully put it up with pins to climb along
the wall. Never has it been thrown since!

The day we moved out of Mélèzes to our next chalet farther
up the mountainside, Fran took two things of special memories with him and replaced them in the new chalet exactly as
they had been in the old. One was a door. One door of our
bedroom, his closet door, had fastened on the inside of it pictures of his parents, our children, and then grandchildren,
which covered it solidly from top to bottom. He wanted this
gallery of memories with him in the same form, so he took
the door off the hinges and spent an hour — in the midst of
moving men carrying in things, yelling up the stairs, chaos
and confusion — kneeling on the floor and transferring the
pictures one at a time to the same position on the inside of
the door of his little attic office in the new home. This was
to be his first office in Switzerland, and he wanted it to have
what our bedroom office had always had, the family pictures
to be seen when he opened the door to get his papers. Second,
he took the ivy. And after the door's pictures had been trans-
ferred and the old door gone back down the hill, the ivy
(which had been tenderly brought up on Fran's lap so that no
frond would break) was put painstakingly up while he teetered
on a stool and was oblivious of any other pressures. That ivy
had to go to a final pot, be placed on a three-cornered shelf,
and be pinned around two sides of the wall. An enormous
amount of ivy covers the wall of this attic office with the warm

sunshine flooding the unpainted wooden walls, and that ivy says a number of things silently with its variety of sizes and shades of green leaves spreading, flourishing, and continuing to be a thing of beauty. It says that it didn't die from being thrown, because the repotting took place so quickly, water wasn't forgotten, and loving care was given the rest of the time. It demonstrates something of the whole family, generation added to generation, as the leaves are added to the plant. As the ivy has grown and spread and yet has "stuck together" in a continuity of plant growth, so the family has grown and increased in number and "stuck together" — still a family, in spite of the variety of branches and leaves and shades of green represented! It also demonstrates the fact that perfection which is held up as an ideal can be destructive. One needs to resolve, "I am going to do better; I won't do that kind of thing," and one needs to know that changes and discoveries of how to avoid flare-ups can help a new family not to repeat the old mistakes. But such a thing as that "ivy masterpiece" in the museum of memories can be a tremendous safeguard. When some new little family is frightened of the emotions of anger, disappointment, disgust, or dismay because of what one or the other has done, the remembrance of the ivy can remind both the calm one and the upset one, "This doesn't need to be the end; just think how many times the ivy was thrown, and how many times it all got cleaned up and repotted. Our human relationship can continue to get better and stronger just as the plant continued to grow with a sturdy, healthy growth." There can be a "repotting and watering" of a human relationship, too.

Your museum of memories will not all be made up of chosen memories and understanding the better use of time, but there will be both good and disturbing memories which will help your children to have a realistic understanding of human beings, of life in a fallen world where sin continues to spoil things, and of the fact that there can be a rebuilding after an "earthquake," and that it is worth it all to go back and make a new start.

"How many times shall we forgive?" Jesus is asked. "Shall it be seven times?" asks Peter (*see* Matthew 18:21, 22). *Shall we forgive each other seven times?* — Peter wants to know as practical preparation for knowing when to say, "Okay, this is the last time." And the answer of Jesus comes to Peter and to us, "Jesus saith unto him, I say not unto thee, Until seven times: but, Until seventy times seven." And when we couple that with what Jesus taught us to ask God in day-by-day prayer, "Forgive us our trespasses as we forgive those who trespass against us," it becomes very sobering, even frightening. Jesus is saying something real when he goes on to say, "For if ye forgive men their trespasses, your heavenly Father will also forgive you: But if ye forgive not men their trespasses, neither will your Father forgive your trespasses" (*see* Matthew 6:12, 14, 15). "Put on therefore . . . [a heart of compassion], kindness, humbleness of mind, meekness, long-suffering; Forbearing one another, and forgiving one another, if any man have a quarrel against any: even as Christ forgave you, so also do ye" (Colossians 3:12, 13). This is talking about relationships within the family, as well as with other people. God means us to pay attention to His warnings. There is meant to be, in our dealings with each other, a consideration of what He has done for us. Who of us is so perfect as to stand in condemnation and judgment and say, "I won't forgive," to a child or to a husband or wife or to brothers or sisters or to grandparents or aunts or uncles? Forgiveness is meant to be *experienced* in a two-way manner in a family, and memories should contain memories of forgiveness. If the weakness, fault, mistake, or sin has never been acknowledged or noticed, then the forgiveness cannot be given or become a reality.

*Memories ought to be put in the budget.* This is a sentence to underline in red ink in your mind. How do you put memories in your budget? Of course it involves a choice, but this time it is a choice in which the spending of money must be definitely faced. You have a little fund or box or an envelope in which you have tucked away bits of saving when you have economized, or when birthday presents have been given to you. Perhaps you have in mind a few possibilities of what you want to use it for — you could get a rug for that old stained linoleum floor on your sewing-room office or new linoleum for the kitchen or even a new winter coat.

Then you get the Music Festival programs for the summer and fall, and notice that there is to be an unusual concert — the Philharmonic Symphony soloists playing as a quintet of strings at Castle Chillon. (It depends on where you live in the world, but I have to use illustrations of my own experience.) The question comes to you and to me: "What is more important, the rug, my linoleum, or memories that will last a lifetime for my children and grandchildren? How long do we have before war makes concerts an impossibility? How long do we have before the family circle will be broken?" And the determination comes — to choose seats, to send off a letter for reservations, to pay the staggering amount! Are you crazy? You go off with little girls dressed in their last year's family-reunion dresses, with adults dressed up and happy, looking forward to being transported into Bach's, Beethoven's, and Brahms's world, being carried off into another century as we all enter the castle. Four-year-old Jessica has just whispered excitedly, "I don't even know what a concert looks like. This is my first one, but I'll keep very quiet." People look a little astonished, but you hear a dignified gentleman whisper to his wife during intermission, "I wonder who those charming-looking little girls are, they are so quiet and interested." They do make a picture in their dark Scottish-plaid wool dresses to the floor, with the collars and sleeves of their white dotted-swiss blouses setting them off, and the black velvet ribbons tieing up their shining braids or curls, or as a band on shorter hair. Will the adults of the family ever forget the evening? Will the children? Who could forget the full moon behind the Castle Chillon, with floodlights illuminating the old moss-covered rocks? Who could forget crossing the covered bridge and peering over to see the dark water rippling below, imagining the days of captive prisoners and the deep intrigue centering in this very place? Who could forget the togetherness of sharing such an experience on the various levels on which it has been shared? What has the money been spent for? Anything tangible? *Memories.* Memories which cannot be taken away from any person who has made up the family group that night, memories which will come back to lull each one to sleep during some restless night of tossing with worries of one kind or another. Memories help to sort out the reality of what God has given us in beauty, to share horizontally in our capacity for enjoyment. Memories help children to realize the contrast of what they were being lured into with promises of "fun," when the fun includes drugs and the dangerous spoiling of the tomorrows with ugly hangovers of some kind. An evening like the one at Chillon, once in memory's museum, is a tremendous protection against false judgments as to what a great evening is like. "The blessing of the Lord, it maketh rich, and he addeth no sorrow with it" (Proverbs 10:22). How better can you really teach children what this means — than by spending money for memories which illustrate this fact?

"What is the use of having tea [milk, hot chocolate, orange juice] in this lovely tearoom? Let's save money and go home and have our tea [or whatever]." At times the saving comes first — but there are other times when you need to recognize that you are not really paying four times the price of what you are having to drink. It isn't the actual thing you are drinking that is at the bottom of the need to say, "Okay, let's stop here and have something to drink." It is the opportunity for a very special memory. You suddenly realize that stopping is going to add an opportunity for a completeness to the day that would not otherwise be there, and you spend your money for the memory — to be put in the family museum of memories and looked at for years to come.

Constantly you need to think of the memory value as well as the practical monetary value of what you are using money for, as you bring up a family. Constantly you need to think of what will last longer, with greater results, a new car or a memory! What about schedules, sleep, school, meals on time, and the usual standard of values as to how to use time day by day? There are times when memories are in danger of being *un*recognized and the time is going to be wasted or lost, with the memory uncaptured! What sorts of memories need to be recognized, protected, captured in the nick of time, before they are lost? Here are a few reminders:

"It will be after your bedtime, but, yes, you can go to the airport and say good-bye to Grandfather. You may never get to do just this again."

"There is a fantastic double rainbow. It doesn't matter whether or not supper spoils a bit. Never mind it, let's all run outside and watch until it fades."

"Mr. Q. is going to bring his slides of African jungles with him to supper tonight. Let the children stay up to see them. They can get their baths first and watch in pajamas."

"We have these little pieces of smoked glass ready to look at the eclipse of the sun. You can all wait for it; never mind the music lesson this time."

"The parade is going right by the house. We'll have sandwiches and ice-cream cones ready and eat them outside so we won't miss it — then save for tomorrow our meal that was ready."

"It's Grandmother's birthday party and we may never have this kind of togetherness again. Let's take Fiona wrapped up in blankets, but give her the antibiotic first. She can lie on the couch, and I don't think it will hurt her."

"It doesn't matter if we *are* all alone. The extra time it takes to put a candle and this African violet on the tray will make a memory of our midnight snack in bed."

"Yes, I do think the children should be allowed to take flowers to Grandmother's bed and put them around her body. Quite the opposite from being shattering, it will help them understand death — and the body being here while the person has gone to heaven — more vividly than anything else. The memory will be tremendously important. Of course, let them pick flowers and go in that room two at a time. Now — you can't decide later."

"Take someone along to take care of little Matthew outside the hospital, after he has had his peek through the nursery window at his baby sister. It takes one extra person's time, but has a value you couldn't assess. Even if he can't go inside for the length of time his father can, the few moments will be a memory all his life."

What is a family? Oh, what *is* a family? — *a museum of memories.*

"What do *you* do? You're just a housewife and slave, aren't you? A nursemaid to a bunch of kids?" — "No, I have a fantastic job, a terrific career. I am a curator in a museum — a museum of memories!"

"You're tied down by a whole family. What a bore! Don't you wish you could get away with the fellows for a real good time?" — "No, I can't waste my time that way. I'm a collector, you see. I have to spend my time collecting, whenever I'm not tied up in work. I am collecting memories for our family museum!"

# 10

## A Door That Has Hinges and a Lock

There are all kinds of doors — from openings without even a flap to make a shield, or openings with strings of cheap beads to give some kind of vague separation from being outside and inside — all the way to heavy, bulletproof, padlocked entrances. When one says the word *door,* many ideas may come to mind. If the idea of a family being an "open door" is set forth, it is needful to determine what kind of door that is meant to be. Does it have to be an opening that has no way of being shut, with no need to knock to pass through? Or should there be a deep moat filled with water, a drawbridge which is only down part of the time, with no way of signaling in an emergency? Is a family to be a secret garden with a door hidden under ivy on an old wall, which can only be found if stumbled upon by accident? Is there to be a bell to ring or a knocker with which to knock?

When asked "What is a family?" and the answer comes, "A door," it seems to me the more accurate definition would be, "A family is a door that has hinges and a lock." The hinges should be well oiled to swing the door open during certain times, but the lock should be firm enough to let people know that the family needs to be alone part of the time, just to *be* a family. If a family is to be really shared, then there needs to be something to share. Whatever we share needs time for preparation.

If we are going to share bread, we need to be provided with the flour, eggs, yeast, sugar, milk, and whatever else we might put in it, and we need to have time to make the dough and bake it before it can be shared. If we took flour, sugar, a cake of yeast, some milk or water, and an egg or two, and tossed them out the window for someone begging for bread, a nasty mess would fall at his feet in a form that would do him no good. It seems to me that there is a danger of having a door so open that there might just as well not be walls, so that there is no shelter at all to enter. In the same way, the family to be shared can also be in a state of just being the raw, scattered ingredients of a family, which need time to become the "bread" which could be helpful to the hungry one needing the reality of a family to share. The kneading and molding and mixing and blending are things which go on throughout a lifetime of putting a family together, but if a certain amount of the togetherness of the ingredients has not taken place, there is nothing at all to share, and the one seeking help comes to an "empty table." The door is the same thing, in the sense that one thinks of people — who are looking for a door — as needing shelter. If there is no lock on the door, there has never been a shelter for anyone. The family cannot be sheltered, nor does it have protection, if there is no possibility of locking itself in and others out — at certain times of need or special danger. If the storm can blow in the door, and the rush of rain can flood the house; if wolves can follow the dogs into the house, and there is no real protection at all — how can the home and family together be sheltered or become a shelter for anyone else needing help or a place of refuge?

If people think, "We'll wait until we are always sweet and lovely to each other, with no faults showing through. Then we'll invite people in," they will never be ready for the first person. On the other hand, the danger is that people will think they are "ready" — in some measure of thinking they will be strong enough to be calm, sweet, kind, patient, long-suffering, gentle, without envy, and *expecting* a kind of per-

fection from each other — and may suddenly be horrified at
the difficulties which will come from the strain of having
strangers around. To expect to be perfect is to fall into
confusion and despair, and to expect each other to be perfect is to put a strain on each other that will add to the possibility of some kind of breakdown in family life or an individual's psychological balance. God speaks to us of this as
He says: "My little children, these things write I unto you,
that ye sin not. And if any man sin, we have an advocate with
the Father, Jesus Christ the righteous" (1 John 2:1). This
has followed right after the last verses of the previous chapter:
"If we confess our sins, he is faithful and just to forgive us
our sins, and to cleanse us from all unrighteousness. If we
say that we have not sinned, we make *him* a liar, and *his*
word is not in us" (1 John 1:9, 10; *italics* added).

No, we will never arrive at the state of being a perfect
person or a perfect family ready to share something of our
"perfect home." God shows us the hour-by-hour need of remembering His formula of how to live together. We are to
confess our sin to the Lord — we have an Advocate, a
Lawyer who pleads for us — we are forgiven on the basis
of the atonement which the Advocate Himself died to give
us; we are cleansed and we go on. Moment by moment this
needs to continue. The trouble is that people want *more* than
the Lord promises; they want the state of perfection that will
not come until Jesus comes back again to change us. Wanting more than we can have now, we have another case of
"everything or nothing," and so many times it ends up "nothing." This happens when there is a demand on the marriage
relationship which is more than two people are capable of,
and a split results or is in danger of happening. But it happens also when people open the door of their home with too
romantic an expectation of being ready for everyone else's
problems, forgetting they are going to continue to have their
own hour-by-hour problems in the midst of it all.

We are very clearly taught that we are to present an open
door to other people, as Christian families. "Use hospitality

one to another without grudging [or without murmuring]"
(1 Peter 4:9). This is the same admonition as is given us
about sharing our material goods — to do it without grudging, to give cheerfully. So our sharing of our homes is to be
without complaining all the time that we are doing so.
This is further underlined in Philippians: "Do all things
without murmurings and disputings" (2:14). If any warning
or command is needed by each of us as we let the hinges
turn and swing open the door, it is this — one of the two
(parents) and the children (as they are a part of the family)
are not meant to buck the others in complaining with either
all sorts of mumbling murmurings or openly arguing and
disputing the giving of this hospitality. In Titus 1:8 the elder
of the church is being spoken of as one who should be "a
lover of hospitality." It is to be with an emotion that is
positive, if one is to be a true *lover* of hospitality. As in the
whole concept of love, this love needs to be long-suffering.
It won't be *easy* to be a lover of hospitality toward a variety
of personalities, some of whom may come barging in without
sensitivity and appreciation, but there needs to be a recognition that, before the Lord, we are meant to be striving for
that kind of attitude. First Timothy 3:2 says that one of the
things an elder needs to be (among other things) is "given
to hospitality." Since he is also to be "husband of one wife,"
this is to be an open home, with the wife having a part in
the hospitality!

Romans is clearly speaking to all of us who are born-again
children of the Lord. Many things are pointed out to us in
detail as to what it means to present our bodies as a "living
sacrifice" to the Lord, and to "be not conformed to this
world," but to be "transformed by the renewing of our minds"
(*see* 12:1, 2). Among other things is this verse: "Distributing
to the necessity of saints; given to hospitality" (v. 13). As
that is followed by "Bless them which persecute you: bless,
and curse not," you can see that it is not in a list of easy
things to follow. These are all things which we can only do
in the power of the Lord, and in His strength in our weakness.

To plunge into having an open-door kind of family, as if it were going to be something like deciding to raise strawberries, is to miss the point altogether. Having hospitality is as difficult as (and really includes): "Therefore if thine enemy hunger, feed him: if he thirst, give him drink . . ." (v. 20). The kind of hospitality the Lord asks us to give is that which is filled with surprises — and might call for us to sit down to eat supper with "an enemy," as well as with those seeking help or coming as old friends.

The element of surprise in opening your door to strangers is given us in Hebrews in a very special command concerning hospitality: "Be not forgetful to entertain strangers [or forget not to show love unto strangers]: for thereby some have entertained angels unawares" (13:2). We are told to remember, to not forget to entertain — which can also mean to show love to *strangers*. The fact that these are not old friends and neighbors is clear; these people are so unknown to us that they might be angels. We don't know their background and origin as we open the door and say, "Come in." We don't have their family history and credentials as we start showing love (long-suffering, gentleness, meekness, kindness, lack of envy — all these things in some form). We are showing a compassion for the lost world in a practical way by showing it to some specific individuals on our own doorstep. The surprise element is always meant to be there. Someday we *might* entertain an angel. We are told so. Some have.

Often in the last twenty years of having at *L'Abri* an open home which turned into many open homes, I have said to the children or someone helping me, "I can't face one more person today — and just want to run." So often what has happened when I have dished out the last of fifty-two desserts and decided I was going to dash away to a quiet spot, the answer to my cry to the Lord — in the midst of throwing the spoon into the sink, and pouring the next cup of tea — has been a knock on the door! Cruel? No, it has so often been a sudden answer on the part of the Lord in the direction of showing me what it was all about. It was as if He said,

"My child, it isn't fifty-two dinners en masse that you have been serving. This isn't a restaurant. Stop!" And the stopping has been in the form of what happened one Sunday in just that kind of moment, when I went to the door and there stood a lovely Indian girl with a hopeful question, "Is this *L'Abri?*" The story tumbled out as I sat with her over one more meal dished out and one more cup of tea. (No, two, because I took one, too!) She had bought a copy of the book *L'Abri* from a ship that had stopped in Mombasa. She had read it and had become convinced of the truth of Christianity and had been born again out of a Hindu background. She was on her way to England when the flight stopped in Geneva for some hours of wait-over, and had arranged an even later plane to give herself a full twenty-four hours. She had left her cousin in Geneva and set forth to find *L'Abri* with no address. She had stood asking strangers in the Geneva railroad station, "Where is *L'Abri?*" and received dozens of scornful answers, "Never heard of it." — "Oh, Lord, I'll ask once more," she prayed, "and if the answer is *no,* I'll go back to my cousin and fly on." One couple came close to her after that prayer, and with courage to ask this last time, she stopped them, "Do you know where *L'Abri* is?" They had just come from there, they said, and went on to give directions.

Now here she sat with me and began to pour out questions from a Hindu background, having lived all her life in Africa and been educated in twentieth-century thinking. Could the Lord have given me a better supply of what I needed at that particular moment? It was like a shake — and a pointing to something I was in danger of missing in the sunset, "Look, this is what you have forgotten to look at!" The evening was given to that girl; she slept in our home and the next day was gone. Sequel? There isn't any to this story. I don't think she was an angel, but there is no doubt that for whatever reason the Lord brought her to us for *her* life. He gave *me* a fresh lesson that day in how He answers prayers by asking for His will to be unfolded, and His choice of people to be brought to us for care.

Yes, there is always the surprise possibility in entertaining strangers, but each one is not an angel, and in the case of each one we do not always see any clear results or any obvious reasons why we have shared our family with that particular person. In hospitality, as in "distributing to the necessity of the saints" — in going to the place the Lord wants us to go, traveling great distances to help people, or in staying right at the kitchen sink and opening the front door to allow more to come in (to make more dirty dishes) — the basic ingredient is saying, "Lord, I'll do what You want me to do." It is asking for His guidance, rather than rushing in to fulfill an ambitious plan of going or staying in one's own strength. We can't have any of the realities of what a family can be, without the Lord's help, and we certainly can't have the reality of *a family as an open door with hinges and a lock,* without constantly praying that the Lord will help us to be ready for the ones whom He sends. Yet we are not presumptuously to plunge into sharing what we don't have to share. There is a delicate balance here, of willingness to sacrifice the praise of others for being "so wonderfully open," when we are meant to be giving privacy to each other, to our children, or to the Lord Himself.

We must never forget that there are times when we are meant to shut out everyone but the Lord. To pray in our closets, as we are told to do in Matthew 6:6, is an admonition to pray alone with the Lord, shut away from others. Jesus went out into a desert place to pray alone. Others went alone to be apart with the Lord for a time. There is a specific need to be private from time to time — with a lock to keep everyone out — in our relationship with the Lord. Otherwise that relationship cannot grow in a way which can give freedom to praying with others, being two or three together asking Him for something, or worshiping along with others whom we are told to join by "not forsaking the assembling of ourselves together" with other believers (*see* Hebrews 10:25). Both things are commanded as needed in the relationship with God, our Father, and with Jesus, our Bridegroom.

We can share our time with God with other people, and are meant to, but we are also called upon to spend time alone with God the Father as our Guide, our Counselor, our Friend, our Shelter, our Strong Rock, and we are to spend time alone with Jesus as our Saviour, our Advocate, our Shepherd, our Elder Brother, our Prince of Peace. There should be aloneness to listen to His Word without distraction as we read the Bible in the woods, in a dry field, shut into a bathroom because there is no other solitary place, or shut away by invisible walls as we sit on a train or bus and ask Him to give us an aloneness in the midst of the crowd. We need to be alone to talk to Him and to have two-way communication as we read His Word. The aloneness is important if there is to be a growing relationship. This does not shut out spending time studying the Bible with others, nor having fellowship with others, nor praying with others, but is something that has no substitute if we are really to come to know the Lord better. We can't know anyone without spending time with that person.

Being finite, limited human beings, we cannot spend time alone with everyone in the world, nor can we spend time alone with a very large number of people, one at a time. But however many we are to get to know in a deep personal way in a lifetime, we have a need, a responsibility, and a command to spend time alone in marriage. We are to be one physically — that takes time *alone!* We are to have our physical oneness continue to be a reality in the same regular way our eating is to continue. This is not a book on marriage, so no more on the subject will be covered, except that it takes time to have a continuing physical relationship, just as it takes time to be imaginative about menus and cooking and serving food in a variety of ways, with or without candle-light, in the sunshine, on grass mats or linen tablecloths. It takes time to be imaginative through years of married life in the area of physical oneness, and that means time *alone*. It takes time to be one intellectually, as it means some amount of conversation, some sharing of reading books, listening to lectures, and discussing. To grow together intellectually takes time alone. It takes time alone to grow together as one spiritually. It takes time reading the Bible together, praying together, and whatever else you arrange. Over a period of a lifetime of marriage, there have to be some *alone* periods for spiritual growth together.

In addition to two people who are married needing to have time alone together, just as each of us must spend time alone with the Lord for our relationship with Him, then also a *family* — mother and father and children, along with the wider family of grandparents, aunts and uncles, and so on — needs to find some time alone, in order to develop the true family relationships which are possible. They do not simply burst forth by pushing a button marked BE A FAMILY! Time must be taken to be alone together — time spread out all through life, not simply taken for one year at the beginning. Relationships are not like a house which you buy and consider to be for a lifetime. Even a house needs a new roof and repaired pipes, but a family has far greater need of regular attention. This is the whole matter of taking time to have something to share. This is what I wanted us to be forceably "hit with" in the illustration of the shower of flour, eggs, yeast, sugar, salt, and milk, falling around the heads of people asking for bread. Too many families are trying to share the raw ingredients and they don't ever expect to take the time to mix them together. They seem to expect to pass around little piles of raw ingredients for a lifetime of having an "open house"! Immediately we need to refer back to the fact that we will never be perfect as a family — in case there comes a shrug of the shoulders and the thought that we can just let the stranger at the gate stand and knock forever with no expectation of ever opening the door.

Perhaps you have never heard of *L'Abri,* but twenty years ago God brought us to a physical place in a chalet in a tiny Swiss Alpine village, and to a place in our own family life when we had made a decision together with our children to live by prayer alone. There was to be an "open door," and we were praying that God would bring the people of His choice to us. That is not the subject of this book, but it is important to say that *L'Abri* is not and has never been a "commune." That is to say it was a shared home, but not a house which had no basic family with its own basic personal possessions. It had rooms which were each child's own room — for privacy and to give a certain amount of shelter to the individuals in the family, as well as being a *whole* house — the family home. Now, twenty years later, with about twelve homes in Switzerland as well as homes in France and in Holland and England which have this same kind of "open door," there are still real families — separate in identity, with their own possessions, their own ideas of menus, their own interior decoration — all a part of *L'Abri,* but not a communal kind of huge "family." We believe strongly that single people in *L'Abri* as Workers ought to have their own apartments or little houses when possible, and that these homes are theirs to share. We very firmly believe that each family should feel that the chalet or apartment or house which is its home is really its own in every way possible.

It seems to me that there are many different kinds of counterfeits in the area of families, as there are many counterfeits of every other true thing. There are communal families in which six or seven women live with five or six men, and no one knows who is the father of which child. However, not speaking of such confusion as this (and other things such as "open marriage" which makes the bed communal, or wives leaving their husbands to take their children to live with another women who has also left her husband — in the new homosexual type of "family"), there are also blurred false pictures given of what a family is meant to be, under the name of Christianity.

When I was attending a Christian conference in a certain place, a young woman with a fifteen-month-old child was slapping him and scolding, "Share, share, share," when he pulled his little toy back from the grasp of another tiny toddler. I couldn't stand this kind of discipline and took the girl gently by the arm and led her out of hearing distance from the group (listening to a lecture) and then asked, "Just what were you doing to that baby?" — "Teaching him to share!"

"But who gave you the idea that slapping would teach a little fifteen-month-old baby to share? Don't you know he needs to learn the meaning of the word? He can get the idea that your slap is the meaning of the word *share,* as easily as anything else. You give a baby a bite of your cookie and say, 'Mommy is sharing this with you. Mmmm, isn't it nice? Mommy shared cookie with you.' You give your baby a bite of your banana and say, 'Here, share this with Mommy. I am sharing it with you.' Day by day you share things, and one day the baby will hold up his precious little bit of cake or apple and press it to your mouth with a gurgle of delight. He has caught on; he is sharing something of his own."

The mother was sobbing by now, "But the leader of the commune, the one who is head of our home, says I have to *hit* him for everything. I have to hit him if he doesn't share!" — "Who is this person — your husband?" — "No, he is only twenty-one-years old and isn't married, but he is the spiritual head of our commune." I discovered that two married couples and a few single people lived in this commune they called a "Christian family," and the young twenty-one-year-old lad was the authority, not only telling this couple what to do with this child, but with their twin babies only six weeks old. Now the girl was pregnant again, because — "The head of the home doesn't believe in birth control."

Varying types of combinations (some with nothing immoral such as sharing husbands and wives) are living in groupings and calling themselves "families" and trying to urge others to come and live with them, as if this were the biblical idea of a family. The responsibility of each parent is to his own children, to give them the personal care and teaching when they "rise up, lie down, walk" as Deuteronomy teaches. To throw open the doors in this manner is to have no walls at all, to have no shelter for the original family group, let alone for anyone who comes in; and to serve, day after day, a horrible mess of raw flour, salt, eggs, milk or water, margarine or other fat, yeast — and call it "bread." This is not a family which has decided to be an open door with hinges and a lock. This is a grouping of people with no door, with broken walls, desperately trying to copy family life without any understanding of what they are trying to copy.

Every Christian is called upon to be hospitable and to care for strangers as well as lonely people and those in need. God says to us that He takes special care to put lonely people in families: "God setteth the solitary in families . . ." (Psalms 62:6). That does not mean that every *solitary* person is going to be picked up and put in a family permanently, any more than every sick person is going to be healed immediately. When Jesus comes back, the problem of being lonely, as well as being ill, is going to be cared for once and for all. Permanently! The people in the Family of the Lord are going to find fantastic sufficiency for every single person who will be there in eternity. But we who have human families need to take some care and have some concern for someone whose husband has just died or whose husband has deserted her completely. We need to remember that a girl who is in the hospital having her first child, and whose husband has left her to live with someone else permanently and wants a divorce, is in tremendous need of being invited for meals, being given time to be with us for tea and conversation, or having the feeling that there is an "open home" nearby that has an interest in seeing how the new baby is getting on. A man whose wife has just died (or a man whose wife has deserted him) should find within the Christian families at least one that is full of understanding and compassion as to what it would mean for him and for the children to have some kind of shelter to go to, or at least an understanding person to write to. We are meant not only to think of the need of strangers and of others needing hospitality, but of the most solitary of solitary people.

Old people, orphans, handicapped people, survivors of a tragedy, lonely people, disappointed people living alone, people in hospitals who have no families — myriads of people need hospitality or an open home. No one person can take care of them all (except God Himself), no one family can take care of them all. No matter how consistently your door or mine is open, everybody who knocks *cannot* be cared for, let alone all who are in need. But because "too much" *is* too much, does not mean we should do *nothing*. Therefore, to more or less degrees, our homes should be places where *some* people can come to find comfort or to find the answers to their seeking questions about the existence of God.

How do you open your door and yet lock it at other times? What practical hints can be given? Each family must work out the details of its own life. There is no list to be followed which will bring about perfection of balance. However, there are some strong imperatives which we have learned in the years of experience in *L'Abri*. We are still learning!

A family with an open door and with people often sharing meals and fireside discussions, teatime on the balcony, or potato peeling in the kitchen, must have at least one day off a week when they are alone as a family together. The day should not be shared with anyone else. Whether the family goes to the zoo, a park, out in the country for a picnic, to a city to shop and stop for a meal and a walk through a museum, or whether the family goes to a good flat sidewalk (away from people who know them) where the children can ride on tricycles or kiddiecars and be sure of their parents' attention — whether the family goes for long walks together, with the baby on Mother's or Daddy's back and the picnic in another sack — whether the family locks the door and sits isolated from the outside, reading books aloud, or playing games or putting together a jigsaw puzzle — whatever it is, the day off ought to be kept for the family alone. Why? Because if you have many shared meals, the parents and the children need to answer each other's questions, keep in touch with each other's problems as well as enjoy some relaxed

time together. One day a week should be the minimum "alone
time" together as a family, if parts of other days are being
shared.

If there is a special planned trip as a family together (for
a birthday, let us say) and you are just ready to go off for
the looked-forward-to event, and suddenly a foreign student
you have had for Sunday dinner arrives on the doorsteps and
says, "Can I go, too?" you have a hard thing to face. If your
children's faces fall (or there is the slightest hint of disappointment), I would say, "No I'm awfully sorry; do come back at
[such and such a time]. Today we have promised the children
a day alone together with no one but ourselves. We do keep
our promises to our children when we are able, and we feel
this is important."

In addition to the one day a week, certain hours or at least
one hour of each day should be given by one of the two
parents — unbroken time, not to be interrupted — for the
children or one child alone to read books, talk over their
questions, read the Bible portion for the day, and pray together. No matter what visitor is in your home, he or she
can wait for that hour to be up and must not join in to
hear what you are doing, or else the whole point of being
alone is spoiled. Naturally, if the whole family can be together, that is splendid, but this much is minimal: at least
one parent giving full attention and sharing book after book
together with the child or children.

"But I thought you shared family prayers with people who
are there in the home?"

Yes, that is right, and children love to have family prayers
shared with other people who are there for the meal. One
child perhaps sits on the father's lap during the Bible reading,
another on the mother's, the oldest leaning against one parent's shoulder or staying in his or her place. Questions should
come from any age person, and the child should feel free to
ask them in front of other people, knowing that they have
important questions, too. But these general family prayers
do not take the place of reading alone from *Alice in Wonder-*

*land, Winnie the Pooh, Sunshine Country,* and all varieties
of books, with time set aside afterwards for the Bible and
prayer. This "alone time" lends an important security to each
day, and there can be a substitute only when Mother and
Daddy are away for some reason.

The longer period is the vacation, once or twice a year,
which all *L'Abri* Workers have, and which we believe is
important for any families who are sharing their homes. The
vacation will, of course, be very different for different families. We are not all alike in what we enjoy, and as we
pray for the Lord's provision, God does not treat each of His
children alike, so where and how the vacation is spent will
be different. Pris and John like to go camping with a tent
on top of their car, reading books aloud (that is, Pris reads
and John drives) that the whole family will enjoy, while they
go eighteen long hours (with stops for picnics and a nap at
some grassy spot along the way) all the way to southern Italy.
They find a nice but inexpensive camping spot and have their
own "pioneer life" there by the sea, swimming, cooking over
a campfire, sometimes sleeping in puddles when it rains, but
thoroughly enjoying the change. Sue and Ran go to an English
farmhouse which takes boarders, where they have meals
cooked by the farmer's wife, help with the milking, and go
off to Cornwall's beach where the water is icy cold, a fire is
needed to warm up enough to eat the picnic lunch, and they
come back to a blazing log fire before dashing up to cold
bedrooms!

Whether you live in the United States or Canada or England or Europe or Japan or Africa, the vacation possibilities
and your own tastes would differ, as would the "provision."
I think it is a very important thing to pray for a vacation
that will help year by year to keep the family close together
and to make a reality of something to share. It is not just the
physical, psychological, and emotional rest that is needed,
it is a great help in discovering gaps in our relationships
which need mending or real loneliness that is growing because of never having time to talk about certain things or to

make discoveries together. To play together in sand, swim together, discover new fish together, hike in the mountains together, read books in strange and new places together, eat strange foods in new surroundings together, bicycle through winding roads together, walk through old city streets together — whatever it is you like to do gives an atmosphere which will melt away some of the "scratchy places" in your relationships, and which will remove you from some of the ordinary irritations of day-by-day life. But don't expect too much! If you expect perfection, then a vacation can be the most dismally disappointing time of the year.

A family is an open door with hinges that close, and a lock that fastens for the vacation period! This is one of the times during which the raw ingredients are getting kneaded and readied for the baking of something fresh to share! — not a time to share with others. There are no relationships which do not need new beginnings. Even in our relationship with the Lord, because of our own limitations, sins, hindrances, and failures, we need to have new beginnings in the sense of saying, "Lord, I'm sorry I seem to have stopped reading the Bible every morning, and now I want to tell You that I am going to try to read it at lunchtime for a half hour." — "Lord, I've found that reading alone each morning has shut me away from my husband, and now I'm going to start listening to his Bible reading, following along with him, so I'll spend other moments of the day alone with You, Lord." — "Lord, I need a new closeness to You, so I'm going to take a lovely picnic lunch with chicken sandwiches and apples, and go off alone for some hours of eating and praying — taking a picnic with You, Lord, with Your Word along, so that You can talk to me."

New starts, new ideas of being with the Lord, fresh surroundings and atmosphere for your time with Him are needed to keep your relationship growing. Time after time in your lifetime of being a child of the Lord, of having God as your Father and Christ as your Bridegroom, you will need to get away from ruts and from other people and be alone with Him in a slightly new context.

Our relationships within the family are also in need of new starts. What can be done practically? You know what your ruts are and what the hindrances are to your being together and doing things together. Military families have problems, government people have problems, news-media families have problems, as well as pastors' families and doctors' families. It is easy to think that your own set of "impossibilities" are the only problems that exist, without realizing that the task of keeping up family relationships is a battle for the "artist" who has taken on this career, in tremendously varied but equally difficult ways. The thing to do first of all is to think of the possibilities of starting a "new thing" which might not be appropriate later on, and which couldn't have been done before, but which will fit in for a "together interest" right now. Have you ever done bird-watching? Do you live where it would be easy to get out for a few minutes with a pair of binoculars and a bird book and try to see what birds there are nearby? Would your family pitch in and become interested if you got the books, put on a record of birdcalls which would likely be familiar ones in your area, and began to find excitement in recognizing a birdcall or in discovering a nest nearby? Another possibility open almost anywhere people live is learning the position and names of stars and planets, and spending a short bit of time, week by week, on the roof, out on a hill, down by the river, a little bit out of the city — just to try to find stars. Charts can be bought, articles read, and the changes through the year noted and discussed and looked for.

Whether it is taking a half-hour walk together before going to bed, starting a custom of eating fruit and milk as one reads a book aloud just before bedtime, playing checkers or chess, putting together a jigsaw puzzle which is left on a board to be worked at when there are a few odd moments to spend together, deciding to collect old family pictures to make a

family history book with pictures from two or three generations, or taking up a new sport, it is necessary to give a new
dimension to your togetherness from time to time, while the
children are growing up — and also after they leave home.

Naturally, if you live where you never have snow, you
couldn't take up our new sport, cross-country skiing. Fran and
I were given cross-country skis as a gift two years ago, and
since I had a problem with my knee, it seemed a good substitute for downhill skiing. As grandparents we find we love
this sport which is a cross between skiing, skating, and hiking, and we can go for miles and miles through woods and
fields, around barns, and across little bridges. There is no
waiting in crowds for ski lifts (and no lift to pay for), but
it is also an occasion for getting away and into the midst of
nature, with exercise which gives one's arms as much as one's
legs a workout, while there is the companionship of walking
together. It really is a whole new dimension to life. Naturally,
you can't (nor would you want to) find new things too often,
but there needs to be an attitude of expecting to find fresh
interests — in the same way there needs to be the realization
that education never stops! When do you do all this? Oh, not
so often. But the memory continues through the weeks when
it isn't possible.

At any time when you as a family are sharing your home
with others and you realize that you yourselves are growing
apart, some kind of new way of being together in a fresh interest should be tried. Perhaps you will meet for tea every day
at five and talk over the news! (And perhaps that will be seen
to be impractical after three days of trying it out!) Whether
you begin new gardening projects, raise goldfish, collect
stamps, go for a five-day hike with backpacks and stop each
evening in a small hotel, take a walk at midnight every night
to feed ducks and swans, play Ping-Pong at ten P.M., read
mystery stories together (one chapter for a half hour or so
at a certain time each day) — whatever it is, some new togetherness is needed, so that the continual having of people
around you does not become an escape from being together

as a married couple or as parents with children. Sensitivity to each other's needs should be developed gradually, so that the urging, "Let's go for a short walk after lunch or supper," should come from one person who suddenly senses the need of someone else in the family to get away. Even as a baby also learns what *sharing* means by having things shared with him or her, so the sensitivity to each other's needs develops when one person in the family continues to be sensitive and to do things for the others.

This awareness of the need of someone for a pickup in the area of doing something to bring you together spreads spontaneously to other people with whom you are sharing your home. Rather than neglecting people outside of the family whom you are trying to help, care for each other speaks to them. It is easy to make the mistake of sacrificing family togetherness to the extent of spoiling what you could be demonstrating to other people.

"Do read a book or listen to this record, we'll be back in an hour, but I like to take the children to do a bit of bird-watching at this time of the afternoon." This can be a sentence that will mean much more to the young people you are trying to help, than just sitting and talking to them and telling them, among other things, how important family life is! My husband had come home on the late bus from Lausanne one evening when a couple had come to have me talk to them about marriage. What to do? My solution was to explain, as I stopped to prepare a tray, that I felt there were priorities to be observed in married life, and that right then a very attractive meal was important. "See how quickly I can prepare a salad with a round of pineapple on lettuce, a split banana, this orange cut in slices, a piece of cheese, some nuts on top — and this omelet! Now I'll top it off with a small pot of tea, this piece of cake, and a candle in this brass candlestick. And it doesn't take more than two seconds to add this bit of ivy. Here, see? Now this is an object lesson for the talk I'll be giving you in a little while. Fran will be happier by far to have me talking to you, once he has had his supper, and

I have spent a bit of time talking to him. I'll see you in a half an hour."

Then I took up the tray and spent time with Fran as he ate in our bedroom, feeling the aloneness that he needed after a particularly long day, before he went on to do a piece of work for the rest of the evening. To have thrown together something not very attractive and given it to him in the room next to where we were talking, would have been an irritation. Anyway, the reality of that object lesson probably would remain in the couple's memory longer than much of what I would later be saying.

Our own decision, twenty years ago, to pray for the people of the Lord's choice to be sent to us and to ask Him to give us that which they needed us to share with them (not just physical food, but the answers they would need), started with our having three, five, seven, ten, and gradually more and more people in our home for weekends, three days in midweek, and then longer periods of time. As months went on we were having people sleep in the living room, on balconies, on the kitchen floor. Our sharing developed into *L'Abri,* as people came to ask questions from fantastically diverse backgrounds and find answers that met their needs. Many have become born-again Christians through the years, and as *L'Abri* has developed into many open chalets, naturally many more are being cared for. It has been a "costly" kind of life in many ways, for us and for all those who have come as single Workers (or couples) to help for short or longer periods of time. The sharing of homes, the seriousness of table conversations, the readiness to answer questions in kitchens, gardens, and while chopping wood — which have developed into more specific study periods interspersed with discussion times — has come about in answer to prayer, as we have also asked God to unfold His plan to us in this day-by-day work.

Should what we did be the *norm?* Should others try to do exactly what we did? Is there a formula to be copied? I would say, "No, a thousand times no." Our God is a God of diversity, and He has diverse plans for the lives of His children. It is no more spiritual to be a pastor than a dentist! If the Lords wants you to be a dentist, then that is His plan for you, and to be anything else is going against His will. To show forth hospitality in your home is following a biblical command, but to what extent that hospitality will take up your time, and how many are to come and go, will differ tremendously from home to home and from time to time in your own history. What God wants you to do this year may be very different from what He wants you to do next year. Whatever it will be, it will not be static.

There is something basic, however, in the teaching of the Word of God, which is the same for all of us who are born into His Family. We are meant to be *tellers of the Gospel, the true truth,* and we are meant to be compassionate and really care for people who are in need, and we are meant to be hospitable and ready to care for people in need, strangers as well as ones we know. Therefore, to some extent, every Christian family is meant to have a door with hinges to swing it *open.* No Christian family is meant to live behind a moat filled with water and a drawbridge swung up out of reach! To protect your family life to this extent, to save your family life in complete selfishness, is to *lose it* in the end. To be willing to lose it is to *find it* in the end, in the same way as other portions of life to which the Lord refers when He tells us that if we are willing to lose our lives for His sake and the Gospel's sake, then we will find our lives. Not only do we care for strangers and people in need, but the Lord says strongly to us that when we give a cup of water in His name, we are giving it to Him. So we are really putting the Lord on our couch, finding space for Him on the kitchen floor, and preparing a meal at midnight for Him as he knocks late at night on our door (and even letting Him break our teapot as He helps with the dishes), while we do these things for others.

How many people? How often? This is something which needs prayer on the part of the family. There must be a oneness among the family in willingness to share. Pray for the people of the Lord's choice to come, one at a time, two at a time, however many He knows you can care for, not just as far as physical food goes, but in the area of answers that they need — spiritual food and shelter from the kind of storm that is destroying them. People with whom a family shares their home should be from all walks of life and from all kinds of backgrounds and nationalities. There should be old people as well as young people. "Lord, send whoever You know would be helped by having an evening with us" should be a prayer you really mean without limits. There is a need to trust the Lord to be able to send the kind of questions you can help with, as well as the number you can care for. If your children feel your honesty and willingness to help people, they will feel a reality as they talk outside the home, which will be a terrific help in their own spiritual growth. To be able to say, "You can come home and discuss things with us some evening; our family likes to have someone for supper and really talk over his questions and problems," is more helpful than any moment of formal teaching in making your own children feel that it is all real and that there is nothing phony about Christianity. There is a need to treat each person as a human being, even as you treat your own family as human beings. Personal needs should be discovered, and the family should discuss later what might be done to help a "destroyed" person.

"I bet," David might say, "that person has never had anyone send him a bunch of flowers." Or Steven might ask, "What do you suppose he would think if we sent him a little personal present on his birthday?" There is a great difference between having people as a duty (and giving a kind of set program for the evening) and getting to know people as *people*. There is nothing that is more helpful for your own children than their becoming involved in compassion for people. There is nothing more beneficial for your children than discovering how exciting it is to know that someone has "passed from darkness to light" because of the times spent in your home. To find that happiness really comes in the midst of seeing someone else helped — especially if helped to find eternal life, as well as to begin to have a changed life here — teaches the whole family what life is all about. To discover an excitement that is more intense than anything that can come in ordinary adventure — watching someone else's excitement in seeing and hearing with eyes and ears of understanding when they have been blind and deaf before — is a great discovery in childhood!

However, an open door can bring disappointments, too, and sometimes it is ten or fifteen years later before results are discovered from what has cost a great deal of patience and sacrifice on the part of the whole family. Sometimes there is no visible result. Therefore, it is important not to be expecting a series of thrills and satisfaction when we pray, "Lord, send the people of Your choice and help us take care of them," but to be wanting to do what the Lord wants us to do for His sake, for His glory, because we love *Him*.

In our finiteness and limitations, as we groan at times over being able to be in only one place at a time, doing one thing at a time, or as we moan over needing to stop to sleep — because there are more people than we have time or strength to see personally and care for — it is imperative to remember that it is not sinful to be finite and limited. That is the way God made us. He will give us what He has for us to do, and that is all He expects us to do. However, *He is infinite and unlimited,* and He is able to do all things. Jesus is able to say, "I am the door: by me if any man enter in, he shall be saved . . ." (John 10:9). Day or night the Heavenly Father is everywhere and is always awake, and *whosoever will may come.* Jesus can say, "In my Father's house are many mansions [many rooms]" (*see* John 14:2). Later we find in Revelation that no man can number them — these multitudes who include some from every tribe and nation and kindred and people and tongue (*see* 7:9). Every family line will have some people in the Lord's Family! What a tremendous Family we belong to, and it will go on forever and forever.

The "sharing now" has something to do with what extends into that time ahead. What is a family? A family is an open door with hinges and a lock — being prepared for its own oneness now and forever and having an effect on some other people's entrances through another door — *The* Door!

# 11

# Blended Balances

Seesaw, Margery Daw,
Jacky shall have a new m-aaa-ster,
And he shall have but a penny a day,
Because he can't work any f-aaa-ster!

*Whish — bump — whish — bump — whish — bump —
creak — creak — whish — bump!*

"How well they balance each other, Margotty and Elizabee. Look at them go!" — "Now it's our turn. Hurry up,
Kirsty, you get there and let me hang on to it here — ooops
— Help!" Becky finally gets herself astride, too, and off they
go, hair flopping up and down, the singsong chant coming
out in breathless little jerks, *"Seesaw, Margery Daw. . . ."* —
"Push harder, I almost don't go up again. Push with your
feet when you hit; I can't get down!" — *"And he shall have
but a. . . ."* — "Now put Giandy on with Jessica — ooops
— It won't work otherwise. Look, just one big thud, and
Jessica is up in the air and can't come down. You have to
balance the weight. It's just no good without a balance of
weight!" — *"Seesaw, Margery Daw, Jacky shall have a new
m-aaa-ster."* — "You need a little help there to keep the balance right. Here, I'll help, because I can give just that extra
little push at the right moment. There you go!" *Whish —
bump — whish — bump — whish — bump!* "A little help

was all you needed to get your feet off the ground again, and to bring the other one down again. It's the *balance* that counts."

It's the balance that counts all through life. It's the balance that matters in the Christian life. It's the balance that matters in human relationships. It's the balance that matters in *family life*. There is a delicate balance, like the equal weight of two people seesawing, or like someone walking a tightrope. Too much on one side, too much on the other, and there comes the thud of one person on the seesaw or the fall of the person on the rope — the continuity of what was going on comes to a sudden stop. Balance is the very important ingredient in every area of life. We see unbalanced people ruining their own lives by being exaggerated in one area or another. We feel upset when we notice a person we love going off on a tangent of one kind or another. We criticize Christian positions or political views which we feel are lopsided and all out of balance. Yet, so often we are in danger of being blind to the lack of balance in the places where it makes the greatest of difference to ourselves as personalities — to the person closest to us, to our families, to our children if we have them, to our parents, to our grandparents, to our friends. We are not only in danger of hurting or disturbing other human beings by our lack of balance, but we can, as children of the Living God, bring dishonor to the Lord in our lack of balance.

We are meant to be representing the Lord as His children. Look at Malachi 1:6: "A son honoureth his father, and a servant his master: if then I be a father, where is mine honour? and if I be a master, where is my fear? saith the Lord of hosts unto you, O priests, that despise my name. . . ." When we accept Christ as our Saviour, we become sons of God as well as servants and priests, and in each of these capacities we are meant to bring honor to God by the way we represent Him to others. If we make no attempt to be balanced in our Christian lives and in our family lives, we are very poor representatives and are in danger of bringing dishonor to the Lord. Second Corinthians 5:20 says we are also "ambassadors for Christ," another vivid description of our need to represent Him well before a watching world. Proverbs 13:17 declares to us, "A wicked messenger falleth into mischief: but a faithful ambassador is health." It isn't simply what we *say* with a good balance which matters. Our lives, our actions, our relationships, our family life, and the wider influence which our family can have as an example to others, *must* have some balance which does not leave one thing "up in the air" and the other "flat on the ground" like a seesaw with two unmatched people as far as weight goes!

Are any of us perfectly balanced? Do I think *I* am? No, of course not. We are imperfect, sinful, full of mistakes, with much to learn until Jesus comes to take us to be with Him, in changed bodies with the sins and imbalances gone! But in this, as in other imperfections, we are called upon to strive for growth and change, and we are meant to help each other "get off the ground" or "come down out of the air." Does nagging and pointing out faults help? A thousand times *no,* but through prayer and gently adding weight on one side or another, we can sometimes help each other — without being obnoxious. As mothers and fathers of children, as grandparents or aunts or uncles, we have responsibility in the area of the need for balance to pray with an awareness and to try to help with as much sensitivity as possible. Parents need to realize that their children, even very young children, can sometimes come out with very wise words in pointing out an inconsistency or an imbalance. There is a humbleness needed in all directions as we live, "each esteeming the other better than themselves" (*see* Philippians 2:3). The *other* can be child, parent, father, mother, grandmother, grandfather — in two directions! The call of the Lord is for us to be sensitive to our difficulty in keeping a balance, and to look to Him for help. Surely the need for balance is to be taken literally in His promise: "If any of you lack wisdom, let him ask of God, that giveth to all men liberally, and upbraideth not; and it shall be given him" (James 1:5).

We are also warned to remember literally, "For the wisdom of this world is foolishness with God . . ." (1 Corinthians 3:19). There *will* be ideas concerning family life and family togetherness which will be infiltrating us, as Christian parents, which come from *this* world and are complete foolishness with God.

As a Christian who believes the Bible to be really true, I do believe we are in a battle and that we have an enemy — Satan. If it is true that Satan hates God and wants to destroy everything that God has made, then *of course* Satan would want to destroy the family. The family is basic. God made man and woman. The first balance that was given was before sin entered into the relationship, a *perfect* balance of two being one, spiritually, intellectually, and physically. All the imbalances have come as a result of sin upsetting the perfect balance, whether in ecological areas of nature or in human relationships. Anytime there is any "danger" (in Satan's way of looking at it) of anything having a possibility of being back *in balance,* Satan, of course, would strike out to destroy that balance. All the disrupting influences and twisted, warped ideas of what a family ought to be, are not simply "chance results" of the century we are in because of the process of evolution! It is quite the opposite — there is a plan behind the devastating falling apart of the family. There is a person behind the plan who wants the family units to fall apart.

One of the most clever blows to the existence of the family is the attempt to destroy the antithesis (or the reality of opposites existing) in the very basic polarity that was made by God — the existence of male and female as different, but fulfilling each other and having the possibility of being one, with the added possibility of bringing forth new human beings who are a blend of the two. The blow against enhancing and enjoying the *differences* between men and women, making it a "dirty word" to say that there *are* differences, and striving for "unisex" in every aspect of personality, is a blow against one of the most beautiful and delicate of all balances. What is being done to men and women is to push one "up in

the air" with the other one "down on the ground," with
Satan's foot planted on the end of the seesaw, so to speak!
Satan is laughing his head off at the struggle to get free from
his foot, as he watches Christians as well as non-Christians
fall into the confusion of the declaration he sets forth in a
flood of books, papers, magazines, movies, lectures — all saying that there is no male-female difference, and that there
*must* not be. Poor, trembling people on top of the seesaw,
hair blowing in the breeze, fearful as the breeze whips into
a wind, not knowing how to get down! People are "up in the
air" because of the lack of balance in anything they have
been taught, and struggling not to recognize what they feel
inside of themselves — struggling against the feminineness
of being a woman, struggling against the masculineness of
being a man, trying to feel neuter. The unfair weight is being
put on by a clever intelligence who can slip out of sight!

As Christian couples, as Christian parents, as Christian
grandparents, as aunts and uncles who are Christian, we have
a responsibility to help in keeping very clear the beauty of
the balance of differences. Marvelous to have a father who
is a rock, a strong tower, a defense against attack, a counselor, a shelter against enemies. Wonderful to have a mother
who is able to concentrate on teaching, being sensitive to the
child's need, compassionate and warm and cuddly and providing the atmosphere of home in the very way of serving
food, of making clothing, of doing some of those things
pointed out in Proverbs 31 as making a woman the kind of
person she should be. Wonderful to have communication with
both parents contributing, in agreement, yet with slightly
different angles of understanding. What a need there is for
teaching little boys that it is great to be a boy "because you
will be a father and love and care for children of your own."
What a need for teaching little girls that it is wonderful to
be a mother "because you can bring forth a baby that will
grow in your own body, and feed it at your breast." — "No,
the father can't feed the baby at his breast, and no, he can't
bring it forth out of his body after nine months of growing

there, because God made man and woman to have different parts in the matter of being parents." — "Yes, the baby is half of each person because the seed is planted by the father and is as much a part of him as of the mother. While the father is doing other things to get the home ready for the baby and preparing wonderful things for the baby to enjoy, and ways the baby can learn, the mother is free to have the baby right inside her, and have that be one of the very important things she can do." — "Just think, Jonathan, every person who has ever lived has had a mother and a father involved in making him. And the only person who has ever been different is Jesus — who *always* lived and who did something amazing in coming from heaven to be born of Mary, but without a human father." There is a balance — men *and* women. There is another balance — each individual with something of each of the parents.

God shows us that the Heavenly Family, the people who will be in heaven, has two relationships that are meant to be understood easily because of our knowing something true in this life. We will all be one Family, with God the Father as *our* Father, and we will all be the bride of Christ, a composite bride made up of the whole body of believers. Christ is masculine in this teaching of what is ahead of us, and also of our positions *now* as Christians — and we are all feminine, all believers.

What then is to be the *balance* in the truth of the man being the head of the home? The pastor (or undershepherd) of a church should represent Christ who is the Head or the Shepherd. The representation is of the masculine: Bridegroom, Shepherd. The husband is to be the head of the home. How does the head behave? Insofar as possible in ways that represent Christ who is the Head of the church. "Husbands, love your wives, even as Christ also loved the church, and gave himself for it" (Ephesians 5:25). What did Christ do as He gave the commission to His bride, the church, when He left to prepare the place for us to go? His commission was: "Go ye into all the world, and preach the gospel to all creatures [or to all nations]" (*see* Mark 16:15). Christ as the Head gave the most important work that could possibly be done through the centuries to His bride — not to angels, not to Himself in a series of trumpet announcements, but to the church. What loving confidence and trust Christ puts in us — "the bride!" Husbands are to treat their wives as Christ treats the church, which means a very special balance of giving important commissions and handing responsible decisions to the wife. Wives are to reverence their husbands and be subject to them, but as the church is to Christ. It is to be real and to be practical, but with an amazing reality of communication and trust. There is another balance that has to be combined at the same time — the balance of our being "brothers and sisters in Christ" — all one in the Family of God. Husbands and wives are to pray together and with their children in this relationship of being brothers and sisters in the Lord's Family. To do other than this is to usurp the place of God as our Heavenly Father. Of course a child must grow to a place of being old enough to understand the Lord's guidance, but certainly that is not to be when life is almost over!

In some universities no man can become "Professor" until the head of the department dies or retires. Then one man can move up to the top place. In some banks there is a line of hopeful "future presidents" waiting for someone to die, so that they can move up. This is not the understanding of what it means to be able to behave as a child of God, with freedom to ask His will to be unfolded directly to you. You do not need to die before your child can look directly to the Lord. The husband does not have to die before his wife can ask the Lord to show the family His plan, and to ask that the husband will recognize it, too. Our mouths are not covered with adhesive tape in our communication and pleading with the Living God. He is our Father, Christ is our Bridegroom, and we *do* have an Advocate, *now*. The beauty of a family

—hand in hand and praying together, having communication together, with this factor recognized insofar as it is possible in the midst of human weaknesses — is marvelous.

An earthly father and mother should *tremble* to take the place of the Heavenly Father or the Shepherd Jesus or the Holy Spirit in telling their children what to do or whom to marry, what university they must attend, what profession they should follow, or whether or not they should go into Christian work. Obedience to God is not a matter of waiting until one's parents die. My father is ninety-nine, and had I needed to let only him make my decisions, I would not yet be ready to ask God what His plan was for me or my family. The balance is delicate; there is a very fine line of difference in weight when suddenly the seesaw flops down and one realizes that the time has come for the "brother or sister in Christ" (one of our own children) to stand directly before the Lord.

Which of us has the wisdom to plan another's life? I feel strongly hit by God's powerful words to Job and to any who would usurp God's direction of His own children, "Then the Lord answered Job out of the whirlwind, and said, Who is this that darkeneth counsel by words without knowledge?" (Job 38:1, 2). What a picture of each of us when we try to plan another person's life, as we "darken counsel by words without knowledge." It couples itself in my mind with, " . . . If therefore the light that is in thee be darkness, how great is that darkness!" (Matthew 6:23). Yes, I know that false religions are the "dark light," but men's certainty at times of what someone *else* should do can also be a very dark light handed to another person for the path ahead. Who but God can know the future and choose His place for any of His children? Who but God can weave the thread of our lives where they belong in His tapestry?

> Where wast thou when I laid the foundations of the earth? declare, if thou hast understanding. . . . Where is the way where light dwelleth? and as for darkness,

where is the place thereof . . .? Knowest thou it, because thou wast then born? or because the number
of thy days is great?

Job 38:4, 19, 21

Do any of us pretend that we have understanding that can
compare to God's? How *dare* we try to be the Holy Spirit or
the Father in heaven, in our telling others that we know what
they should do! People are so prone to tell their own children
(but some deign to tell others' children, too) when they should
*go* or *stay* or *do this* or *do that*. Is there then no place for
talking things over together, for praying together, for helping each other in the area of decisions? Yes, of course, and
this is one of the next balances to discuss.

One of the places in danger of becoming pushed out of
balance in this century of family relationships is the area of
*dependence* versus *independence*. Some accept without questioning the drive for independence as being necessary and
good. Some parents feel their greatest responsibility is to
teach their children independence. They push a child off their
laps with a feeling of great virtue, "I'm teaching him to be
independent." Later these same parents don't bother to
answer letters when their children are away: "They have to
learn how to get along without us." They push a child away
when he comes in fear or with questions: "Run along now,
you have to find things out for yourself." They pointedly go
away when a child is weeping, and never try to find out what
is wrong: "Put out your light and go to sleep," and then
feel proud of saying to some other adult within hearing, "I'm
making her self-sufficient." All signs of dependence are
squashed by some parents as quickly as possible: "Give the
baby a cup as soon as possible, so he or she won't depend on
the bottle for comfort." Breast-feeding is put aside by some
as an unnecessary beginning of dependence upon the mother.
"Get in a baby-sitter who is new every time, and walk out
without any explanation!" is the method some use in order
to wean the child away from depending on the mother or

father. Any tiny leaf growing on the little plant of communication is pulled off as a sign of dependence.

Yet later in life these *same* parents will sit alone in old-folks' homes or in nursing homes or in lonely apartment houses, while their "independent" children let the parents also be "independent." Is this what a family is all about? Isn't there something upside down — in the call for men to be independent of their wives, wives to be independent of their husbands, children to be independent of their parents, and vice versa? People — afraid of dependence on people. Where is the balance?

"Hearken unto me, O house of Jacob, and all the remnant of the house of Israel, which are borne by me from the belly, which are carried from the womb . . . and even to hoar hairs will I carry you: I have made, and I will bear; even I will carry, and will deliver you" (Isaiah 46:3, 4). God is speaking to Israel, but also to all who are in His Family, His own children. God is stating very strongly that from before birth and to very old age we can be dependent upon Him, and are meant to be dependent upon Him. "Then shalt thou call, and the Lord shall answer; thou shalt cry, and he shall say, Here I am . . ." (Isaiah 58:9). Not only are we to be dependent, but we can cry out to Him, and He will listen and *answer* — not just yell, "Go to sleep." — "For this God is our God for ever and ever: he will be our guide even unto death" (Psalms 48:14). And in Romans 4:20, 21 we find that Abraham didn't stagger at the enormity of God's promises because he believed that what God promised, He "was able also to perform." Abraham lived depending on God.

Family life through the years should be a beautiful and blended balance of dependence upon each other. The security that comes in the midst of dependence gives birth to the right kind of independence. A child is meant to learn by the dependability of the mother's and father's interest and concern that God is a Father who can be depended upon. When God promises guidance, His strength in our weakness, availability, comfort in our sorrows, love, understanding, compassion —

these things should have been found on a human level as real
elements in the relationship with parents. A very false picture
is being given of God when parents push children away in
a frenzy of teaching independence as the greatest thing to be
learned. What's wrong with dependence of husband upon
wife, wife upon husband, child upon parent, parent upon
child, grandparent upon grandchildren, grandchildren upon
grandparents? All the hue and cry about a "separate identity"
and "I don't know who I am apart from this circle of people,"
is adding weight to the other side of the seesaw and brings the
danger of "throwing you up in the air," out of balance.

"I can always depend on my mother understanding what
I want to do." — "Really? You mean your mother will let you
make that tent with her blankets?" — "Yeah, she understands
what we're playing. She just — well, she just understands.
Wait and see. I bet she'll give us something to eat, too — to
eat in the tent."

"I can depend on my dad to see how much I need to be
with him next week. He'll take me along. I just gotta talk
because I'm all mixed-up about something!" — "You mean
your dad would believe you need to go that bad? He knows
it when you need him? Boy!" — "Yeah, there are times
when he needs *me*, too; he says so. We like to be together."

"I've got a terrific idea. I want to talk it over with you,
Mother. It's an idea for making these. . . ." — "Hey, Mom,
come and see what I just made!"

Do you drop things and go? Is it important to you? Are
you available? Are you glad for the dependence on you
and not afraid of it? Are you dependent, too? Is there someone you want to have see the picture you painted, the book
you wrote, the cake you baked, the garden you planted, the
doghouse you built — and get his or her opinion on it first?
Do you have someone you depend on for understanding and
giving constructive criticism, but never "missing the point"
altogether?

Who am I? I am a human being made in the image of
God — who needs horizontal relationships and horizontal

dependence on other human beings, just as I need dependence upon God. I don't need to spend my whole life in isolation wildly looking for an identity apart from everyone else. What's wrong with being interrelated with the people my career puts me with — my career as an ecologist, an artist who is involved in making a mobile (living, changing, never the same for two days in a row), my career as a collector for the museum of memories! What's wrong with my identity blending in a mélange, a beautiful mix as mother, wife, sister, friend, counselor, nurse, artist, cook, interior decorator, and so on! Why can't I be interwoven with *people,* since I am a *person?* The impersonality of a separate identity can be terrifying in the way it is carried out in some people's drive to be independent.

The thought that warm, loving human dependence on other members of a family through the years is a "crutch," is a parallel to thinking that if human beings need God, that too, is a "crutch." Both thoughts are born out of an impersonal base, a universe of chance which has no personal Creator in whose image people have been made. In such a universe each person is an independent collection of molecules.

Another balance that is important to consider — as your children play, fight, or squabble, and you sigh, wish for ten years to pass, look at the clock and wish it was night, or lie in bed wishing the day to pass because you have the flu — is the balance between the danger of wasting the "now," or of considering that everything is going to be static, with no future! It is so easy for people to let their children grow up without being taught to think of the preciousness of "today" and "this hour." I used to stop my children and say over and over again (so many times that each one remembers it as one of the outstanding sentences heard in childhood), "Don't waste this hour. Don't waste today. Stop fighting for a minute and just think! You are getting older every day, and you won't be four, with an eight-year-old sister and a tiny baby sister for very long. Think hard — what can you do now in this combination that you can't do in ten years, in five years, even next year? Then *do* it!' "

"You won't be fifteen with an eleven-year-old sister and a seven-year-old sister and a new baby brother for very long. Think! What does this summer have for you and what does today have that you can do, that won't be possible five years from now, two years from now, next week?"

"Figure out what you might wish you had taken time to do. Enjoy each other now. Someday all that you can do today or this week will be only a memory. Let it be a memory of what you *did* do — not of time wasted in fighting."

"What if we have to move; what would you want to do first? What do you enjoy about this garden, this house, these books, that if it all were taken away, you'd wish you were here to do for just one hour? Pretend that this is your last day together in this house, and think what you'd want to play together or look at together. Don't waste the 'now.' "

"I wish I were rid of diapers. Ugh! When this stage is over I'll be glad!" — "I wish I were rid of the preschool years. I'll be glad for a free number of hours!" — "I wish I were finished with teenagers. I can't wait till they all go off and I can start a new life!"

Diapers also mean a baby stage that is all-too-soon finished, of dear "first" things — first responses, first words, creeping, bits of personality showing through and making you eager for the next stage of finding out who this new person is! Each stage goes so quickly, and life is soon gone. The danger of wasting the "now," because of sighing, quarreling, or being irritated into disregarding any of the positive things which will soon be gone, is a danger of being down at the bottom of the seesaw in an important balance.

What is the opposite danger in this particular blend of balances? *Whish — bump — whish — bump.* What should be balancing the sensitivity to the "now?" It is the recognition that life is not static, that there are things to be discovered in each other, in our selves, in hidden talents and new interests, in freedom to do things which cannot be done now. The attention to be paid to the "now" should be balanced by the inner realization that there is a future with new things ahead. What is the "now" simply won't last, and the changes ahead should be like contemplating wrapped gifts with hidden contents!

"Optimist," I can hear someone say. Perhaps the changes are illness, accident, war, or death. Yes, realistically, yes! This is a fallen world, and the future is not promised as a rosy one, but as Christians we look forward to a final future which is to be fantastic — and until that moment we look forward to God's unfolding of His plan, day by day, in *whatever* set of difficult circumstances. The balance to be considered is the importance of the "now" versus the fact that this present situation isn't static. Within a family, help is needed by each in remembering this. And the toddler can get the idea and help Grandmother, as well as the other way around.

"Who do you suppose Grandfather will want to see first when he gets to heaven?" — "Maybe Grandmother or maybe his parents, because they died so very long ago, or maybe his little boy who died when he was a baby. I guess he might want to see that baby first." — "I don't think so," said Samantha, with her brown eyes round and solemn. "I think he'll want to see God first, 'cause he's never seen Him before." This is the balanced expectation of a four-year-old's view of Grandfather's future!

Another balance needed in the family circle is a planned withdrawing back into another century, balanced by understanding today's world and the philosophy which permeates it. There should be times of reading aloud together books which take the whole family into another period of history, so that a particular historic time becomes as vivid as the newspapers and the news magazines make today's moments, day by day. It is important to discuss and to consciously bring out things of past periods, not as "golden periods" when there was perfection, but to show what is being lost, and what totally wrong standards are being accepted today — accepted simply because they are taken for granted. This doesn't need to be a lecture, but a balancing which is planned by choosing books and times to read them together. Past, present, future — with a blend of understanding based on biblical standards. Balance to help judgment.

The balance of understanding that we need each other across the age gaps is something to teach by seeing that there are some periods of "together times" for the three or four generations of your own family, or by bringing in other people of different ages for your children to be with. It is important to experience being needed by children on the part of old people, and being needed by old people on the part of children, as well as important to find out that there is much to learn in cross-conversation.

The togetherness of generations must also be balanced, however, by a very hard-and-fast rule of never telling young families how they are doing it wrong, if the "mix" is to continue. "Don't give that child that dish of food. Half of it goes on the floor!" is simply no sentence for a grandmother or mother-in-law to say. It's the mother's business if half the food is lost, and a sister or a friend or anyone else has no business in making such a suggestion. The beauty of generations enjoying each other can be destroyed by this kind of interference. Does it work both ways? Well, someone has to be willing to bite his or her tongue and not snap back, and it *ought* to be the older and more experienced person who realizes that the relationship is more precious than showing how "inconsistent" the younger ones are being in their criticism!

Balance must be kept between "putting the Lord first" as someone else might recognize it, and "putting the Lord first" by sufficiently putting the family first. For a family to break up — because the husband or wife or both are "putting the Lord first" in some kind of Christian work — to the extent that the children are never "first" and the marriage relationship is never "first" — is *not* "putting the Lord first."

He has given us the responsibility of caring for continuity in oneness and family life.

God speaks to us clearly of fulfilling the sexual needs regularly in marriage, ". . . that Satan tempt you not for your incontinency" (*see* 1 Corinthians 7:1–5). And Deuteronomy 6:7 — "And thou shalt teach them diligently unto thy children, and shalt talk of them when thou walkest by the way, and when thou liest down, and when thou risest up" — means that children are to be *with* parents. These two passages specifically put the togetherness of husband and wife and the togetherness of the family in a place of *balanced* importance. People seem to ignore the need of thinking of this balance and act as if all Christian men are eunuchs, Christian wives without sexual need, and that the children can be put aside in the press of "first things first." The balance of what is "first" is pretty tragically upset in the overall picture of a particular family's history, and there may be the kind of crash which takes place when someone jumps off a seesaw while someone else is up in the air!

Children need to grow up having the example of responsibility which is exhibited by the father and mother not deviating from a task that has to be done. However, that must be balanced by putting absolutely everything aside for a moment when the whole family or one individual has some special need. Is this "putting everything aside" to be saved for severe illnesses, accidents, death, and funerals? No, but it must be something important and take place infrequently enough to be really impressive as to the importance of what was put in place of the normal work. When Franky was about fifteen, he and his father were having a stormy discussion during which Fran suddenly decided that he had not spent enough time with Franky. Since his trip to Florence with the three girls had been the summer of Franky's birth, the time to go with Franky was not "when it might be convenient," but right away. "But, Dad, would you cancel everything you were going to do in your work for a whole ten days just to go with *me*?" It was such an unusual putting aside of normal

responsibilities that nothing could have been as great a demonstration of really caring. That father-son time of seeing
the museums of Florence and Venice together — discussing
and talking alone over a tremendous variety of things without interruption — was priceless in their relationship. Nothing but time, taken when it is needed, can fulfill a need that
takes *time*. Giving a piece of time is much more of a gift in
a human relationship within a family than giving a sum of
money.

The "putting everything aside" can be a very drastic necessity when the marriage is threatened, and there is a break on
the horizon! Years ago Fran visited a couple and found that
the husband was packing to leave in the morning. His inten-
tion was to go off with a girl from his place of work with
whom he was infatuated. Fran stayed all night talking. Not
that he was very welcome! But he was able to point out some
of the complications of the breakdown of continuity in life:
being separated from the children, trying to keep two homes
going, grasping for "happiness," when very obviously the
problems in the marriage hadn't been discussed, nor had any
solution been looked for. By morning the answer was, "Okay,
I'll do what you've suggested and give it a try." Because the
basic trouble was withdrawal and coldness in the physical
part of the marriage, and a seeming lack of understanding in
that area on the wife's part, Fran's advice was, "Let Edith
talk to your wife, and then you go and *give up your job*, go
away for a three-week honeymoon. Go somewhere you've
never been before and really do the things you'd enjoy together — without your children for this time. Give your wife
money to buy a 'wedding trousseau' and whatever Edith tells
her to get."

The next day I spent several hours with the wife while I
did my washing and ironing, talking about the biblical view
of sex in marriage, not an ascetic view, but one of fulfilling
each other's needs. Hers had been a stiff Mid-Victorian upbringing. I advised her to get an exotic black nightgown and
others, some sexy underwear, some very different types of

daytime clothes, have her hair done in a completely new style, buy a new kind of perfume, and go off on *his* planned second honeymoon determined to really forgive her husband. She was to start with the realization that she had also been at fault and was prepared to make a completely new beginning. It was a drastic putting aside of job, time, and bank account — with no security for the future together. But — there took place the most amazing discovery of each other as almost unknown people. "Wow, I never knew my wife before! I don't know what was the matter with me." For both it was a willingness to do a seemingly foolish thing for a very wise reason. The balance of putting the most important thing first, and of being willing to lose everything materially, in order to find each other, was a balance that anyone looking on without understanding might call an "irresponsible act" — or an "unbalanced decision."

These people are grandparents today, with a beautiful family. The material insecurity plunged into at that time has been balanced by the wonderful security of a continuity of family life into the third generation. It is worth it to fight for a variety of *blended balances,* so that the continuity of family life doesn't suddenly come to an abrupt stop! If a job is taking you into dangerous waters as far as your family life goes, be willing to have a lesser job, rather than push on heedless of the greater price to be paid — coming to a split which incidentally breaks the whole picture which families are to *be* of the continuity of the Heavenly Family.

The holiness of God and the love of God are perfectly balanced.

. . . God sitteth upon the throne of his holiness.

Psalms 47:8

We have thought of thy loving-kindness, O God, in the midst of thy temple.

Psalms 48:9

God hath spoken in his holiness. . . .

Psalms 60:6

Hereby perceive we the love of God, because he laid
down his life for us. . . .

1 John 3:16

In the death of Christ as He took our place, the love of God
and the holiness of God met for us. This God is our Father:
"At the same time, saith the Lord, will I be the God of all
the families of Israel, and they shall be my people" (Jeremiah 31:1). He is our Father and the God of our families
as we become His children.

> For this cause I bow my knees unto the Father of our
> Lord Jesus Christ, Of whom the whole family in
> heaven and earth is named.

Ephesians 3:14, 15

Fear thou not; for I am with thee: be not dismayed;
for I am thy God: I will strengthen thee; yea, I will
help thee; yea, I will uphold thee with the right hand
of my righteousness.

Isaiah 41:10

For this God is our God for ever and ever: he will be
our guide even unto death.

Psalms 48:14

We have a perfectly balanced Father who is also our God,
and who has promised us the help that is needed. He knows
we are weak, and He promises us His strength. What a
balance — His strength in our weakness! He knows there will
be times when we will be afraid for ourselves and for our
children — and He promises to be with us so that we don't
need to be dismayed. He knows we are in danger of falling
flat — and promises to "uphold" us! He hasn't promised us
an easy time without suffering, but has promised comfort to

balance the suffering. He hasn't said our lives will be smooth, but has promised to give victory in the terrific varieties of battles ahead of us. As we contemplate what a family can be in the twentieth century, there is no need to turn away in discouragement: *For this God is our God for ever and ever: he will be our guide* [yours and mine] *even unto death.*

The original Artist of the mobile — the perfectly balanced art form in constant movement, the living, changing family — is God who made people in His image and placed them together in families held together by invisible threads! Satan, the vandal, has been working at destroying this artwork ever since! The need to "work at it," as with any other art form, is augmented by the need to give protection to the family, to place "guards" to keep the destructive attacks away, and to keep sensitive watch for any approaching army with swords raised to "cut the threads."

A family — for better or for worse, for richer or for poorer, in sickness and in health! Dirty diapers, chicken pox, measles, mumps, broken dishes, scratched furniture, balls thrown through the windows, fights, croup in the night, arguments, misunderstandings, inconsistencies, lack of logic, unreasonableness, anger, fever, flu, depressions, carelessness, toothpaste tops left off, dishes in the sink, windows open too far, windows closed tight, too many covers, too few covers, always late, always too early, frustration, economies, extravagance, discouragement, fatigue, exhaustion, noise, disappointment, weeping, fears, sorrows, darkness, fog, chaos, clamorings — families!

A family — for better or for worse, for richer or for poorer, in sickness and in health! Softness, hugs, children on your lap, someone to come home to, someone to bring news to, a telephone that might ring, a letter in the post, someone at the airport or station, excitement in meeting, coming home from the hospital with a new person to add, someone to understand intellectually, spiritually, emotionally, happy shrieks of greeting in which you are involved, beloved old people, welcomed babies, increasing togetherness, blending ideas of interior decoration, blending musical taste, growing interests, fun, satisfaction, enjoyment, clean washing, ironed clothing, tulips up, flowers arranged, rugs vacuumed, beauty, dogs, cats, candlelight, firelight, sunlight, moonlight, fields with someone to walk with, woods with someone to picnic, sharing food, imaginative cooking, exchanging ideas, stimulating each other — families!

A family is a mobile strung together with invisible threads — delicate, easily broken at first, growing stronger through the years, in danger of being worn thin at times, but strengthened again with special care. A family — blended, balanced, growing, changing, never static, moving with a breath of wind — babies, children, young people, mothers, fathers, grandparents, aunts, uncles — held in a balanced framework by the invisible threads of love, memories, trust, loyalty, compassion, kindness, in honor preferring each other, depending on each other, looking to each other for help, giving each other help, picking each other up, suffering long with each other's faults, understanding each other more and more, hoping all things, enduring all things, never failing! Continuity! Thin, invisible threads turning into thin, invisible metal which holds great weights but gives freedom of movement — a family! Knowing always that if a thread wears thin and sags, there is help to be had from the Expert — the Father — "Of whom the whole family in heaven and earth is named."